CHANGING THE WORLD WITHOUT LOSING YOUR MIND

Also by Alex Counts

When in Doubt, Ask for More:
And 213 Other Life and Career Lessons for the Mission-Driven Leader

Small Loans, Big Dreams:
How Nobel Prize Winner Muhammad Yunus and
Microfinance Are Changing the World

Voices from the Field: Interviews with Microcredit Practitioners for the Poor

Give Us Credit: How Muhammad Yunus' Micro-Lending Revolution Is
Empowering Women from Bangladesh to Chicago

Praise for *Changing the World Without Losing Your Mind*

"If you have heard of microcredit, you have benefitted from Alex Counts's determined drive to give this idea global wings. In the process, he showed all of us how to market and spread a social innovation everywhere—which is, in itself, a 'how-to' breakthrough. This remarkably open, honest book explains how he did this. It will give you many tools, both programmatic and personal."—Bill Drayton, CEO, Ashoka: Everyone a Changemaker

"Do you have an idea that would help others that you don't know how to implement? Are you worn out from working in the nonprofit world without achieving results? This book will give you the confidence and skills you need to make a real difference. Alex Counts has been there and done that. Now he shares his vast experience on how to save yourself while you save others."—Mike Enzi, U.S. Senator from Wyoming

"Alex Counts brings us insights on social impact with thoughtful reflection and generous advice. With verve and wit, he distills key leadership lessons from his decades of service building one of the great pioneering organizations in the financial inclusion movement."—Michael Schlein, CEO, Accion

"Remarkably candid, self-reflective, generous, and practical, this book is part memoir, part self-help. Alex Counts is an astute observer whose amazing memory helps him recount his own healing journey in vivid detail, offering stories, lessons, and sage advice that will benefit many readers. You'll love this book, and you'll laugh out loud as you read it!"—Susan Davis, co-author, *Social Entrepreneurship: What Everyone Needs to Know*, past chair, Grameen Foundation, and co-founder, BRAC USA

"Nonprofit leaders and managers need great mentors. Alex Counts's new book lets you experience conversations with a brilliant mentor whose candid sharing of his mistakes and accomplishments will help you avoid pitfalls and multiply your success."—Sam Daley-Harris, founder, RESULTS, Microcredit Summit, and Civic Courage

"Effective social entrepreneurship is both an art and a science. In this book, Alex Counts generously shares what he learned during more than 25 years addressing pressing issues such as poverty. It will be an invaluable resource to the next generation of entrepreneurs, both social and traditional, especially as it addresses not only how to make an impact but also how to ensure that it does not come at great personal cost."—M. R. Rangaswami, founder, Indiaspora

"Alex Counts has led a major organization, taken principled moral stands, and made decisions that have helped humanity on a grand scale. As all-consuming as that is, he has also led a life of balance. If you need to get world-changing things done, but you don't want to ruin your life at the same time, Alex is the perfect person from whom to seek advice."—Mark Levy, founder of Levy Innovation LLC and author of *Accidental Genius*

CHANGING THE WORLD WITHOUT LOSING YOUR MIND

Leadership Lessons from Three Decades of Social Entrepreneurship

REVISED EDITION

ALEX COUNTS

Copyright © 2019, 2021 by Alex Counts. All rights reserved.

No part of this book may be used or reproduced by any means, graphic, electronic, or mechanical, including photocopying, recording, taping, or by any information storage retrieval system without the written permission of the publisher, except in the case of brief quotations embodied in critical articles and reviews.

Printed in the United States of America • May 2021 • I

ISBN-13: 978-1-953943-03-3
LCCN Imprint Name: Rivertowns Books

Rivertowns Books are available online from Amazon as well as from bookstores and other retailers. Orders and other correspondence may be addressed to:

    Rivertowns Books
    240 Locust Lane
    Irvington NY 10533
    Email: info@rivertownsbooks.com

To Emily, my bride of twenty-five years,
who has been there for me
through all the ups, downs, and lessons learned

Contents

Foreword by Muhammad Yunus — xi

Introduction to the Revised Edition — xiv

Why This Book? — 1

PART ONE: GETTING STARTED

1. Deciding to Make a Difference — 11
2. Choosing to Be Bold — 30
3. First Lessons in Leadership — 40
4. Learning to Tell My Story — 51
5. Laying a Foundation — 64
6. Running My Own Show — 81

PART TWO: LEARNING TO LEAD

7. Fundraising as a Win/Win/Win Proposition — 91
8. Managing Up — 110
9. When Leadership Is a Struggle — 134
10. Turning Points — 153
11. Coping with Success — 163
12. Building a Great Board — 182

13. Forging Partnerships   198

PART THREE: CARING FOR YOURSELF

14. Life in Balance   217
15. Beginner's Mind   230
16. Learning Acceptance   239
17. Living Generously   251
18. Letting Go   266

Epilogue: Leading in a Time of Crisis   275

Acknowledgments   291
Index   297
About the Author   305

Foreword

by Muhammad Yunus

MANY YEARS AGO, an unusual letter crossed my desk. It was from a college student in the United States who said he wanted to come to work with Grameen Bank because he admired what we were doing and wanted to learn everything he could about microcredit. The author of the letter was Alex Counts.

At that point, we had had foreign visitors coming to us to stay a few days at a time. Although I was not sure what he intended, I sent him a letter welcoming him and giving a him a list of advice. My first advice was that he should learn Bangla as much as he could before coming, because English would not be useful in communicating with Grameen borrowers.

I also told him we couldn't pay him anything, and that he might not like the work. Furthermore, we might not be able to offer him interesting and useful things to do. I thought if he was not serious about his intentions, I might never hear back from him.

I did hear back from him. He arrived in Dhaka eighteen months later, with his degree from Cornell University in hand and speaking Bangla at a reasonable level. He spent a total of six years living in Bangladesh, the first part as a Fulbright scholar. Over time, he learned to speak Bangla beautifully, with a noticeable accent from the district of Tangail. If someone were blindfolded and listening to Alex speaking in Bangla, he would bet Alex was a native from Tangail.

Alex spent many of his formative months at a remote branch office of Grameen Bank in Tangail with few of the facilities he had grown up enjoying, such as running water and electricity. He got fond of spicy Bangladeshi food. Everybody in the village forgot that he was an outsider. For them, he was a young man from their village. He was a friend and an ally.

Ultimately, when he was leaving Bangladesh, I asked him to take the responsibility of Grameen Foundation in the U.S.A. in 1997, which existed basically on paper at that point of time. Alex injected life in it and led its growth from its modest beginnings into a powerful institution.

Alex has always been there for us during times of crisis. For example, when a cyclone hit us in 1991 and we were facing other difficulties, Alex worked around the clock without any sleep for several days trying to be helpful. One of the results of his efforts was an impressive and supportive article he wrote that was published in the *Washington Post*. There have been many other times when he devoted himself to helping us address some need or seize an opportunity. He earned our respect and trust.

In this book, he reflects not so much on what he accomplished during his career and life, but on what he has learned. His ideas on managing and leading people, fundraising, and attending to his well-being are in some cases not the same as my own, but I am sure that they will be useful to many people. In some respects, he has adapted Grameen's philosophy and applied it to his own life and work in creative ways. His impressive accomplishments in the areas of microcredit and social business, some of which are chronicled in this book, speak for themselves.

I have come to believe that while making money may lead to happiness, making other people happy leads to super-happiness.

A life of service to others and to society can be deeply fulfilling. Anyone who seeks to live a life informed by this insight will benefit from this exceptional, and highly readable, book.

Professor Muhammad Yunus
Dhaka, Bangladesh
March 2019

Introduction to the Revised Edition

EVERY TIME I'VE HAD A BOOK PUBLISHED, it has been an emotional experience. What if no one likes it or even reads it? In the case of this book, which contains deeply personal stories from my life that are organized around the most important lessons I've learned about nonprofit leadership and self-care, the intensity was magnified.

My intention in writing *Changing the World* was to provide valuable ideas, tips, and "hacks" to mission-driven leaders. While a handful of people I'd mentored had found value in some of my insights, I had no idea how a much larger audience might respond. I hoped that sharing my adventures and misadventures and the lessons they'd taught me would be instructive to a new generation of changemakers, but I had no idea whether they would be.

Happily, the feedback from readers has far exceeded my expectations. For a few months after the book came out, I received an average of one message per day from someone in the world who had just finished the book. Many of these messages were generous and soulful. Some were quite creative. One young woman who purchased the book at an event in Portland applied my idea of sending handwritten letters to donors while travelling abroad (described in chapter eight) by sending *me* an appreciative post card from Spain. She taught me that there is no better way to bring a smile to the face of someone who has written a how-to book than to demonstrate one of the techniques that they wrote about.

Encouraged by such gestures, in the fall of 2020 I set the goal of having forty five-star reviews of my book published on Amazon.com by the end of the year. As December neared, it looked as if we would fall far short. But a flurry of activity during the final days of that dreadful year ensured that the target was reached. The last review of the year, published on New Year's Eve, concluded with these generous and humbling words: "This timely book by Alex Counts, part confessional, part inspirational, is full of helpful insights and perspectives. Counts' many anecdotes and words of wisdom serve as useful antidotes to the despair, uncertainty, and frustrations that can accompany the field of social entrepreneurship. Any leader who wants to stay the course through a lifetime of service should add this book to her/his library."

Of course, this reviewer's praise pointed to another fact: the world had changed dramatically since the first edition of this book was published, and not for the better.

I RECALL READING ABOUT THE CORONAVIRUS starting in mid-January, 2020. You may have had a similar experience. Each successive article seemed more ominous. At first, I tried not to worry too much about the possibility of a global pandemic. After all, it was completely out of my control, and there was a chance it might never rise to the level where it would impact me or our society in a significant way.

But by the time March rolled around, the world had turned upside down. Like most people, I had to make some difficult decisions quickly with few guideposts to help. I squeezed in a trip to Obion, Tennessee, to bury my stepfather in his family's cemetery.

After I spoke at the outdoor service under threatening skies, I exchanged my last handshakes of the year with family members and well-wishers. Around that time, my wife Emily, whom you will meet in chapter five, was being evacuated from Geneva, Switzerland, where she had been meeting with officials at the World Health Organization. A few weeks later, Emily was departing for what ended up being a seven-week stay in New York to care for a relative. None of this had been planned in advance.

The disruption to our lives was significant, but it paled in comparison to the pain and stress experienced by others. Our many friends in the service and entertainment industries, including a number of musicians and waitstaff based in Key West and Nashville, saw their incomes drop dramatically. People we knew contracted COVID-19, and one died. An avalanche of depressing statistics confirms what we saw amongst our friends and family: the people with the least savings and the lowest incomes suffered the most and recovered the least in the months that followed. Social and economic inequality in America, already obscene, became decidedly worse.

Nonprofits and the people who work for or govern them were also terribly impacted. Revenues dropped even as society's need for nonprofits grew. People who had dedicated their lives to mission-driven organizations saw their jobs become more stressful or vanish entirely in a matter of days—this at a time when many were also struggling with home schooling and other disruptions. As one might expect, some organizations handled layoffs with fairness and humanity, while others struggled to do so amidst the tumult.

The sheer scope of the devastation was difficult to for me, or anyone, to fathom. Wide swaths of the population were set back even as a long-overdue reckoning on racial injustice was confronted with indifference, cruelty, and conspiracy theories from leaders in the federal government, a fact-challenged political party, and too many other Americans.

Once I stabilized my personal and family situation as best I could, I began mining my past experiences for lessons that could help those leading mission-driven organizations through this difficult time. I advised people and wrote blog posts. I've now synthesized the best ideas into an epilogue titled "Leading in a Time of Crisis." It is meant to complement the chapter "When Leadership is a Struggle," which deals more with self-inflicted organizational wounds than with the impact of society-wide crises on nonprofits and how leaders can effectively respond.

While it may be difficult to imagine as you read this—particularly if you are leading a struggling organization with a noble mission during the waning months of the 2020-21 pandemic or some future crisis—things *will* get better. Boom times and favorable conditions will return. Your job is to survive until then, doing the best that you can and retaining as many of your top staff, volunteers, and donors as possible.

More favorable conditions, when they come, will allow you to have a bigger impact on underlying systemic issues while stockpiling funds and talent for future crises—which are, sadly, inevitable. So you should seek to make peace with the boom-and-bust cycle of nonprofit management and, by all means, avoid the trap of complacency when times are good.

ONE OF THE HAZARDS OF PUBLISHING a how-to book on topics as complex as nonprofit leadership and self-care is that you are constantly reminded of the ways that you fall short of your own ideals and fail to apply success strategies you have publicly advocated. On the other hand, writing a book like this provides the kind of little nudge to follow your own advice that can make a positive difference in matters big and small.

One of the ideas in this book that has generated more attention than I expected is the recommendation to relish being a novice at something you truly care about (described in chapter fifteen, "Beginner's Mind"). People attending my author talks often lit up when I told the story of how I learned this technique after volunteering to establish a fan club to support a bluegrass band that I loved—something I threw myself into despite being totally unprepared and doing it poorly for the first year or two. As I discussed this discovery with readers, I had a related insight: As most people age, they gravitate towards things that they either find comfortable (such as watching reruns of their favorite television show) or that they have some expertise in. I have come to believe that this creeping midlife trend breeds complacency, self-importance, and a kind of intellectual laziness. Seeking out opportunities to be a novice is a way of combating this human tendency.

At the time, I didn't know that there is an empirical body of evidence suggesting that learning new skills as an adult improves the quality of your life and your performance as a professional. But I subsequently read the important book *Beginners: The Joy and Transformative Power of Lifelong Learning* by the journalist Tom Vanderbilt (Knopf, 2021). His research and experiences as a midlife novice strongly reinforce my own insights and have significant implications for nonprofit executives.

One of many insights I gained from Vanderbilt's book relates to what you can learn from your own mistakes, either during the process of learning new skills or while applying well-developed ones. Throughout this book, I openly discuss many of the errors I have made—so much so that a former board chairman told me he thought I was "too hard on myself" in these pages.

Vanderbilt describes the power of mining mistakes for insights while learning new skills like singing, drawing, and surfing. "What's curious," he writes, "is that all these errors I made loom much more vividly in my mind than any tangible moments of progress, which seems important: These were inflection points, moment when I was standing up against the edge of my knowledge and ability . . . I was running an ongoing experiment, and mistakes gave me raw insight." Expect many similar inflection points and raw insights in the pages to follow.

By the time I was discussing this concept during book events in the summer of 2019, I had become better at running the bluegrass band's fan club. My growing proficiency required me to identify *new* activities that I could be a novice at. So I talked about learning to cook and serving as a court-appointed special advocate for a child in the foster care system. When I remarked, with mock anger, that I wished someone had warned me that you could never, ever have enough garlic in your house, I always got a laugh—and it prompted an Indian woman speaking alongside me at one event to extol the wonders of *her* essential spice: ginger.

Today I've moved into two new areas: following a rather haphazard meditation practice and engaging in climate change activism based on my growing involvement with an organization called Methane Action, established by Peter Fiekowsky (a bold visionary if there ever was one) and led by a dynamic woman named Daphne Wysham. How appropriate to pair those two new priorities given the overarching theme of this book: one that deals with being a changemaker in the world, and the other with personal well-being, or changing my *internal* world.

I suppose I now have the blessing—or curse—of forever feeling pressure to apply my own insights given the existence of this book. Since I have no choice in the matter, I guess it is best to joyfully accept this challenge!

SINCE COMPLETING THE FIRST EDITION of this book, I have continued to learn new lessons and find novel applications of the ideas I discovered previously. In this second edition, I have mostly limited myself to adding those related to crisis management.

At the same time, I realized that I had many more powerful tips, techniques, and ideas for mission-driven leaders than I could fit into this volume. Some readers asked me for a ready reference of my best ideas to have on their desks so they could refer to them when they were confronted with a complex or daunting opportunity or problem.

In response, I gathered some material from this book's cutting room floor in a small book titled *When in Doubt, Ask for More: And 213 Other Life and Career Lessons for the Mission-Driven Leader*. Each lesson is summarized in a few sentences that occupy just a page or two. My friend Mona Bentz described this volume as a "daily devotional" for nonprofit leaders. I think she got it just right. I am grateful to my editor and publisher, Karl Weber, for working his usual magic to make that book happen—and, now, for helping me launch the second edition of this one.

Once the initial shock of the COVID-19 pandemic abated, people started paying more attention to the ideas contained in these two volumes. Many, I think, are timeless concepts that can help a leader navigate good times and challenging ones. Indeed, one of the most common pieces of feedback I have received is that most of the learnings I offer apply far beyond the nonprofit world to arenas that include business, government, academia, and even the arts.

Wherever you are on the landscape of changing society for the better, I hope this new edition helps you to do good and remain well. The world needs your help more than ever, and you deserve to provide that assistance in a manner that feeds rather than crushes your body and soul. It is possible, and I hope this book helps to show you how.

Alex Counts
Hyattsville, Maryland
March 2021

Why This Book?

"HELLO, THIS IS ALEX," I answered hurriedly from my desk in a small office near the U.S. Capitol. It was a Friday afternoon in July, 1990. Back then, before the advent of caller ID, most people just picked up their phones, not knowing who to expect on the other end.

At the time, I was nine months into what would be a three-year interlude based in Washington, D.C., between my two stints in Bangladesh. I was the legislative director for RESULTS, an aggressive, controversial, but widely respected international nonprofit organization dedicated to anti-hunger advocacy. It was a preposterously senior role for someone who was just 22 years old, but my previous association as a Fulbright scholar with Grameen Bank and its illustrious founder, Muhammad Yunus, was already opening doors for me.

"Hi, Alex, this is Mitch Snyder," said the voice on the other end of the line. That got my attention.

Mitch was the driving spirit behind the Center for Creative Non-Violence (CCNV), an organization that served and advocated for the homeless. I had read about Mitch and his battles with President Reagan. In one successful confrontation, he'd gone on a hunger strike in order to pressure the administration into giving an abandoned federal building in Washington to his group for a homeless shelter. Fifty-one days into Mitch's fast, the government agreed to his demands. Like many in the nonprofit world, I considered Mitch Snyder a legend.

"Can your organization sign on to a letter about homelessness that we have prepared?" he asked. I was a bit surprised—and impressed. Here was a celebrated provocateur and activist doing the spade work of calling around to get cosigners on a rather mundane advocacy letter. I've always admired leaders who don't delegate all of the unglamorous, practical parts of their work to others but rather pitch in themselves.

"Sure, fax it over," I promptly replied. I planned to talk to my colleagues about endorsing the letter after reviewing it over the weekend.

It didn't work out that way. On Monday morning, I read in the *Washington Post* that Mitch had hanged himself over the weekend.

The news left me shocked, dismayed, and confused. How could Mitch be diligently plugging away at his latest project one moment only to take his life a few hours later? I wondered whether I had been the last person he had spoken to.

It was a sobering lesson about the psychic toll that dedicating your life to a noble cause can sometimes take. But seeing what can happen to another person isn't always enough to make us change our own behaviors.

In little over a decade, I found myself facing my own existential crisis. I had returned from my second tour in Bangladesh, which had lasted five years. I was running Grameen Foundation, an organization that I had founded a few years earlier to advance the humanitarian ideals of Muhammad Yunus, the iconic Bangladeshi social entrepreneur, which I'd adopted as my own. On the surface, things were going well. But just below the surface, trouble was building fast.

Starting during my final years in Bangladesh, when I was behind a desk more and exploring the realities of the rural countryside less, I had been gaining three to five pounds per year. This was just one symptom of the contradictions I was living. I exercised fairly regularly, but not enough to stave off ballooning weight and borderline high cholesterol. I had the job of my dreams, but often was a bundle of nerves. I was driving my employees and family crazy, and I had virtually no interests beyond my work. I'd been successful at raising more money than ever before, but I was also feeling increasingly insecure and anxious.

From time to time, I wondered whether I might I end up like Mitch, plugging away on some project to advance the common good one moment, hanging from the rafters the next. My worries only deepened as I observed other nonprofit leaders battle depression, adopt unhealthy habits, get divorced, belittle their own achievements, and become enveloped in cynicism.

My crisis came to a head in December, 2000. At Grameen Foundation's annual holiday party at a Washington, D.C., restaurant, I rose to give a thank-you speech to the staff. I attempted to strike a balance between our big fundraising successes that year—most notably pulling in $1 million for our work in India with the help of Steve Rockefeller, Jr.—and all the things we had not yet accomplished. Sometimes I give very effective speeches to teams I have led, but this was one of my worst ever. The team members in attendance applauded politely, then went back to partying.

At around nine p.m., someone announced to everyone still at the party that we had paid for more alcohol than we had consumed. The bar was open for business, big time! Seeking some fun and release, I started drinking shots with colleagues. For the first and only time since my college years, I concluded the night by throwing up.

The next morning, one of the first people I saw was Howie Erichson, a brilliant law school professor who was in town on business and had stayed overnight in our basement apartment on Capitol Hill. Howie had served as a mentor of mine since I was fourteen, and he's one of the people I most admire. I was deeply embarrassed to let him see me stumble home and, the next morning, in my hung-over state. After he left, I did something else I had never done before: I cancelled a business trip I'd planned for that day. I was feeling too miserable to travel.

A few weeks later, it was New Year's Day, 2001. After a morning workout, I jumped onto the digital scale in the Atlantic Health Club on the Jersey shore, and I saw a really big number shouting back at me. My years of self-neglect now meant that I was 25 pounds overweight.

Driving back to Washington later that day gave me a chance to reflect on what had happened to me.

I was a mess. My mental and physical health was fragile, at best. My wife Emily and I had little in the way of savings. I had a small but stubborn credit card debt that I never seemed to be able to pay off. I buried my worries in a pint of Ben and Jerry's ice cream each night and then rallied myself to show up at work the next morning to pump the adrenaline needed for me to play the part of the leader who had all the answers—despite the fact that I sometimes felt as if I had few answers to give my small but growing staff team.

This profile of inner stagnation and decay wasn't unfamiliar to me. Mitch Snyder wasn't the only gifted social activist I'd seen in similar straits. I had once sat with a microfinance legend, often mentioned in the same breath as Yunus, who lamented to me that he felt that everything he had done for the past 40 years had essentially failed. Now he was hoping to make up for all that carnage with one final Hail Mary pass—a domestic lending initiative that ended up being a fiasco. It was a tragic waste of money and energy, and a needless blot on what had actually been an admirable and accomplished career.

I observed another leader pick up a succession of bad habits due to the stress of running an activist organization. At one point, she had to change jobs—but not before letting her health insurance lapse and experiencing a health crisis that has caused her to suffer from intense pain and be unable to work ever since. Years later, over a cup of coffee with me, she reminisced about her journey from being a nationally recognized advocate for low-income people to someone who sometimes had to choose between buying food and medicine.

Now, at the age of thirty-three, I was becoming one of those leaders: successful enough to attract some funding and talent, clever enough to make even modest accomplishments sound significant, but unhealthy and unhappy to the core.

I realized it was past time for me to turn things around.

My first job was to convince my wife Emily, a trained dietician, to put me on a sustainable weight-loss program. She initially resisted, based on all the times she had designed similar programs for hospital patients only to see them never sustained or even tried. But she finally gave in, and within a few months my weight was back to 155 pounds, where it has remained ever since.

I also began taking steps to learn more from mentors and inspirational books, and to loosen up as a boss. I employed my sense of humor more, which had been missing in action at work for quite a while. Above all, I resolved to distill what I was learning from all my professional and personal accomplishments and failures, and then to develop habits that would make putting those lessons into my day-to-day life as natural as possible.

Over the next 20 years, I experienced many ups and downs. So did the humanitarian causes to which I'm dedicated. Yunus and Grameen, and everyone associated with them, had the winds at their backs after the 2006 announcement that they'd been jointly awarded the Nobel Peace Prize. But just a few years later, a wave of unjust and inexplicable persecution that targeted Yunus in his home country cast a pall over our entire movement and at times sapped much of my idealism and energy. It was a bumpy ride that included moments of unhappiness and occasional despair.

But the downward trend was reversed, and my professional accomplishment, success in working with others, and personal fulfillment grew and advanced each year. My life has been increasingly characterized by robust mental and physical health and much more appreciation for what I have accomplished—despite the things I have failed at. Now, at age fifty-two and just beginning my fourth decade working as a leader in the battle for social change, I can look back at fifteen years of consistent health and relative happiness. I've carved out time to pursue hobbies from running marathons to promoting bluegrass music.

My pathway from despair to contentment was not based on a single moment of epiphany, but rather on hundreds of incremental insights that I often struggled with initially but ultimately was able to integrate into how I led organizations and lived my life. The lessons and habits that turned my story around are things that I wish I'd learned earlier.

Leading social change is a life work that is full of contradictions, paradoxes, and traps. Some of them are common to any highly demanding job, but others are unique to working in the nonprofit or humanitarian sectors.

I've seen far too many middle-aged nonprofit leaders who were overweight smokers and whose cynicism and jaded perspectives lived right below the surface of their ossified idealism. Some took risks that seemed rooted in a sense that they had not accomplished what they had expected to by that point in their lives, gambles that sometimes endangered their organizations and all who depended on them. Theirs seemed to be a quiet desperation that I came to understand during my own leadership journey—and which I ultimately learned to escape.

This book is an attempt to share my story, and the lessons it taught me, with a new generation of leaders dedicated to social change and environmental justice. I hope it will benefit those who doubt that they will ever become unhealthy and jaded, as well as those who have already turned that corner and wonder if they can reverse the trend before it is too late.

The book is divided into three parts. Part One, "Getting Started," recounts some of the key moments from my personal journey of leadership. It describes how and why I became drawn to a career dedicated to world-changing ideals; the various steps I took—some well-planned, others more haphazard—in my search for a mission that was suited to my talents and passions; the people I encountered along the way; and some of the first lessons I learned about how to be an effective leader. Part One concludes with an account of the first few months after my launch of Grameen Foundation, the organization to which I have devoted the bulk of my nonprofit career.

Part Two, "Surviving at the Top," delves deeply into many of the specific leadership challenges I had to deal with as president and CEO of Grameen Foundation—challenges that most other nonprofit leaders are likely to find familiar. The chapters in Part Two offer advice and ideas for mastering skills such as fundraising, forging strong relationships with supporters, working effectively with your board, and crafting partnerships with outside organizations in support of your mission. Whether you are an aspiring leader in the nonprofit world, a newly-appointed manager, or a veteran executive, you should find information in this part of the book that will provide food for thought and help you bring added value to your leadership work.

In Part Three, "Caring for Yourself," I address the kinds of personal issues that have derailed the careers of so many gifted nonprofit leaders, and that have sapped the energy, happiness, and effectiveness of many more. Those of us who pursue careers dedicated to missions larger than ourselves are very fortunate; unlike many of our counterparts in the for-profit world, we rarely have strong doubts about the importance and the value of our work. But the downside of a mission-driven life is that it's all too easy to become obsessed with the mission and as a result neglect your own well-being—a misguided approach that helps nobody in the end. The chapters in Part Three describe the insights and practical strategies I developed over many years that enabled me to rediscover and then to maintain the mental, physical, and spiritual balance that allowed me to keep going—to be a high-energy, high-intensity, truly dedicated leader without falling prey to burnout, anxiety, depression, exhaustion, or any of the other ills that might have ended my work prematurely.

The privilege of a career spent pursuing goals that are deeply meaningful and inspiring has been the great gift of my life. My hope is that the ideas in this book—ideas that I wish I'd known when I started my journey many years ago—may be my gift to the rising generation of nonprofit leaders, as they pick up the torch and carry it to new heights of achievement.

ated to produce an appropriate output — fixing this is a primary challenge for empirical research in the field.

PART ONE: GETTING STARTED

PART ONE: GETTING STARTED

1

Deciding to Make a Difference

How early experiences shaped my commitment
to a life and work centered on
making the world a better place

THE SIGHT TOOK MY BREATH AWAY. It is still etched in my memory thirty-five years later.

On one level, it was just a bunch of middle-school kids running around playing games on a field. But to me, it was so much more than that.

As a sports-crazed kid, I had missed not being able to play team sports when I was in the seventh and eighth grades due to school policy. So during my senior year, when my friend Paul Hilal was elected student body president, I hatched a plan with him to organize an intramural sports program for the lower schoolers. With Paul's support, I began methodically securing permission from the school administration, and the idea quickly became a reality.

To this day, I have an intense memory of looking down the main sports field with four frenetic games being played simultaneously by scores of kids, contemplating what I had done. Despite always feeling a bit out of place at my high school, I had made something happen! A hundred-something of my peers were doing something that Paul and I had brought into reality. They were not just going through the motions to humor me. Clearly, they were having fun. I had never experienced a sense of agency like that before. The program even continued after Paul and I graduated later that spring.

Ever since then, it has been difficult for me to hatch an idea about making things better for myself or others and then pooh-pooh my ability to make it happen if I set my mind to it, even if it involved hundreds, thousands, or tens of thousands of people and millions if not billions of dollars. (And years later, Paul became a Grameen Foundation board member who helped me create things much bigger than an intramural sports league.)

The lessons I took away from this teenaged accomplishment have profoundly shaped my character and career. Complaints can be turned into tangible plans and progress that benefit one's peers and future generations. Things can be improved, often simply by getting motivated, designing a plan, enlisting others, and following through. Watching others benefit from your achievement can feel satisfying, even glorious, even (or especially) if most of the beneficiaries don't realize that you are responsible, allowing you to remain anonymous. Reinforcing your sense of agency and power to change things can propel you into a virtuous cycle of ambition, action, and results.

At the same time, I think that this pivotal moment has occasionally made me overconfident in my ability to right wrongs, especially since I occasionally misjudge what is actually wrong. Sometimes you can misdiagnose a problem and then implement a flawed solution. Other times, trying to solve a problem without enough skills can backfire. If it is another person's job to deal with an issue, jumping in can make it appear that you are showing them up. Experiencing success can lead to an exaggerated sense of agency which can then cause overconfidence, hubris, and overreach. Solving a problem in an ad hoc way might retard efforts of others to come up with a permanent and sustainable solution.

My willingness to stand up for what I think is right, even at personal risk, is both one of the qualities I am proudest of and also one that I need to better calibrate and use more thoughtfully during the remaining years of my life.

An Activism Focused on Practical Solutions

I LIVED PRIMARILY WITH MY FATHER and stepmother after my parents divorced when I was 8 years old. They were both enormously influential even though their parenting style was decidedly hands-off. My mother was also an important part of my life growing up. Above all, she nurtured her children's creative and entrepreneurial gifts. (And she had the good sense to marry a wonderful man named John Fox who was, like my stepmother, a great stabilizing force in our extended family.)

In recent years, I have credited my career choice in part to being brought up in a family that included many helping professionals. For example, my father was a psychiatrist, and my stepmother and older brother Doug were social workers. People working in professions focused on helping people overcome mental health issues frequented our home. Their worldviews shaped my younger brother Michael and me in subtle ways. Dinner table conversation sometimes included my stepmother Norma and my father discussing issues that arose in his practice. Occasionally I offered my own views.

Once, my father told me that he sometimes told patients who were struggling to find meaning and motivation in life the magnificent quotation that was part of a poster of Martin Luther King, Jr., that has hung in my room or office since I was in my teens: "If a man hasn't found something he will die for, he isn't fit to live." I felt proud that something I had brought into our household had made it into my father's healing sessions, and I still feel that way today. (Another thing that has struck me is how many African-Americans who've visited me have been astonished that I idolize Dr. King so much that a large poster of him is always in a prominent place in my home—a potent reminder of how powerful images can both build and burn bridges between people.)

I was born in New York City and spent some early, formative years living first in Brigantine, New Jersey, which at the time was a sleepy little island off the shore of Atlantic City. Our family moved to the upper east side of Manhattan when I was nine years old, into an apartment that my stepmother still lives in and that I continue to visit regularly. I attended a public primary school through sixth grade, then switched to Horace Mann School in the Bronx, one of four private schools that my father picked out as options for me. He let me make the final choice, a typical thing for him to do; from the time I was quite young, he showed an unusual degree of respect for my independent judgment, which I am sure helped me to grow up into a self-confident person.

During my senior year at Horace Mann, three things happened that sowed the seeds of the kinds of things I would involve myself in during college, and beyond. One was the opportunity to create the intramural sports program that I described a moment ago.

Another was sitting through several assemblies and films about the Holocaust, which the school's largely Jewish alumni network was interested in sensitizing all students about. It helped me to understand the great evil human beings are capable of.

On the other side of the spectrum, some of my fellow students urged everyone to fast for one day in November and give the money they would have spent on food to Oxfam America, to support anti-hunger programs. Like many of my peers, my closest friends and I avoided the cafeteria more out of peer pressure than solidarity with the poor—in fact, we ate lunch in a local restaurant—but the idea that there were things that could be done to fight modern-day injustice left a mark on my psyche. I also got involved in something called the Tutoring Project, where every

Saturday I would help a handful of younger students from nearby low-income schools prepare for college. This would involve my travelling two hours by subway round trip, which I was happy to do since the students seemed so grateful.

It was during my sophomore year at Cornell University that my social conscience began to develop beyond what it had become in high school, and move towards reformist activism grounded in idealism and practical solutions. This awakening was catalyzed by observing a nationwide divestment movement that began at Cornell and Colombia Universities. Our own anti-apartheid activists campaigned to get Cornell to divest its endowment of all investments (then totaling about $120 million) in companies that did business with South Africa. At one point, 211 of my fellow Cornellians were arrested. Those brave kids and many others constructed a vast replica shantytown on the Arts and Sciences quadrangle. It was meant to drive home to all of us the abysmal living conditions of blacks in South Africa, and Cornell's complicity. I never lifted a finger to help those activists, who were criticized by some but who nonetheless cowed the administration into not demolishing the eyesore of all the rickety houses until after the semester was over.

Still, while not moved to taking action against apartheid, I began to construct my own activist paradigm and strategy. I gave presentations that I had been trained to deliver on world hunger to fellow Cornell as well as Ithaca College and Ithaca high school students, and I led a campuswide fast to raise money for Oxfam America similar to the one organized by my classmates that I'd lamely observed while in high school.

I felt most drawn to approaches that were practical and positive. I asked myself the question: What would need to be done when apartheid was over in South Africa, and when the senseless proxy wars the U.S. was waging in Central America concluded? Poverty would remain. Could it be solved? I went on a journey spanning classes, lectures, and my own personal research to see if there were existing solutions to poverty that addressed root causes, rather than just Band-Aids that dealt with symptoms. My curiosity was heightened when someone said that all of the major problems facing humanity had been solved somewhere; the major challenge was adapting and scaling those micro solutions to scale of macro problems such as poverty, environmental degradation, racism, overpopulation, and so on.

Time and again, people pointed me in the direction of the Grameen Bank of Bangladesh and its founder, Muhammad Yunus. This was pre-Internet, and there was not yet much written about Grameen; what was published was not easily available, even at Cornell. Yet my increasing commitment to pragmatic activism prompted me to learn everything I could about the success of Grameen, and thus became a launching pad for what became my career.

Stimulating classes and romances, which had about equally long shelf lives for me during college, began to take a back seat to my involvement in social issues, poverty in particular, during my sophomore year. Over lunch one day, not far from the "model" shanty town on the Arts Quad, my friend Julia Plotnik asked for help in starting a Cornell chapter of RESULTS, a scrappy grassroots advocacy organization founded by Sam Daley-Harris that focused on lobbying Congress to allocate more U.S. foreign aid to effective anti-poverty solutions.

She explained how her mother and stepfather had led the Bronx chapter for years. Its focus on creating the political will to end hunger and poverty by advocating for known solutions to receive a bigger share of the U.S. foreign aid budget seemed practical and exciting. In fact, it resonated strongly with two blue-ribbon commissions' reports on world hunger, which both found that existing technologies would be capable of ending world hunger—which meant that the overriding factor preventing us from getting the job done was the lack of political will.

RESULTS had a standard formula for starting groups (and for much else, as I would learn; this was part of the genius and also the limitations of Sam Daley-Harris's approach). The people trying to start a group would write letters to their friends inviting them to a kick-off presentation featuring a RESULTS staff member (of which there were exactly three at the time) or an experienced volunteer, who usually flew in (or, especially in the early years, arrived by Greyhound bus) for the occasion. Late in the fall semester, Julia and I spoke to Nick Schatzki (a volunteer leader from the Manhattan group who would later figure prominently in my life) on a Radio Shack speaker phone. He gave us pointers for writing our letters.

Two things attracted me to RESULTS. First, it promoted practical and positive solutions. I never could develop more than momentary passion for handwringing and oppositional types of activism that focused on stopping things that were bad, rather than promoting things that were good. Second, RESULTS was winning—and still is today. Modest though the triumphs were in the grand scheme of things, they were moving the ball down the field in terms of getting Congressionally mandated spending increased for what it had identified as proven anti-poverty programs. With each passing year, the scale of the victories achieved by RESULTS seemed to be growing. Not only did this reaffirm the responsiveness of our political system, but it fired up my competitive juices. Like many people, I liked being on a winning team and being able to help it do even better.

So I spent the winter break of 1985-86 crafting my letter inviting friends to the kick-off presentation. Soon after we returned in January, Julia, one or two others involved, and I had another speaker-box call with a staff member named Cameron Duncan (who would sadly die of complications from AIDS a few years later). His gentle and affirming voice calmed all of us as he went over the basics. Then he asked those who had written letters to read them aloud. I went first. My letter was over-engineered and much too detailed. I did not yet understand that excessive information could overwhelm clarity and readability, wisdom I still neglect on occasion today. Julia's letter, on the other hand, was much shorter and more effective.

In the nicest way possible, Cameron said he thought Julia's letter was stronger and urged us in any case to get our letters delivered as the meeting was only a few weeks away. (I was too embarrassed to admit to the group that I had already delivered mine to scores of friends around campus.) His gentleness with me and my flawed letter evoked my father and how he passed on nearly every opportunity to rebuke me, and seized most opportunities to affirm me.

As the kick-off presentation approached, I studied RESULTS advocacy materials. In the past, campaigns conducted by fewer than seventy chapters around the country in support of more funding for immunizations and Vitamin A supplements for children had saved hundreds of thousands of lives. Fewer deaths led to fewer births, so these solutions did not contribute to overpopulation. It all seemed so simple, positive, and practical. I was hooked—and remain hooked three decades later.

On March 16, 1986, Nick Schatkzi flew up from New York City and delivered a three-hour workshop for thirty-two fellow students. There was a big educational component, but the highlight was writing a letter to a member of Congress in support of one of the solutions RESULTS staff had identified for support that year. While students were provided with the information needed to write their home-state member of Congress, Nick emphasized that the local representative, Matthew McHugh, sat on a key subcommittee allocating foreign aid and that sending an appeal to him might make a bigger impact. I felt a sense of euphoria when I sealed my letter, which was further heightened when sixteen people held up their hands at the end to say they wanted to be part of the group, despite the requirement that all members commit to attending three meetings per month. Since the minimum number of partners was four, we were in business! Success felt sweet.

There wasn't much time left in the semester to hold meetings, but we squeezed in as many as we could. As co-founder of the group, I was in a position of leadership for the first time, and I struggled, despite my experience managing people as a student supervisor at Cornell Dining. (I worked there fifteen hours per week for my spending money.) Perhaps the difference was that this work was much more meaningful for me than getting 1,800 fellow students fed over a four-hour period. In any case, members of our group started to leave due to my uncompromising and inflexible style. Still, letters got written, and, as classes ended, we still had a core that made us one of the bigger chapters in the county in terms of the number of active members.

It was the end of my sophomore year at Cornell, and even liberal arts students like me needed to choose a major. (I had been amazed when many of my fellow students arrived on campus at the start of freshman year being crystal clear about what they wanted to major in.) I had a vague sense that the discipline of economics was central to the battle against world poverty, so I opted for that. Immediately I realized that I was short on credits in that subject area, so my father indulged me by letting me take summer classes, which he paid for.

A highlight of that summer was attending my first RESULTS national conference in Washington, which included an inspirational banquet with great speakers whom Sam introduced to the delegates only after he had introduced the delegates to the speakers by asking each to stand up if they had hit certain advocacy milestones. The next morning, we all headed to Capitol Hill to lobby for various pieces of legislation related to reducing poverty. I recall emerging from Rayburn building with Julia after having visited with Rep. McHugh's staff member Gary Bombardier. My excitement and high sense of purpose had not been dulled at all when, at the last minute, we did not get to meet with McHugh himself.

I kept the Cornell RESULTS chapter alive over the summer, as a few students who were involved stayed in the area, and we had by then attracted a handful of members from the local community. The lobbying approach of RESULTS at the time was organized around monthly actions—usually letters to one's senator, U.S. representative, or the editor of the local newspaper. The first meeting of the month was a nationwide conference call lasting two hours. Partners in all the cities with active chapters gathered around the inevitable Radio Shack speaker phone and listened to updates from staff on the current month's action as well as past campaigns. The highlight was hearing a guest speaker, usually an international development expert or an ally in Congress. These took place on the first Saturday of the month. It was thrilling to hear people chime in from cities and states I had never visited, knowing there were people coordinating their letters and other advocacy with mine. That created a sense of community as well as plausibility that our individual actions could add up to big changes (which was reinforced by the track record of success in the organization's first five years of existence). Activists who are atomized and uncoordinated usually lose influence and interest, but ones who are powerfully connected to a well-coordinated network can feed on each other's wins and learnings.

The second monthly gathering was called the delivery meeting. Just the partners huddled and practiced speaking concisely about the issue of the month using some simple but effective exercises. The third was the action meeting, where partners and invited guests came together to learn about the issue, see a related video whenever possible, and then take action through writing a letter. (There was often discussion of a follow-up, in-person meeting with one's elected representatives or newspaper editorial board—though in practice those usually involved only the partners.)

The July, 1986, action meeting was held in downtown Ithaca, to make it more convenient for our growing number of community members who were not affiliated with Cornell. I was proud of the fact that nearly twenty people came on a sweltering upstate New York evening. But more exciting still was the topic. Until then, RESULTS had mostly focused on health and nutrition interventions as well as famine relief. Many volunteers, including me, felt that these were an important but incomplete response to the global hunger crisis. Malnutrition resulted from poverty, and poverty was fundamentally an economic issue. Unless people had opportunities to earn more money, health and nutrition deficits and crises would remain the norm, if perhaps less severe.

The RESULTS staff had sensed this gap in their choices of issues for us to lobby for as well, and had been searching for an advocacy campaign related to self-help economics. Staff from the International Fund for Agricultural Development (IFAD), a U.N. agency focused on rural poverty that owed its post-1985 existence to a RESULTS campaign to save it from being shuttered, had provided RESULTS an emotionally evocative video about the Grameen Bank, which was just coming on the scene as an innovative institution. (IFAD was dedicated to improving the condition of the rural poor in the developing world, mainly subsistence farmers, and RESULTS support of it was its first major attempt to go beyond advocating health, nutrition, and famine relief measures.)

When Ben Gilman, a liberal Republican from Upstate New York, introduced a bill to promote this kind of work, which it termed "microenterprise development," that was all RESULTS needed to begin a new line of advocacy. Sam Daley-Harris had mentioned on the conference call that this would likely be the first of many actions related to microenterprise, which I shared with our Ithaca action meeting attendees. Little did I know that within a year, I would be taking concrete steps to dedicate my life to supporting the founder of the Grameen Bank, the leading practitioner of microenterprise development.

Geeking Out in D.C.

MY JUNIOR YEAR AT CORNELL was something of a blur. The fall of 1986 was spent working on another Fast for A World Harvest to raise money for Oxfam, keeping the RESULTS group going and my grades up, and chasing after attractive young women. Under my leadership, several thousand students signed up to give up their meals at Cornell Dining on the Thursday before Thanksgiving, with the understanding that Cornell would donate the value of those meals to Oxfam America. I did everything I could to make sure that year's campaign was successful—it had been done annually for years—but I left out an important follow up: verifying that a check had gone to Oxfam. I did not know who to call and with each passing week my omission weighed on me more, but I never placed any calls, and feel guilty about it to this day. Perhaps the payment was made, but I will probably never be sure. This error, after so much work by so many people, continues to motivate me to this day to never take follow-up for granted unless I confirm it myself.

After having lived in the fraternity house my sophomore year (as was the rule), I moved back into the freshman dorms into a single room. My best friend, Rohit Bakshi, had graduated and left for medical school, and I had not invested enough time in the friendships and planning needed to end up with roommates off campus or in the frat house. I was a bit lonely, but it turned out to be a good thing. During the middle of that semester, I heard about the Cornell in Washington program and immediately applied with the idea that I would do my obligatory internship in the RESULTS national office. Like the Fulbright program that I would get connected to the following year, I was lucky and just diligent enough to take advantage of an excellent program set up to encourage idealistic and energetic young adults to get outside their comfort zones and prepare for lives of achievement and service.

Before I knew it, I packed up my Honda Civic—my second one, after having crashed my first during the summer after my freshman year—and headed to Washington, oblivious to the snowstorm that lay ahead of me. I arrived on a wintry night in mid-January, 1987, and moved my belongings into a modern apartment that I would share with a premed student named Craig Fishman. I had been assigned to Craig randomly, but he would become a close friend. From a middle-class family on Long Island, his gifts included a keen intellect, restless curiosity, and a wry sense of humor.

When I awoke that first morning in Washington, the city was essentially shut down by a snowstorm that no one in upstate New

DECIDING TO MAKE A DIFFERENCE

York would have paid attention to. I got on the metro (which, then only a decade old, was in terrific shape) and headed to the RESULTS office for my first day. No way I would miss that! Virtually all of the other students stayed in the Cornell building in Dupont Circle. When I arrived, I found Sam Daley-Harris, a bit surprised that I had made the trip, working on a mailing to be sent that day to RESULTS chapters around the country. Since my internship supervisor, the recently hired legislative director Michael Rigby, had stayed at home in Gaithersburg, Maryland, all I could do was pitch in with the mailing.

Sam was an unusual character. I idolized him as the founder of such an impressive, accomplished and aggressive organization. I had seen him on stage from the back of the room at the national conference the previous summer. On this day, he struck me as purposeful, a bit remote, and charmingly simple (the latter quality symbolized by the fact that he wore socks on his hands since he did not own gloves).

During my internship, I geeked out in ways that still make me laugh, even today. I went through the cassette tapes that Sam kept capturing moments from his work, and I studied many of them, including conference calls of the RESULTS board of directors. As I listened on my Sony Walkman, I silently applauded when he told the board that he had declined an invitation to fly to Rome to attend a reception in his honor by the president of IFAD. Sam felt that IFAD should spend its money on fighting poverty, not on buying him an airline ticket—and RESULTS didn't have enough money to send him there itself. Such principled stands, like many that I would see Sam and Yunus take in the years ahead, influenced me for years, and still do today.

I was thrilled to learn that my main assignment for the semester would relate to microenterprise development, which all the volunteers had been intensively briefed on by Michael Rigby and board chair Ernie Loevinsohn during regional conferences held around the country the previous fall. We were all excited to learn that microenterprise development, in the spirit of Grameen Bank, would be the focus of the first true "RESULTS Bill," in the sense that it was something that our staff worked on collaboratively with a congressman's team. Previously, RESULTS had mostly tagged along with initiatives of like-minded representatives and more established humanitarian advocacy groups, adding oomph, and a certain idealistic impatience, to their lobbying efforts.

When a plucky volunteer in Cleveland who worked on the reelection campaign of his congressman cornered Rep. Ed Feighan on election night and asked him if he would introduce the RESULTS bill to promote microenterprise development internationally, it led to a series of meetings and ultimately, to the introduction of the Self-Sufficiency for the Poor Act of 1987 (H.R. 910). Sam and Michael negotiated all the details with Feighan's chief of staff, none other than a young George Stephanopoulos, a few years away from the fame he would achieve as an advisor to Bill Clinton and then a television news host.

Despite strong lobbying from the staff of Foreign Affairs Committee Chairman Dante Fascell to not put the legislation forward—opposition that was softened by effective advocacy in favor of the bill by a hardy group of Miami-area RESULTS volunteers backed up by Sam (a South Florida native) and Michael—the bill was introduced in late January. (Rep. Gilman also reintroduced his less-sweeping bill, H.R. 1032, which we had written letters in support of the summer before.)

My job was twofold. First, I had to personally visit the offices of members of Congress who did not have RESULTS chapters in their districts and were not on the Foreign Affairs Committee. (Michael would handle the offices of those who were on the committee but did not have a RESULTS chapter.) Each day I would leap out of bed and head into the office with Craig, who was interning with Rep. Charlie Rangel's office doing research on domestic health care policy, which was also the focus of his thesis. (Of course, mine was on microenterprise development.) On several occasions, Craig commented to me that he felt as if we were the new generation, taking Capitol Hill and indeed the country by storm. He said it with equal measures of humor and gravity, and perhaps a touch of awe. Such are the pretensions of young adults in enriched learning environments.

I met with dozens of Congressional staff. I was a bit surprised that they generally would agree to meet with me, an intern barely twenty years old, and even more that they would listen to my arguments in favor of the legislation. (As I later realized, the foreign affairs staff of members of Congress who do not specialize in that area get few visitors except when some issue is in the news and/or up for a high-profile vote.) When a few of those offices co-sponsored the bill, I was overjoyed. Ultimately, 105 House members co-sponsored the legislation by the time it was integrated into a larger bill passed by Fascell's committee. I had been part of getting more than a dozen of them on board. By that point, Senator Dennis DeConcini had introduced a companion bill in the Senate, and the initiative had real momentum.

My other task was to find examples of other microenterprise programs besides Grameen Bank, especially since some were prone to write Grameen off as a fluke that was mainly a function of its founder's charisma. I located some studies about other programs in Bangladesh as well as a large one in Indonesia, the Badan Kredit Kecamatan, and a handful in Latin America and Africa. These weren't much, but they were enough to parry the "fluke" critique.

I watched in horror as USAID, the agency that would be tasked with implementing the bill's call for $50 million in new spending, as well as some more staid humanitarian groups who got millions in dollars of grants from USAID, pushed back fiercely against Sam. They called him misguided, in over his head, and much worse. Despite having a tiny staff and being opposed by dozens of consultants, lobbyists, and USAID allies, RESULTS rebutted the key critiques effectively and kept its key Congressional allies on board.

Picking Up the Trash

LOOKING BACK ON MY FIRST FORAYS into social activism as a RESULTS staffer, some of the lessons that I gleaned stand out for me.

I suppose my tendency to feel as if I had the answer to every problem and the responsibility to try to apply my solutions goes back to my days working for RESULTS (which I did a couple of years after my internship there described immediately above). I felt woefully underprepared for my job as RESULTS' legislative director which started in October 1989, but I learned how to fake a sense of confidence. In time, I even learned to fool myself; I would feel competent even when I knew, deep inside, that I was not. It's a pitfall of the fearless fake-it-till-you-make-it posture that sometimes feels like the only way to survive when you are in over your head.

My feigned overconfidence worked well enough, in combination with my (very) raw intellect and my ten months of field experience in Bangladesh, which gave me some credibility. I tended to impress RESULTS staff and people in Congress despite my youth and inexperience. Being a solid and occasionally excellent public speaker helped enhance my standing. But at my core, I felt out of my depths, an imposter.

With the benefit of hindsight, having to fake a sense of confidence took its toll on me. I imagine it does on many young professionals who take positions that entail significant responsibility and leadership demands, and where their peers are mostly ten to twenty years older than they are. It almost felt as if I was living a double life. On the one hand, I knew that I was a twenty-two-year-old with limited life and professional experience and rough around the edges in everything from table manners and personal grooming to my diplomatic and problem-solving skills. On the other hand, I was someone expected to confidently and calmly provide solutions, inspiration, strategy, and dispute resolution to hundreds of people, many of whom were much older than I was.

I responded by putting in long hours, reading voraciously, and adopting mentors. It all worked fairly well, even during my six months of depression during the second half of 1991 (an episode I will return to later), which resulted from a confluence of personal and professional issues, not least among them being a crisis Yunus and Grameen were facing in Bangladesh that seemed existential and that I felt a great responsibility to help combat.

All of these challenges brought out some of my darker qualities, which were more pronounced in my younger days. I was overly sensitive to negative feedback. When a few people criticized my presentations at regional conferences, rather than shrug it off I complained to people about it for weeks. I was impatient and controlling, and picked unnecessary fights with colleagues. My desire to look competent and confident during my time at RESULTS propelled me into trying to solve problems that were way over my head in terms of my experience and skills.

That connects naturally with another of the lessons I took from my RESULTS experiences—my belief in the power of taking the initiative to fix (rather than simply complaining about) societal problems of any size and shape.

Here's a tiny example that illustrates how thoroughly this attitude permeated my life. At some point during my early years living in Washington, I began to pick up garbage on the street when I walked from my basement apartment to RESULTS global headquarters, where I worked. I would hold onto it until I passed a trashcan on the street, and then drop it in. Perhaps what prompted me was something I read or saw on television. I honestly can't recall.

During a time when I was deeply insecure about my work, doing this was a kind of service meditation. Like so much effective international social justice work, I was working on policy changes and far removed from the places and people who I hoped would benefit from my efforts. It was activism that was too conceptual and often felt unreal. It lacked the satisfaction and immediate feedback loops that work at the grassroots can provide (though working on the front lines has its own limitations and frustrations, as I was to learn). Doing something tangible on my way to the office brought a bit of balance to my work to leave the world better than I found it.

I didn't really think about what others made of this odd habit. I did take notice, however, when my friend David Schnetzer mimicked me once and picked a discarded newspaper off the street as we walked together.

I discontinued this practice during my five-year stint in Bangladesh in the mid-1990s. I suppose the fact that there was so much garbage in the urban areas there, and no place to put it, and that picking it up would have made me look weird when I was trying my best to fit in, all contributed to not doing this anymore. But when I returned to the United States in 1997, I didn't resume picking up trash here and there. I was too busy and too overwhelmed (again!) with the reality of being in over my head.

But as I worked on this book and thought through my success strategies, I was reminded of this habit from my twenties. And then I started doing it again, first during training runs as I prepared for my third marathon, and later whenever I was walking around anywhere. Just as this practice had in an earlier era, it gave me a sense of accomplishment and satisfaction that either substituted for, or enhanced, whatever I felt I was (or was not) accomplishing professionally. Perhaps this serves as a reminder that periodically inventorying your success strategies provides opportunities for reviving positive habits that have fallen into disuse.

Other examples of the same attitude are strewn throughout my life. When I felt inadequate in answering questions posed by ambitious young people about how to get jobs in the humanitarian sector, I thought about a solution: pull together a handful of young professionals who had recently broken in, have a roundtable discussion with them about what they learned and how they counsel others, record the conversation, and then publish an edited transcript of it. It took me a few years to break through the inertia I felt and to make it happen, but with the help of John Weiller, a high school intern and son of a friend from my teen years, I got it done in the fall of 2013. Even now, six years later, I refer people to it several times each month.

Here's another example: When friends began asking me how best to enjoy Key West, Florida, as they knew I loved it there, I used some downtime around the Christmas holidays one year to write a quirky guide to the city, which I have periodically updated ever since. Many people report how useful it has been. One final case: When I met Danny and Tim Carter, two terrific musicians who were struggling to make a living playing their remarkable blend of bluegrass and blues, after thinking about it for a year I formed a fan club to support them.

Seeing a need, designing a response, and acting on it can take seconds or years, depending on the scope, but I find it to be grounding, satisfying, and even spiritual. On occasion, I also think it can inspire others to get off their butts and do something they have been talking about for years. It's a way that we can each exert a positive influence on the world around us—not necessarily through any grand gestures, but often through small efforts that encourage others to join or mimic you, or do their own thing to make society at least a little bit better.

2

Choosing to Be Bold

How I had the courage to reach out to my hero, Muhammad Yunus, and the lessons for others who want to dedicate themselves to nonprofit work

LIKE MANY OF THE TURNING POINTS IN MY LIFE, my initial connection to Muhammad Yunus involved following the advice of a mentor, being bold and perhaps a bit presumptuous, following through, and leveraging my ability to write. I wrote a letter offering my talents to someone I had never met but whom I had come to admire. It all happened because of a conversation that would change my life.

Michael Rigby, my internship supervisor at RESULTS, was a brilliant, largely self-taught man who grew up in Liverpool, England, and had a gift for seeing the potential in other people and in powerful ideas. He took me aside one Friday in April, 1987, in a way that impacted my trajectory forever. Indeed, his words over the course of fewer than ten minutes would end up shaping the next three decades of my time on earth.

"Alex, what Grameen Bank is up to is truly revolutionary, and we are in the position to bring it global, to its full expression," Michael said. "But none of us have even visited it or met the man behind it. If I wasn't married and didn't have one daughter and another child on the way, I'd go to Bangladesh myself for a year to work as a loan officer and then return to this job."

At this point, Michael stopped for a dramatic pause and took a sip of water. "So I can't serve as this ambassador, this bridge. But *you* can, Alex. Go there for a year after you graduate, and become the champion of what these two organizations can do together."

I can't recall what I said in response, if anything. I do remember spending the weekend that began a few hours later feverishly contemplating this bold and flattering proposal. I didn't sleep much. Could I, Alex Counts, be the ambassador that Michael thought I could be? It was a thrilling and daunting opportunity. Was I up to it?

I composed a letter to Muhammad Yunus over the weekend. I left a draft on Michael's desk on Monday morning before heading to Capitol Hill to meet with congressional staff on the microenterprise bill. When I returned in the afternoon, the letter sat on my desk with these three handwritten words: "Great! Send it."

That afternoon, I dropped the letter in a mailbox on Second and D Streets NE, very close to the Dirksen Senate Office Building. I still walk by that mailbox several times a year and always think about the moment I sent my first message to Bangladesh.

Six weeks later, I received a letter from Yunus by airmail. He invited me to come join him. He expressed both delight and enthusiasm, but also some wariness. I ignored the more ambiguous messages and focused on the positive, and immediately began seriously thinking about and preparing myself for life after college for the first time.

Within twelve months, I learned the fundamentals of Bengali—after having struggled terribly to do the same with German and French—and crucially was awarded a Fulbright scholarship to support my first nine months in Bangladesh working for Yunus.

I would end up spending six of my first nine post-college years there with him, and the other three focused on advancing Yunus's agenda by working for RESULTS, again with Sam Daley-Harris in Washington, since their agendas by then were very closely aligned.

Writing that letter was the result of two habits or techniques that I would continue to develop throughout my career: applying the advice of mentors, and having enough of a sense of agency, courage, and boldness that I could confidently ask people—even complete strangers or people in positions of great authority—for things that many people would consider outlandish.

Winning the Votes

MY SENIOR YEAR OF COLLEGE passed quickly. It turned out that Cornell's excellent modern languages and linguistics program was one of only five in the country that taught Bengali as a for-credit course. It was the first time I demonstrated some skill (or at least sustained interest) in a foreign language. I applied for a Fulbright scholarship and two other, smaller sources of funds to support my work in Bangladesh.

Sam helped me book a personal meeting with Professor Yunus in Washington, for which I skipped classes for a day and drove six hours. Yunus was impossibly warm, treating me less like the twenty-year-old novice that I was, and more like a senior RESULTS leader who had been nominated as an ambassador to Grameen (which I guess I also was).

During the summer, Sam was the subject of torrents of criticism that had a kind of elitist tinge to them: Who was this former musician and substitute teacher who thought he could browbeat the foreign-aid establishment into falling in line behind a success story they had almost entirely missed? Over time, these attacks began to wear him down. Nearing despair, he read *The Different Drum*, a just-published book by M. Scott Peck, the author of *The Road Less*

Travelled, a monumental bestseller in the self-help genre. Peck's book urged people to form communities in which intimacy would be developed through each person sharing their "brokenness"— their hurts, their fears, their tragedies.

Impressed, Sam pulled together the regional coordinators of RESULTS—about twenty senior volunteer leaders, of which I was now one—in Evergreen, Colorado, in order to try to apply the lessons of *The Different Drum*. The goal was to create the more loving, intimate community needed to withstand the growing opposition as the RESULTS bill gained momentum. The meeting was led by Dorsey Lawson, a retired school teacher who was our main grassroots organizer based out of her home in Pasadena, California. Everyone had read the *Different Drum* and came ready to apply its lessons to deepening our collective intimacy and our commitment to seeing the bill through. It was a triumphant exercise that readied us for the final weeks of the campaign.

However, there was one dark cloud hanging over the meeting: A staff member we all admired and depended on failed to show up. We wondered what kind of personal crisis he was dealing with. Some of us speculated he might have attempted suicide. It turned out that the stress of the campaign and some personal issues had been weighing on him, and within a few months he left the organization. It was a stark reminder that advocating change aggressively can create great amounts of stress—something that I would see again, a few years later, when Mitch Snyder killed himself.

That fall, the larger piece of legislation that the RESULTS bill was attached to died, but there was a backdoor way of getting it passed through the appropriations process, where committees allocated funds to various programs. A bill like that should have been incorporated into so-called authorizing legislation, which sets the policy for individual programs, as opposed to an appropriations bill, which simply provides the funds for those programs. However, with the breakdown of the authorization process due to partisan gridlock, the appropriations bills by necessity began to incorporate policy language where needed, especially for new programs.

The Foreign Operations Subcommittees of the House and Senate Appropriations Committee were key to getting the RESULTS bill passed. Under Michael's guidance but with a lot of freedom to act independently, I lobbied Senator Alfonse D'Amato's office relentlessly, and in September he agreed to co-sponsor Senator DeConcini's bill. As a result, for the first time a majority of the subcommittee had signed on. At that moment, I felt as if I had been the pivotal advocate within the RESULTS national network to push the legislation over the top. Only a few months later, the full appropriations bill was passed with language mandating a new $50 million program in support of microenterprise development for the poor.

I was ecstatic. The thrill of this success gave me an adrenaline jolt and filled me with a sense of power that would help drive me through future years of hard work on behalf of the causes I believed in.

As if I did not already have enough to do, I created a new, unsalaried position for myself at RESULTS—that of campus coordinator. I started four student groups in upstate New York and New England, and one community-based group in Woodstock, New York. That entailed a lot of driving around and talking on the phone. In the meantime, I took some graduate-level courses and continued my run on the dean's list, which had begun during my Cornell-in-Washington semester the previous spring. (Prior to finding my passion, I'd been just a middling student.)

I spent my winter break in Washington with Jennifer, a high school beauty from the Tulsa RESULTS chapter, whom many people assumed I would marry (and I nearly did). We worked as volunteers in the RESULTS office and stayed with Michael and his family for a week. I spent the rest of my time in Washington that month immersing myself in Bengali language and culture.

The story of how this brief exposure to Bangladeshi culture came to pass reflects South Asian hospitality and, perhaps, an earlier and simpler era. A few weeks before arriving in Washington, I had written a letter out of the blue to the Bangladeshi embassy, innocently asking whether I could stay with one of their staff for a week in January in order to accelerate my learning of Bangla (as Bengali is generally called in Bangladesh). Humayan Kabir, then the second secretary of the embassy, a fairly junior role, wrote me back and said that he and his wife Ruma would be delighted to host me—which they did, extending the best of Bangladeshi hospitality and introducing me to their infant son. (Years later, Kabir would return as the Bangladesh ambassador to the U.S. and host me once again, which allowed him to reintroduce me to his son, who by that time was an adult.)

Soon after winter break ended, I received notification that my Fulbright application to study and work in Bangladesh had been given preliminary approval. But soon after that I received another letter, saying that my application was not among those accepted, though as a highly rated applicant I was put on a short waiting list.

By this time, my father had taken a strong interest in my plans to move to and work in Bangladesh. Initially skeptical, he and my stepmother pressed me on my reasons for going during a long lunch at our Jersey shore home at the end of the summer. That afternoon, my conviction won them over, and from that point on, every few weeks until my scholarship for the year in Bangladesh was confirmed, my father sent me cash in the mail to help me build up a nest egg to allow me to go. That helped me keep faith when the Fulbright grant looked uncertain.

In the meantime, I received an award given each year by the Cornell class of 1964 to the senior most committed to public service, which included a $1,000 cash prize and a full-page congratulatory message in the campus newspaper. I also received $3,000 from a fund that supported students wanting to study overseas. Finally, I got a call from Walter Jackson, an amazingly diligent and conscientious staff member at the Institute for International Education (IIE), notifying me that I had been taken off the waiting list and would be given a Fulbright scholarship after all.

My Long Road to Dhaka

WHILE I HAD HOPED TO LEAVE for Bangladesh weeks after getting the news of my Fulbright in June, 1988, the Bangladeshi embassy was slow to respond to the IIE's request to give me a one-year visa. When massive floods hit Bangladesh in August and September, it was even harder to get the embassy's attention. I grew impatient, though I kept myself busy waiting tables at a family-owned and -run restaurant specializing in Jewish delicacies from Eastern Europe and Russia as interpreted by its owner, Leah Fisher. I made some quirky friends there: a twenty-something aspiring actress named Debbie with a flair for the dramatic; Jesse, a black teenager given the job by the owner's desire to push back against the vestiges of racism; Anita, a free-spirited Puerto Rican lady; and Robin, Mama Leah's niece, who'd been found alive after the collapse of the garment district textile factory she had been moonlighting in, after which the *New York Post* deemed her fit for its front page with the headline, "True Grit!" The cooks were all black and quite friendly and good; the dishwashers, who also handled deliveries, were all Hispanic. These ethnic divisions reflected the informal caste system that characterized many restaurants of that era.

I was crushed, and my impatience was further stoked, when, during the fall, a RESULTS activist asked me whether I had *already completed* my year in Bangladesh. I hadn't even left yet! I tried to remain useful. When the members of the Cornell/Ithaca RESULTS chapter expressed willingness to attend the regional conference but lacked transportation, I drove five hours to Ithaca, picked them up, brought them to northern New Jersey, and then drove them back after it was all over.

Channeling what I had learned through RESULTS, I started writing letters to the Home Ministry in Bangladesh, urging them to speed up the approval for my visa, which probably annoyed the bureaucrats there and delayed things more. Finally, the Fulbright administrators decided that I should go on a three-month tourist visa, which the U.S. embassy would help me extend after I arrived in country.

By the time this all got sorted out, it was December. Any rational person would have waited until after Christmas to depart for what ended up being ten months overseas—my first trip outside the Western Hemisphere. But I was so impatient that I got on the next flight after receiving the initial installment of my Fulbright stipend and my visa-stamped passport from the Bangladeshi embassy. It was December 20, 1988, when my parents took me to JFK airport and ushered me to the departure gates for a Pan Am flight to London. As I neared the jetway and waved good-bye to my father and stepmother, fear gripped me. What awaited me in Bangladesh? Would I fit in? I knew I wanted to be there, but there were huge unknowns and I could not predict how I would react.

I spent a day and a half in London. I struck the pose of RESULTS ambassador when I met in person with John Mitchell, the head of the World Development Movement (roughly the U.K. equivalent of RESULTS), and talked to John Clark, a senior policy analyst at Oxfam, by phone.

It was rather jarring to read in the newspaper the morning after I arrived that a Pan Am flight had blown up over Lockerbie, Scotland. I wondered whether it was the same plane I'd flown into London on hours earlier. Finally, as I headed to the airport on the London Underground, an inebriated Englishman attacked me. I was able to fend him off easily, but he did rip the back of my blue blazer right down the middle. After all of this, I was eager to get out of London and set off for the final leg of my trip, on British Airways to Dhaka via New Delhi.

It was time.

As my flight made its way to Dhaka from London, thoughts raced through my head. What would it be like to serve as

RESULTS unofficial ambassador at Grameen? As my spoken Bengali was still quite rough, how many people besides Yunus could speak English? Was my dream of being at the leading edge of taking Grameen global feasible? If so, what would it take?

Arrival at Dhaka's international airport in the 1980s immediately confronted a visitor with all manner of out-of-date technology. However, the petty corruption I had been warned about—and for which I'd brought a carton of Marlboro cigarettes to use in buying off local officials—did not materialize in the airport, or very much at all during my ten months there. I would come to learn that Bengali hospitality ensured that most corrupt practices were only applied by one Bangladeshi to another, unless the amount of money involved was very large. In fact, I would never be asked for a single bribe during my six years living in the country.

After I emerged through immigration and customs, I was faced with one of several turning points during my Fulbright-sponsored time in Bangladesh. I was greeted by a delegation of three senior Grameen officials (two of whom would become lifelong friends), as well as a group from the U.S. embassy. There was some discussion about who I would leave the airport with, as the embassy staff had booked a hotel for me, while the Grameen team had made plans for me to stay in their training hostel within the Grameen campus in Mirpur. Everyone was pleasant, and no one seemed upset that I had not clarified this in advance. (It was long before emails or even faxes could be easily exchanged to iron out such details.)

I decided to go with the Grameen team. From that point onward, I interacted as little as possible with the expatriate community, which was centered in the Gulshan diplomatic enclave. It was a good decision, which helped me build rapport with Grameen staff at all levels, and accelerated my learning of the language and national culture as well as Grameen's organizational peculiarities.

The four of us drove from the airport late on a Friday afternoon. My eyes bugged out at the beggars with horrible deformities and all the commotion on and near the roads we traversed en route to Mirpur, one of the many districts that make up the vast, sprawling megalopolis of Dhaka. At one point, the most senior official, Mohammad Mortuza, with whom I had been speaking mostly in English (as he was fluent), got out of the car and left me with Amir Khosru and Ratan Nag, two instructors in the training institute. (Years later, Ratan would be promoted to the post of acting managing director of Grameen Bank.) We chatted a bit in my rough Bengali and their rough English, but mostly I just gawked out the window.

The first thing I had to do after arriving in Dhaka was to make my initial contact with the embassy and its team that assisted Fulbrighters. (I must pause to say that I consider Fulbright one of the best investments in soft diplomacy and international understanding in our country's history.) I spent the better part of a slightly terrifying day riding around Dhaka in so-called baby taxis (picture small, enclosed golf carts) and rickshaws, trying to find the right office. I traveled to the old U.S. embassy in the financial district (which had just been vacated), the new U.S. embassy, and finally the proper office in Dhanmondi, yet another Dhaka neighborhood. I was hamstrung by my rudimentary Bengali and my lack of knowledge of how the city was laid out, not mention my tendency to use "pure" Bengali words in cases where English words are used in modern spoken Bengali. For example, much to my amazement, even illiterate rickshaw pullers use the English word *building* (as in "office building") rather than the proper Bengali word, *dalan*.

Finally, I had arrived. The impertinent letter I'd dared to write more than a year and a half earlier had paid off at last. I was ready to begin the next stage in my education as a mission-driven leader.

3

First Lessons in Leadership

Insights I gathered during my years in Bangladesh under the wing of one of the world's most idealistic and charismatic leaders

MY TEN MONTHS IN BANGLADESH as a Fulbright scholar proved to be one of the most exciting experiences of my life—a time of amazing personal growth and an enormous broadening of my perspective on life.

One of my first opportunities to learn from my new mentor, Muhammad Yunus, came in January, 1989, when I was informed that I would be able to accompany him on a tour of Grameen Bank branches in the Tangail district of Bangladesh. These were some of the oldest branches of the bank outside of the original ones in Chittagong, and the trip was timed to coincide with the tenth anniversary of their founding. Yunus would have the chance to participate in the celebrations planned for the occasion as well as to observe the operations of the branches to ensure they were continuing to faithfully carry out his vision.

As Grameen did not have many long-term visitors like me, it was no one's responsibility to advise me on such things as what I should pack for the trip. Nor did I have the sense to ask anyone. So I just packed up my large backpack—the kind people use when they are touring Europe by train and foot—with clothes, toiletries, and some linens. Joining Yunus and me were a French film crew, charged with capturing the highlights of the tour as part of a larger documentary project.

We spent about a week visiting two or three bank branches per day, often followed by an evening "town hall" session where Yunus took written questions from several dozen employees for a few hours. Allowing employees to submit unsigned written questions, Yunus told us afterwards, would make them more willing to ask tough questions without appearing insubordinate. At times during my later career, I adopted this strategy for ensuring candor when meeting with staff members who might hesitate to challenge and potentially offend their boss.

The visits to the bank branches were festive in typical Bengali fashion. As the guest of honor, Yunus would be welcomed with rose petals thrown in his path, people bowing down to touch his feet reverently (which would always prompt him to ask them to stand up straight instead), and people chanting Grameen slogans about self-help. He would be led to a small stage with an awning where he could look out on hundreds of women borrowers lined up according to their centers—federations of up to six solidarity groups, each made up of five members. There were a small number of male centers also. Hundreds of onlookers from the neighborhood would watch on the sidelines.

The members of each of the centers would be asked to stand and be recognized. Groups of children, usually about twenty in number, would then perform, mostly by parading in front of the stage to perform traditional dances as best they could, or sometimes simply by lying down and then standing up in unison. Finally, Yunus would address the gathering. I didn't understand all of what Yunus said; my Bangla was not yet fluent. But the festive nature of the gathering transformed into rapt attention when he took the microphone and spoke in a singsong voice, alternating between serious advice, calls to action, and humorous asides. Having seen him handle such gatherings in later years, I surmise that he probably emphasized how each client had the power to ensure their families and their centers remained strong by taking practical, disciplined steps in the direction of self-help. If all the centers did that, it had the power to collectively transform the nation and redeem those who had sacrificed for the country's independence.

I sat through these celebrations bug-eyed and astonished. The last book I had read before leaving for Bangladesh was Dominique Lapierre's novel *City of Joy*, which described the depths of degrading slum life in Calcutta, the Bengali-speaking Indian city near the border of Bangladesh. Now I was expecting to feel a sense of pity for how poor women, even those touched by Grameen, were isolated and deprived. Yet here I stood, watching them utterly dominate my field of vision and create something of a colorful spectacle. I sensed their joy and pride in being part of a respected institution that in turn respected them. As I would learn, these gatherings were like Bangladeshi political rallies except that the slogans people shouted were positive ones about self-help, rather than attacks on rival political parties or chants of support for their own. Most important, the focus was mainly on the crowd and what *they* had achieved, rather than on the guest of honor.

During the evenings when there were no town hall meetings, Yunus held intense discussions with small groups of local staff members regarding issues specific to that cluster of branches. Between these meetings, the film crew and I got to talk with Yunus. I recall being rather starstruck and asking anodyne questions to the extent I dared, though as the week wore on I became more comfortable and a bit more willing to raise more complicated and challenging issues.

At one point midway through the trip, we stopped at the Tangail zonal office, where Yunus conducted interviews with young women who had applied to be entry-level employees—then called bank workers (and upon promotion, bank assistants), though later renamed center managers after a brouhaha related to an attempt to unionize Grameen's staff. The fact that the managing director of a bank serving 500,000 clients was himself interviewing entry-level staff members was a remarkable demonstration of what it meant to be a hands-on leader who wants to remain in touch with realities on the front line—another lesson I took to heart for future application.

The substance of the interviews, which were conducted slowly and in simple language that allowed me to follow them fairly well, was equally striking.

Typically, Yunus would start by asking the interviewee her name, home village, educational attainment, and why she wanted the job. Most of the young women, perhaps overwhelmed by their interviewer and the handful of guest observers including me, answered weakly, almost inaudibly, in as few words as possible. Several who warmed up a little over the course of their interview described having been married off by their families and subsequently thrown out of their husband's home because their father could not supply all of the promised dowry—a common, often tragic process that dimmed life prospects and drove some to depression, even suicide. At this stage in their lives, leveraging what was essentially (in American terms) a high school education into a job was their only hope. One woman was unable to speak at all, simply staring ahead blankly when Yunus posed softball questions. Finally, Yunus told her it was okay to excuse herself from the room, breaking the sad awkwardness we all felt.

Life at Kendua-Madhupur

TOWARDS THE END OF THE WEEK, we were taking part in some final branch anniversary celebrations in the district of Madhupur, known for its delicious pineapples and having one of the few surviving forests in Bangladesh. When I learned that the group would travel back to Dhaka the next day, I asked Yunus if I could stay behind in one of the branches, preferably a remote one with few amenities and characterized by deep poverty, even by Bangladeshi standards.

Yunus agreed. The following afternoon, I was whizzing along on a motorcycle driven by the local area manager, en route to the most far-flung branch in the Kendua-Madhupur district. This was a place I would return to repeatedly over the years.

I was introduced to the staff (six men, including the branch manager, and two women), the townspeople, and, over time, the roughly 1,500 Grameen Bank clients. Some were at first a little wary of me; I was the first foreigner to ever visit this branch (or, possibly, the entire area). My wobbly command of Bengali made things awkward. But in no time I was given a cot in the manager's residence—essentially an oversized tin shed with a dirt floor—and began riding a spare bike as I tagged along with different bank workers as they conducted their morning field visits to take part in weekly center meetings.

During this era in Grameen's history, these gatherings—business meetings with a social and social development aspect—typically took place in a shady part of the small courtyard, or under an open-air structure with a tin roof that had been constructed at the borrowers' expense, and which was used throughout the week for other purposes. Twenty to thirty women sat in rows of five on woven bamboo mats, often with children in their arms and loan passbooks filled with cash for their weekly payments in their hands.

The bank worker and I would sit in front of the group, facing the women, on our own bamboo mat. The Grameen employee would count the money, mark up his or her collection sheet and each client's loan and savings passbooks, noting who had paid their installments in full and who had not. Then he or she would facilitate the discussion of new loans (if there were any that day), and deliver announcements or messages related to changes in policy and upcoming events. Finally, the bank worker would deliver some general encouragement to the members to adopt the principles Grameen's self-help manifesto, The Sixteen Decisions, which had been composed by its borrowers with Yunus's help five years earlier.

The scale of this low-tech outreach by front-line staff was massive. By the year 2000, Grameen Bank had grown to 2.4 million clients, and the total distance travelled each day by bike or foot to reach these center meetings equaled roughly twice the circumference of the earth. By the year 2016, all these statistics had tripled.

The bank worker would also talk with the elected leader of the group of borrowers, known as the center chief. Their dialogue would be a combination of mundane back and forth about loan payments and friendly banter about local happenings such as births, deaths, politics, and the like. Surprisingly, it often took no more than fifteen or twenty minutes for everyone to basically start ignoring me; I suppose that, as the first white person many of them had ever seen, I was so exotic they didn't know quite what to make of me. In any case, they had business to conduct.

On one occasion, a tough female bank worker named Rezia Khatoon took me on a journey to a center meeting that included crossing a river on a rickety boat, for which we paid the boat's pilot a few takas (at the time, one taka equaled about three U.S. cents). At the meeting, one member said she didn't have her loan payment for the week. Rezia calmly but firmly said that payment would need to be made, and she could wait all day if necessary for the client to come up with the thirty-five taka required. I was tempted to pay the amount myself, but wisely resisted. The idea was that the client would somehow "manage" the payment by borrowing from a fellow Grameen member or a relative. Forty-five minutes passed after all the other business was done, and everyone sat around, as no one dared excuse themselves while Rezia sat there, awaiting resolution. Finally, the woman produced the full payment, and the meeting wrapped up in short order.

As we made our way back to the branch, I strung together a sentence to express my admiration for Rezia's patience and her commitment to having the women solve their own problem. She smiled weakly at my compliment, and we returned to the branch's modest concrete building, mostly in silence.

The living conditions at the Kendua-Madhupur branch were very rustic, but I loved the time I spent there. It felt like the real Grameen. With every passing visit, I became more familiar with the people, the rhythms, and the language. Food was initially a problem. I ate dinner with a group of men who stayed in a bamboo hut behind the branch office, and the cook—a woman we affectionately called Chachi, or "auntie"—would usually wait until nine or ten p.m. before delivering the meal, by which time I was generally famished. The food was also exceptionally spicy for my American tastes. Until I acclimated, which took several months, I could barely eat it. I often went into the market to buy some biscuits to sustain me through the night. My weight dropped lower than it had ever been since childhood.

As it was January during my first visit, there was a bit of chill in the air, and the bed I was given had a single sheet and no blanket. I had only sandals and no socks, so my feet got cold each night, prompting me on my second visit to bring a thick blanket—one that proved to be totally unnecessary, since it was February by then, bringing with it the warm, tropical weather that was the norm for most of the year. (Another lesson learned.)

It was on the way home from that visit, with my superfluous bedding bulging out of my knapsack, that I had my first solo adventure in the country. After a couple of weeks passed in Kendua, I felt confident enough to travel home alone by bus. Jibon Chandra Kha, the Hindu branch manager who would teach me so much in the months and years to come, took me to the provincial town of Dhonbari, five miles from the Kendua bazaar, to board a bus bound for the capital. The three-hour ride should have put me within a half-hour baby taxi trip to Grameen's campus by about seven p.m. But an hour or so outside of Dhaka, the bus broke down. At first, the conductor kept saying that it was going to be fixed, but after a half hour of waiting it was clear that this contraption wasn't going anywhere. So the hundred or so passengers began frantically waving down other Dhaka-bound buses, most of which were packed. My large, bulky backpack made it even harder for me to find a space. After a few attempts, I was able to board a bus that never completely stopped but slowed just enough for me to jump on. A passenger already on board helped pull me up.

Relieved, I stood in the back for the rest of my journey.

Insights from Bangladesh

DURING MY STAY IN BANGLADESH, I would visit Madhupur and other rural bank locations periodically. Between these field trips, I spent time in Dhaka chatting with the training instructors (in Bengali), with Yunus's senior deputy Muzammel Huq (in English), and with three other top officials who had been among the first to be named zonal managers, the most senior leadership position in the field: Dipal Barua, Shamim Anwar, and Sheikh Abdud Daiyan. All took a sincere interest in me and my learning journey. But above all, it was my sessions with Yunus himself that instilled in me the confidence and sense of purpose that still sustain me today.

After my first stay in Madhupur, I wrote a report of around ten pages and had it sent to Yunus. He had a secretary type it up and then sent for me so we could discuss it. It was a major, unexpected ego boost to have the person I considered the world's foremost authority on poverty alleviation make the time to read and discuss my ruminations on discovering Bangladesh and Grameen.

I had written about how fascinated I was by the bank workers and branch managers—their devotion to their work, the high standards they were held to, how they methodically memorized the names of hundreds of clients and client family members as one of many gestures to build rapport, and the family and financial stresses they experienced.

I also wrote about how I was impacted by the stories of clients: their simple houses, the horrors many had experienced in their pre-Grameen years, and the pride they took in the assets they had accumulated with Grameen's help. I was struck by how some clients had obviously undergone significant life changes in just a few years, while others seemed to have made very limited progress despite nearly a decade of taking loans from Grameen Bank. Being an idealistic true believer, I emphasized the success cases and paid less attention to those who showed limited or no improvement.

When I returned to Dhaka after my second stay in Madhupur and again wrote up my experiences and observations—leaving out being stranded by the side of the road on my return, lest Yunus give orders to have me reined in—Yunus told me that he thought my writing and analysis had matured in just a few weeks' time. I was over the moon with pride.

Of the dozens if not hundreds of conversations I had with Muhammad Yunus during my Fulbright year, two others stand out.

On a Friday that summer, reflecting on my desire to be at the vanguard of taking Grameen international as well as my steadily improving spoken Bengali, I began obsessing about a new idea: After my Fulbright fellowship was complete, I would move to the Bengali-speaking part of India and start a microfinance program modeled on Grameen to demonstrate that the basic model could be transplanted and adapted. Believing I had a bold and satisfying plan, I walked out of the training hostel and down to the modest, five-story residential quarters, where Yunus lived on the bottom floor with his wife Afrozi, who taught physics at a local university. (Other staff occupied the remaining four floors.) It was Yunus's day off, so I knew he would be at home.

With an absurd amount of presumptuousness, I knocked on Yunus's door and told him I had something I wanted to talk to him about. He welcomed me in. I shared my plan, such as it was, and he congratulated me and offered his support in principle. I stuck around, jabbering about related topics (like how much I had to learn about India), and at some point dinner was served. Yunus invited me to join him and Afrozi at the table. I at least had the good sense to at try to excuse myself, as I was unannounced and his cook had not planned for a third person. But he said, in words that I will never forget, something that roughly translates as, "We'll simply share what there is." I settled in for a simple dinner, feeling exultant about my decision and about Yunus's support.

With my plan for how I was going to contribute and also pay back Yunus's investment in me now settled, I relaxed and got back to my immediate learning and other assignments.

Another experience with Yunus was harder. I somehow was included in a session around the large, oval-shaped conference table in the room that adjoined his office. A half dozen visitors from Sri Lanka peppered him with questions about Grameen after having spent a few days at a branch office (likely one much better equipped to handle foreign visitors than Kendua-Madhupur). At one point, after Yunus responded to one of their questions, I jumped in and added my own perspective on the topic. I felt good to be in a position to share my wisdom about all things Grameen with people from countries that could adapt it. As the conversation wore on, I injected myself into the dialogue several more times. On one occasion, I even provided my answer before Yunus could reply. I was so focused on myself and my growing knowledge that I never bothered to notice whether my mentor was okay with my active participation.

Fortunately, Yunus didn't upbraid me in front of the visitors. But a few days later, when I was meeting with him privately, he told me he did not think it was appropriate for me to answer the guests' questions. They had come to hear him talk—not me.

I initially felt embarrassed and a bit angry at being "put in my place." On the one hand, I had clearly disappointed and annoyed him, which was disconcerting. At the same time, with the youthful arrogance and presumption that sometimes made me insufferable during my 20s (and on occasion even today), I thought that anyone with something to add to a conversation should be able to speak up. (Certainly my parents' indulgence and encouragement of me during family conversations when I was a child had had an impact.) Was this an aspect of Bangladeshi culture? Or was Grameen Bank simply an organization where only the senior-most person in the room was permitted to speak? I fortunately muzzled myself and told him I would honor his request in future meetings.

Sadly, it took me several years of reflection to realize that, especially within the context of South Asia, Yunus was right. In fact, it was very generous of him to delay his critique and to deliver it in a matter-of-fact manner and in private rather than angrily and in public.

As you can imagine, I grew a lot during my time in Bangladesh. I learned about how to observe human interactions and develop sensitivity to what they say about the ways people communicate. I learned to read relationships in another culture very different from the one in which I was raised. I learned about recognizing the differences between the way an organization and a system is supposed to work in theory and the way it actually works in practice.

Most important, perhaps, I learned at a visceral level a great deal about how leadership works—how people are motivated to give of themselves in support of a cause that is greater than their lives. I began to feel that, if I could exercise that kind of leadership in my own career, I could consider my life worthwhile.

4

Learning to Tell My Story

Experiences in learning to articulate my personal passions and communicate them effectively to others

MY WORK WITH RESULTS and Grameen Bank gave me opportunities at an early age to learn the value of being able to communicate clearly and persuasively, and to think about how I wanted to present myself to the world. One of the first of those opportunities arose when one of the most powerful television news programs in the world came knocking on the door of Grameen Bank.

I was on a visit to Dhaka in April, 1989, when Muhammad Yunus called for me to visit him in his office. I was suffering from a stomachache that had dogged me for weeks and would stick around for another month. Amidst the dry heat of a Bangladeshi April—the sort of heat that makes you want to stand still under a whirring ceiling fan—Yunus pulled out a scrap of paper and began telling me that the top-rated U.S. television program *60*

Minutes was coming to do a segment on Grameen Bank. After briefly considering and then dismissing the possibility that they were coming to do an exposé, Yunus asked me to be the host and guide for the advance team. He then showed me the piece of paper where he had written down the name of the producer who was coming in a few weeks. He had written "Patty Hussler," though in fact her name was Patti Hassler. She was one of the most prolific producers at *60 Minutes*, who was going to be working with journalist Morley Safer on the segment.

I crisscrossed Dhaka and Tangail to set up Patti's field trips to see Grameen operations, all the while still fighting off my stomach ailment. I took her to the branches in Tangail I myself had visited as a newcomer to Bangladesh, including Kendua. It was at this point that I realized that even the branch manager had language issues, as he was more than a decade removed from studying at a university where he had been required to learn passable English. Even the local area manager (the position that supervised around ten branch managers), who had good knowledge of English, spoke with such a strong accent that his language would be too exotic for an American audience.

By this point, I was so starved for contact with Americans that I wore Patti down with all my conversation during our car rides around Tangail. But she got the information she needed, some of it through an interview with Susan Davis, a program officer at the Ford Foundation whose vivacious intellect and animated speaking style convinced Patti that she had to be included in the segment.

Morely Safer arrived and conducted some interviews in Dhaka, including one that put the USAID mission director on the defensive as the "bad guy" in the segment. Many of us watched from a distance as Safer interviewed Yunus in a courtyard near his office, but we couldn't hear the back and forth until we saw excerpts on *60 Minutes* months later.

The trip to Tangail with the *60 Minutes* crew was hectic, to say the least. I had told Patti about the anniversary celebrations that I'd attended months before, and when she expressed interest in filming such an occasion, one was hastily arranged to coincide with their visit. A Hindu borrower in that branch would be featured in the segment, showing how she had built a handloom business that was employing five male weavers. The caravan moved to Madhupur, where they met with a woman who had built a movie hall, but the proposed on-camera interview was cancelled when it became clear that her husband had probably earned most of the money to build it through some kind of illegal activities.

The trip to Kendua did not go as planned. The local Grameen officials had arranged for Safer to visit a big celebration of farmers who were being served by a large irrigation pump that the bank had taken over from the government and was running on an experimental basis. I went to the event site by bicycle, over narrow roads that I feared would not support the *60 Minutes* caravan. The afternoon dragged on, and hundreds of farmers along with a dozen or so Grameen staff waited and waited. Finally, torrential rains came, and everyone scattered.

Once the rains passed, I biked three miles back to the branch, and heard that the crew had left for the Madhupur guest house, the only semi-respectable place for foreign visitors and senior government officials to stay in the area. Babar Ali Talukdar, a senior Grameen official responsible for the irrigation program, joined me in a fifteen-mile rickshaw ride in order to join the film crew. By the time we arrived, it was ten p.m. I'd had neither lunch nor dinner, and I was cranky. (Much to my embarrassment, as I recall this episode today, Babar Ali never complained, though he too had gone without food.) Fortunately, there was some curry left out from the dinner everyone else had enjoyed hours earlier, and I gobbled it down.

I learned the next day that all had not been lost. As the caravan arrived at the branch, the road was lined with Grameen borrowers, men and women, chanting self-help slogans, which was caught on film and made it into the twelve-minute segment that ultimately aired. Safer and Yunus got out of the car amidst the raucous welcome and conducted impromptu interviews. Finally, the slashing rain that dispersed our big event three miles away was caught on film to show how difficult Mother Nature could be in this tropical land.

Perhaps as a way of saying thank you for all my advance work, Safer interviewed me the next day. Foolishly, I tried to guess the questions I would be asked and rehearsed my answers, over and over. When Safer asked different questions than I had expected, I was a bit tongue-tied. This was a hard lesson about the dangers of overpreparing for a conversation or interview rather than having a rough plan and then going with the flow.

Despite Patti Hassler's efforts to include me in the segment, her editors cut me out. I was not entirely disappointed, especially once I learned that the Ford Foundation's Susan Davis received all manner of love letters and hate mail (and everything in between) for years after the segment was broadcast with her two compelling interviews. Still, I wonder from time to time whether, if I had not frozen up on camera, I would have achieved more prominence within the microfinance movement earlier in my career, and whether that would have been a good thing. Years later, Patti Hassler herself approached me about the possibility of working for Grameen Foundation as a kind of encore career, but it didn't work out.

The segment aired in March, 1990, by which time I was back in the United States. Some eighteen million viewers watched it when it first aired, and millions more when it was rebroadcast over the summer a few times. For years to come, when I would ask people how they'd first heard of Grameen, Yunus, or microcredit, many would respond, "I saw the story on *60 Minutes*."

In the course of this experience as the host and cultural guide for the *60 Minutes* team, I learned some striking lessons about the complexities of modern communications. I discovered how many people and what complicated feats of logistics and orchestration are involved in producing a filmed presentation for network television, and how crucial it is to capture facts and relationships through vivid, unforgettable images rather than relying on dry recitations of data.

The Power of Story

THE CHALLENGE OF EXPLAINING YOUR WORK and engaging the interest, understanding, and support of an audience comes in many forms to all nonprofit leaders. Indeed, it's probably one of the most important elements of the work, since our only hope of making meaningful change in the world relies on winning the backing of many people for our cause.

When it comes to making connections with an audience, I have found data, like Power Point slides, to be an overrated tool. Storytelling, on the other hand, is underrated and underused. In fact, leveraging a good story has bailed me out of many speaking and writing dilemmas.

Over the course of one month in late 1989, I was asked to speak to hundreds of activists at eight separate conferences about my year as a Fulbright scholar with Grameen Bank in Bangladesh. My first talk was a confusing jumble of abstract concepts. From the second speech onward, I focused almost exclusively on the story of one woman I had interviewed in depth during my final weeks in Asia and how microloans had helped her turn around her life. That worked much better.

Whether in private conversations or public speeches, I find that people often want to know less about the intricacies of microfinance and other social innovations I have helped develop or champion, and more about my personal story, and the stories of the people (mostly women) who have benefitted through the self-help strategies I've helped to advance. The best responses I get often come from telling stories about what I did, what impact those actions had on not just society but on individual people, and what I learned. I attached special importance to what I learned, as I felt I had an opportunity to warn the next generation of activists and social enterprise leaders to avoid the mistakes I made and to benefit from the things I had discovered along the way. While some of the most valuable learning is based on what people experience themselves and the lessons they draw from those experiences, tips, insights, and even tricks from others can also play an important role.

You might feel a little diffident about relying on stories as the heart of your communication style. After all, unless backed by credible data and analysis, stories alone don't prove anything. This can make it seem a bit hollow or even slightly deceptive to use anecdotes to win over an audience. (As many people like to say, rather dismissively, "The plural of anecdote is not data.") But stories have crucial powers that data alone can't offer. Stories can tickle the imagination, help people understand a trend, give someone pause before making a grave and avoidable error, and instill the courage to take a risk or test a new idea. And unlike data analysis, good stories supplemented by distilled learnings have a way of sticking in one's mind for years, even decades. At their best, they can serve as sturdy guardrails against silly errors, unnecessary risks, unproductive conflicts (or conflict avoidance), and mindless adherence to an era's conventional wisdom. My experience through the years has taught me not to be afraid of using stories as a communication tool, but instead to take full advantage of their power.

When speaking to audiences about my humanitarian work, I typically refer to a few early insights that diverted me from expected career paths like Wall Street or medical school and led me instead to dusty villages in rural Bangladesh. One of these insights was the notion that most of the great problems facing humanity have been solved somewhere—often in a small pilot project or in the laboratory. Issues like poverty, infectious disease, climate change, and deforestation have all been studied extensively, and, for many of them, proven solutions exist. Once I came to this realization, I concluded that the central challenge of our time is to bring such solutions "to scale," so that the whole world can benefit from them.

I found this insight liberating, because it made daunting global problems seem manageable. The popular press tends to give the impression that humanity is beset by problems to which there are no solutions and that things are getting worse over time.

The facts say otherwise. For example, the Presidential Commission on World Hunger, launched by President Carter in 1978, found that the persistence of mass malnutrition was mainly caused by the lack of political will to end it. The same is true of most of the other major problems the world faces. Thus, solving critical global problems is more a matter of execution and prioritization than of invention. To me, as someone more comfortable with disciplined action than with creativity and innovation, this insight felt empowering; it gave me a path to action that I could imagine following with success.

Addressing the chronic underutilization of existing solutions and resources became a theme of my life. I came to appreciate how Muhammad Yunus, Sam Daley-Harris, and other mentors of mine focused at least as much on activating overlooked systems, idle assets, and forgotten people as they did on innovation. After all, aren't the very poor people served by microfinance themselves underutilized resources that can be made productive if provided with economic opportunity in creative and respectful ways?

After laying out this basic insight in my speeches, I go on to describe how I went on an intellectual journey to identify the most pressing issue facing humanity—which I decided was global poverty—and then to select a promising solution to that problem that was not operating on a large scale, but could be. Microfinance was that solution, one that I obsessively studied and have promoted for more than three decades, starting in my late teens.

In this way, my personal story becomes an avenue that allows others to share my appreciation for the world-changing power of proven poverty-reduction solutions. When I conclude my presentation by inviting people to join me in the effort to make these solutions more universally available, many respond enthusiastically.

Another lesson I had to learn—and one that I learned too late, and probably did not apply enough even after I learned it—is the importance of tasteful and strategic self-promotion. This is important even inside one's own organization—in my case, Grameen Foundation.

Like many nonprofit leaders, I'm not someone to whom self-promotion comes naturally. As a teenager and young adult, I found myself drawn to people who led by example and who did not engage in much if any self-praise. I am turned off by leaders in business, social change, and politics who spend too much energy explaining or even just hinting at how accomplished, smart, or noble they are. While I certainly disagreed with most of his policies, I preferred the diffident style of President George H. W. Bush, who resisted all the advice he received to weave more boasting into his speeches. (You can probably guess which recent president I compare most unfavorably with the elder Bush!)

However, it's also possible to err too far in this direction. Meredith Kimbell, a terrific consultant who served as my leadership coach, expressed it neatly: "Alex, I think you play the humility card too often." When I responded with a quizzical look, Meredith continued, "Alex, people want to be proud of their leader. If you keep quiet about what you are doing and rely entirely on others to talk about your achievements, you make it harder for them to be proud of you." If I had my life to live over, I would probably be more open about broadcasting my own accomplishments, particularly within the walls of Grameen Foundation, as a way of inspiring and energizing the people I worked with.

Over the years, I have also become a little more aggressive in my external communications about drawing attention to things Grameen Foundation did well, wherever possible by relying on hard data or the testimony of third parties, so as to enhance our credibility. Emphasizing what the organization accomplished, rather than what I did personally, feels more natural and comfortable to me. I have also become more willing to negotiate for more prestigious speaking roles at conferences, or to allow others to do so on my behalf.

Make no mistake, I am no shrinking violet. I have been aggressive and even dogged in speaking up for the ideas, principles, and values that Grameen Foundation embodies, even at times and in places where they are unpopular. On many occasions, my colleagues have urged me to keep quiet on matters of policy and principle, especially when my views were outside the mainstream. One of the greatest challenges of leadership is to stand up for things when no one else can or will, whatever the consequences may be, and I've tried to rise to that challenge as best I can.

I have also learned to accept and appreciate praise rather than fall into the trap of false modesty. But I rarely seek it, especially in public settings. When asked to make a speech or presentation, I always urge the person introducing me to be brief, to avoid citing a long list of my accomplishments, and to stick mainly to sharing a telling personal anecdote (if they happen to know me), and perhaps make a try at humor (even if at my expense), since that tends to relax people

When discussing something from my work that went well, I like to highlight how others, and sometimes just plain luck, contributed as much as or more than my own actions did. When exploring things that went wrong, I prefer to emphasize my own culpability, and most important, what I learned and how it made me a better professional and person.

Rising to the Occasion

NO MATTER HOW WELL you may develop and hone your communications skills, there will someday come a time when circumstances make sharing your story seem exceptionally difficult—perhaps even overwhelming.

Almost a decade after my *60 Minutes* adventure, soon after I had founded and begun to lead Grameen Foundation, I was invited by the philanthropists Craig and Susan McCaw to a rather special dinner. They were hosting Nelson Mandela, the legendary hero of the battle against South African apartheid, for a series of events in Seattle, including an exclusive dinner in their home. Among the guests were Bill and Melinda Gates and Gary Locke, the governor of Washington at the time. Bill Gates's father and various Microsoft executives were there as well. The total number of people that gathered that evening was twenty-four, arranged in four tables of six.

And at the ripe age of thirty-one, I was invited to be one of three speakers. The other two were Mandela himself and the head of a large environmental organization. The McCaws were benefactors of that organization, as they were of my comparatively tiny Grameen Foundation.

I walked into the McCaws' home and promised myself that I would concentrate hard on remembering the name of everyone I met. Overwhelmed by the occasion, I promptly forgot the name of everyone I talked to who was not a public figure or someone I already knew. I introduced myself to Bill Gates, and sensed a small dimension of how strange being famous must be when he seemed unsure how to respond. He certainly did not need to introduce himself to me because, like virtually everyone else on planet Earth, I already knew who he was.

The dinner itself was well orchestrated by the McCaws. I was assigned to a table that included Bill Gates, Sr., and Nathan Myrvhold, one of Microsoft's in-house geniuses. After every course was cleared, people shifted tables so that everyone got to spend twenty minutes or so with Mandela and his elegant wife, Graça Machel.

After the first course, Mandela spoke. After the second course, Craig introduced the head of the environmental organization. How did he do? There is no other way to say it: In the pressure of the moment, speaking to multiple billionaires and Nelson Mandela, he melted down. He could barely complete two coherent sentences in a row. It was excruciating for all of us to watch.

I was the one who was slated to speak next. During the dinner course that followed this episode, Craig took me aside and, with some combination of embarrassment, anger, and empathy, said, "Now, Alex, you won't do *that*, will you?"

I did my best to look him in the eye and said, "No, it will be fine."

I resolved in my mind to not do anything fancy, but rather to give a version of my normal stump speech at the time, with a subtle nod at the end to the potential of the people in the room to advance the cause of poverty reduction through microfinance. My six-minute oration was not spectacular, but it was solid. Certainly, it stood in stark contrast to the struggles experienced by the previous speaker.

Within two years of the Mandela dinner, Craig and Susan's foundation made a $2 million gift to start something we called the Grameen Technology Center, a major new initiative of Grameen Foundation. That big donation built on several smaller donations they had made and was followed by millions more in the years ahead. It took us longer to get Bill Gates to get on board, but within a decade his foundation gave us the largest grant in our history, amounting to $9.9 million, as well as several other donations in the $1 million to $5 million range.

Not a bad outcome from a nerve-wracking evening which represented my first time in a social setting with two of the most dynamic philanthropic couples of our time.

The crucial learning that I took away from this episode was that, when speaking publicly, if anything about the environment is very new to you, and perhaps disorienting, keep your presentation simple, and don't be too hard on yourself if you aren't spectacular. Afterward, take time to figure out how you can be unfazed by a similar curveball if it is thrown to you in the future—because it probably will be.

Here's a second, very different, example from my career.

I looked out into the crowd and assumed everyone was sweating as much as I was. I was about to speak to 800 people, but the real reason I was drenched was that it was late June in Bangladesh, and we were in a facility without air conditioning. Think being outdoors in Florida during the summer.

During this conference held outside of Dhaka in 2011, Yunus had invited me to be on stage with six other international guests to address a crowd that was mostly Bangladeshi. It was the inaugural Social Business Day, and it came at a vulnerable time for the

Grameen movement. The previous year, the Bangladeshi government, which had long treated Yunus with what amounted to benign neglect, had begun a campaign to discredit him and obstruct his work.

In response, RESULTS, under its dynamic leader Joanne Carter and with the help of other allies, convinced all eighteen women in the U.S. Senate to sign a letter to the Bangladeshi prime minister to ask her to back off. The senators pointed to the positive impact Grameen had had on the women of Bangladesh and the importance of its independence from government control. This was the fraught moment in which the first Social Business Day conference was convened.

Most of the audience understood English, and except for a few times where Yunus spoke in Bengali, all the speakers—even the Bangladeshis—used English. Yunus asked me to start the panel with an announcement about the act of solidarity from the U.S. senators. I took the microphone and walked a few steps forward, glancing briefly at the ceiling fans whirring overhead to steady myself.

Before I could start, Yunus said to the crowd, "You might not expect it, but Alex speaks beautiful Bengali." There was a loud murmur. People thought it was strange and wonderful that a foreigner had learned their language, which is little known in the rest of the world. Yunus continued, "Why don't you talk about this initiative in Bangla, Alex, so that the Grameen board members can understand?"

I was horrified. My spoken Bengali had once been excellent, but it had gradually deteriorated, since I'd only used it a few times per year since moving back to the United States fourteen years earlier. Even when I had given speeches in Bengali when I was fluent, I'd had to think ahead of time about how to express things effectively, using analogies and figures of speech that Bengali speakers would recognize.

In this moment, I had a choice to make. I could ask Yunus for permission to speak in English instead (with him translating, perhaps), pleading that I was out of practice or unprepared. Or I could do the best I could, pleasing him, giving the women clients of Grameen in attendance the ability to comprehend without intermediation, and giving the hundreds of other delegates who were bilingual the thrill of seeing a foreigner speak their mother tongue, however imperfectly.

I decided in that instant to take a swing at this unexpected curveball and try to deliver my message in Bengali. The brief talk I gave was not entirely grammatical, and after I sat down I thought of several ways I could have expressed myself better. But it still got a huge ovation from the crowd.

A few days later, I even received an unexpected compliment from Lamiya Morshed, the impressive executive director of the Dhaka-based Yunus Centre, with whom I almost always speak in English. Over tea, to my astonishment, Lamiya remarked, "My colleagues and I were impressed with the vocabulary you used, and how well you expressed yourself, Alex." It was one of the nicest compliments I've ever gotten.

Indeed, one of the hardest and most important lessons I was to learn in my early years running Grameen Foundation was this: In public speaking as in life, being impressive does not necessarily mean being perfect. In fact, sometimes simply being able to think on your feet and do a credible job in a stressful situation is the most important quality to demonstrate to potential donors, partners, or anyone else whose help and support you hope to attract.

5

Laying a Foundation

Developing the skills, knowledge, insights, and
self-awareness that would serve as building blocks
for my budding career as a mission-driven leader

WHEN MY FULBRIGHT SCHOLAR PERIOD in Bangladesh came to an end, I returned to the United States with a stock of new insights about myself, my life goals, and the skills I would need to become an effective leader in the mission-driven work I'd chosen to dedicate myself to.

For the next three years, my life had two basic areas of focus. One was the day-to-day work involved in creating the political will to end hunger and poverty—work that I typically did six and a half days per week, sometimes more. This included my new role as legislative director of RESULTS. My job involved leading, motivating, managing. and educating hundreds of volunteers, colleagues, and allies as well as opponents in Congress and the media.

My other focus was learning how to be a functioning, responsible adult living in my home country, which neither college nor the strange life I'd lived in Asia had prepared me particularly well for. This included my search for romantic adventures and a life mate—something I'd always known would be an important element of happiness for me.

These two demands on my time and energy alternatively reinforced and worked in conflict with one another.

Testing New Tactics

AT RESULTS, MY FIRST YEAR BACK HOME started with getting up to speed on everything and meeting people. Then I set to work distributing copies of our investigative report, *Where Credit Is Due*, which examined how the U.S. government had spent the funds that had been allocated for microenterprise support due to advocacy by RESULTS in 1987. We hoped the report, written by an impressive colleague named Danielle Yariv, would prompt Congress to ask for a study by the General Accounting Office (today known as the Governmental Accountability Office) and ultimately lead to better laws and more focused spending by USAID. I was also involved in crafting a bill to build on the World Summit for Children held in New York in September, 1990. When time permitted, usually on weekends, I would indulge my growing love of writing by producing opinion articles for regional and national papers. I was also trying to turn the letters I'd written to Sam Daley-Harris from Bangladesh, which Sam had shared with hundreds of RESULTS volunteers, into a long-form article for a venue like the *New York Times Magazine*.

The Summit for Children had been spearheaded by Jim Grant, a tireless champion for the UN children's organization, UNICEF. Before it began, RESULTS volunteers canvassed the country asking people to write to President George H. W. Bush, urging him to attend and support the summit. Tens of thousands of post cards were sent, and the president did ultimately go. Building on my suggestion that RESULTS get outside its comfort zone,

Sam Daley-Harris came up with the idea of holding candlelight vigils across the country and the world, on the Sunday before the summit to demand action on childhood poverty. It was a daring, costly, and tiring effort, which ultimately led to more than one million people gathering in vigils on five continents and a special segment on the *Oprah Winfrey Show* that raised more than $1 million. The Summit for Children would ultimately serve as a model for the Microcredit Summit, which became a turning point in my career seven years later.

For me, however, this new focus for RESULTS was discouraging. I felt demoralized by being the legislative director of an organization that had always been focused on legislation but that had shifted, at least for the moment, to public demonstrations and movement building. I sulked even as I worked with allies in Congress to come up with the World Summit for Children Implementation Act, which led, in 1991, to tens of millions of new dollars allocated for proven child survival and development programs.

The key congressional leader who made this happen was David Obey, ranking Democrat on the House Appropriations Committee. I had the good fortune to testify before his committee in an intimate setting the day that a *Washington Post* op-ed piece I'd penned was published. This triumph was a needed balm to make the vigils feel worth the trouble. It also made up for the failure of RESULTS to enact the Global Poverty Reduction Act, which had been the focus of our lobbying in 1988 and 1989. It gave me a feeling of agency and power, which unfortunately led to overreach in my third and final year working for RESULTS.

As if the demands of being RESULTS legislative director were not enough to keep me busy, I joined a group of activists focused on solidarity with Filipino non-governmental organizations (NGOs) working on poverty alleviation and environmental protection. They were in the process of launching a coalition called the Philippine Development Forum, and I was attracted to their methods and the people involved. (I'd enjoyed a brief but memorable visit to the Philippines during my Fulbright year.)

Ultimately, an executive committee of the forum was created and I was appointed to it. When meetings bogged down despite the raw intelligence, passion, and deep subject-matter knowledge of the other members, I volunteered to chair the committee, mainly to help keep the meetings on track. It was my first opportunity to lead a group of professionals outside the Grameen and RESULTS tribes, and it felt challenging and satisfying. That experience taught me the importance of giving people early in their careers different kinds of leadership roles so they can gain confidence and work out their kinks.

With the dawn of 1992, RESULTS was looking ahead to the Earth Summit in Rio de Janeiro as a platform for more and different forms of advocacy. We had tried something new in 1991: getting on board with the Beyond Beef campaign led by some environmental and animal rights organizations. The idea was that beef production was resource inefficient, diverting crops to feed cows rather than people, while also being environmentally toxic, and that curtailing it would be a boon to the world's poor and help to preserve the global ecosystem. This campaign had appealed to some of our activists but generally fell flat. The Earth Summit provided us another opportunity to craft an agenda around the intersection of poverty reduction and environmental preservation.

I followed a two-pronged approach to this challenge, largely on my own—which proved to be a big mistake. First, working with several leading environmental organizations we published a report card for the Bush administration's preparations for the Rio Summit, giving it a D overall and slightly higher or lower grades for individual aspects. The report card got good media exposure when we released it on the eve of the summit, being incorporated into a front-page story in the *USA Today*.

My main regret was how inflexible I was about giving credit for the report card to my co-author, Chris Darling of the National Audubon Society. I didn't want the report card to seem to be the work of renegade individuals within our two organizations—which, in a way, it was—by listing Chris and me prominently. So I insisted that both our names be stricken from the report, and only the sponsoring organizations be listed. Darling was deflated, but ultimately agreed. With the benefit of hindsight, I should have compromised and arranged for the acknowledgements page to mention Darling and me. But, typically for me at that age, I was too self-righteous and inflexible to consider compromise and an alternative option that would have worked for everyone.

In the future, when I found myself digging in on a position, I often thought back to this mistake and reminded myself to take a step back to look for win/win options rather than trying to force my view of what was right onto others.

My other priority was to come up with a new RESULTS bill that would address the shared agenda of environment and development while being as sweeping as the failed Global Poverty Reduction Act, as inspirational as the Self-Sufficiency for the Poor Act, and as tangible as the World Summit for Children Implementation Act. I felt a keen sense of responsibly to come up with something special, and I failed miserably. My biggest mistake was spending too much time reading about the issues involved, and not enough time talking to people in organizations that could help us craft and enact such legislation, finding out what they were passionate about.

The result of my efforts was the Earth Summit Leadership Act. It proposed that some of the funds then going to the Economic Support Fund, essentially a slush fund available for the secretaries of state to use in shoring up the budgets of allies (including some rather unsavory ones), would be diverted to create a new Foundation for Sustainable Development modeled on the Inter-American Foundation, but larger. I did succeed in getting Oxfam America, World Neighbors, and several leading environmental organizations to get actively behind it, and Rep. Wayne Owens, a Democrat from Utah, agreed to introduce it in the House. The RESULTS volunteers were, in general, excited about it. But as the bill came together, Sam progressively distanced himself from it, and I did nothing to change his attitude. In the end, Sam's indifference, and the failure to get the bill introduced in the Senate, doomed the effort. Had Wayne Owens won the Senate seat he ran for in 1992, the bill might have gotten new life, but, alas, he did not.

I was deflated. I had a vision of spurring a microcredit revolution while also writing a book about the nascent movement before I turned thirty years old. Ultimately, I concluded that returning to Bangladesh would give me the best chance of making a unique contribution to that movement. I began plotting how I could return to Grameen and Bangladesh.

My final assignment at RESULTS was to help choose my successor. Michael Rubinstein, a friend and a distinguished RESULTS volunteer from Maryland, was a finalist, as was Joanne Carter, a veterinarian from suburban New York who was likewise a productive and committed activist. I took part in the interviews with both, and with Sam's support we offered the position to Joanne. She went on to occupy the role for nearly twenty years, and later took over as the executive director of RESULTS. She has done a tremendous job leading the organization into a new era and making an impact on hunger and poverty by advancing effective policies by the governments of the United States and other countries around the world.

Discovering Emily

AS FOR MY OTHER MAIN PRIORITY at this time—finding a partner to share my life with—that was a quest that would ultimately end in complete success. Like many people, I found that it happened unexpectedly.

In the aftermath of our candlelight vigils campaign in late September, 1990, the RESULTS staff and volunteer base was in no condition to organize eight regional conferences that fall, as had been the custom. Instead, they were delayed until January and held on four consecutive weekends early in the year. I was one of two staff members who was to attend all of them. That meant visiting two cities each weekend, sometimes speaking at the second conference fresh off a red-eye flight from the other side of the country. Never did we take any compensatory days off—that just wasn't part of the culture of this scrappy advocacy organization.

On a Sunday in mid-January, 1991, I was scheduled to speak to a gathering of about thirty activists from California and Nevada. I had made a big presentation the day before in Omaha. It was a beautiful Northern California winter day, and everyone except the presenter was seated in a semicircle at the international student center on the Stanford University campus. I was introduced briefly by Lynn McMullen, who was destined to play a major role in some later stages of my career, including as a founding board member of Grameen Foundation. I then began my spiel, which focused on how we chose legislative issues for the volunteers to lobby on.

About twenty minutes into my hour-long talk, three women entered the room and sat down. A quarter-century later, I can still remember the positive energy they brought into the session. I noticed their smiles, their gait, and the bouncy head of blond hair on one of them. I knew that once my part of the presentation was over, I was going to try to get to know those women.

Unbeknownst to me at the time, these three ladies had come from Reno, Nevada. They'd been debating that morning whether or not to ditch the conference in order to explore the gorgeous weather and many attractions in the Bay Area. Finally, Barb Scott, the group leader (and the one with the blond hair), said with a laugh over breakfast that they should do the right thing and go to the conference after all.

When my presentation ended, I passed the baton to other speakers and took a seat next to one of the women from Nevada—a six-foot tall lady whose easy smile and winning personality would charm me for the rest of the day. It wouldn't be long until I introduced myself and learned her name: Emily.

I had intended on getting to know all of the three Nevadans that day, but I never got beyond spending time with Emily. She was pleasant to talk to, and treated me like a friendly guy who was nearly two years her junior (not to mention three inches shorter), rather than as an intimidating senior staff member. After her group left for Reno, Lynn came over and said with a smile, "You really connected with the tall one!" At about that time, Emily's friends were gently teasing her in the car about the same topic.

The following week was a busy one. Regional conference season was always hectic; during that period, I went a month without any days off. But despite the demands of that period, I was determined not to lose track of Emily.

On the Tuesday after the conference, I called Barb Scott and meandered through a slightly awkward conversation that was held under the pretense of discussing RESULTS business. Finally, I asked if she thought it was a good idea for me to call Emily. Stifling a laugh, she encouraged me.

It took a few more encounters in various places for me to generate as much interest on Emily's part as I felt from the beginning, but in a while we became a couple. We've remained one ever since.

Becoming an Author

MEANWHILE, I'D DEVELOPED A GNAWING DESIRE to write a book on Grameen Bank. I knew I had some talent for writing, and I felt that producing the first mainstream book about Grameen could be a significant and unique contribution to the microcredit movement.

One day, I got a letter from an editor at Doubleday named Joel Fishman who was interested in a book on Grameen. I responded enthusiastically, and with his encouragement and support I wrote a book proposal. However, a few weeks after completing it, Fishman told me he could not sell the idea to his colleagues within Doubleday. He mentioned in passing that he was thinking of leaving Doubleday and setting up his own literary representation firm, and if he did so he would be willing to take me on as a client.

By the spring of 1992, I'd decided that I was going to move back to Bangladesh to devote nearly my full energies to writing a new book proposal with Joel's help. I hoped this would yield a book contract from a major publisher that came with an advance to cover my living costs in Bangladesh. I really didn't think through all the details as I should have, but youth and a certain self-confidence bordering at times on swagger—something I had drilled into myself as a survival strategy even this early in my career—allowed me to move forward despite all the uncertainties and risks. My only concern was what to do about my deepening relationship with Emily.

Somehow, my harebrained plan to "have it all" worked. I got engaged to Emily, moved to Bangladesh, found some interesting work to do with Yunus to complement my book writing, and was connected to a terrific research assistant named Abdul Mannan Talukdar who had worked at Grameen for a long time. I decided (after a number of arguments with Joel that he ultimately won) to devote a substantial portion of the book to an early effort to replicating Grameen in a U.S. inner city, and I wrote a proposal based on this approach. Three major publishers bid on the proposal, and because Random House offered the most money—$20,000—I signed with them. I raised a bit more money from two foundations—the Fund for Innovation and Public Service established by Bill Drayton, the visionary founder of Ashoka, and the Wallace Global Fund—and I sent in the first four chapters of my book in order to get the second installment of my advance (so I wouldn't go completely broke).

Writing the book allowed me to sharpen my eye for telling detail while immersing myself in the lives of a handful of poor women. I initially chose to write about a branch in Tangail where my research assistant Mannan had worked from 1980 to 1983, during his first four years at Grameen. In many ways it was perfect, and I spent much of the first half of 1993 learning everything about the place.

But an incompetent and ambitious regional manager in Tangail was increasing loan sizes indiscriminately in a way that Mannan and I thought would lead to some major delinquency issues, which in fact came to pass. So, midway through my two-year research program, we pivoted and began anew in the Grameen office that Mannan had founded and managed in 1987. The branch, Shaymganj Deloutpur, was on the banks of the Jamuna River, two hours west of Dhaka. The village we ultimately chose at this branch—Kholshi—had a lot going for it as a place to base my research.

The extended periods in the village of Khoshi gave me a deeper understanding of Grameen's operations and of rural life in Bangladesh than I had gotten from my readings or my time as a Fulbright scholar. The many in-depth interviews I conducted included structured sessions with Grameen clients as well as informal chats at the local tea stall with neighborhood men—always men—and catching up with the bank staff over dinner in their communal kitchen. More important, I had the chance to get deeply acquainted with rural Bangladeshi life and, in particular, the realities of four very different women: two Hindus, Shandna Rani Halder and Nonibala Ghosh, and two Muslims, Amena Begum and Fulzan Begum.

What made the book research even more interesting, but also much more complex and expensive, was studying the replication of the Grameen microcredit method on the south side of Chicago, as mandated in my book proposal and as agreed with Random House. The project was called the Full Circle Fund, and it was run by a local group called the Women's Self-Employment Project (WSEP) based on advice provided by Grameen.

I took seven trips to Chicago, most lasting about ten days but including one that took up most of the summer of 1994. After my second visit, I settled on five African-American women in a single group who were willing to be studied and agreed to keep a diary in between my visits via cheap tape recorders I had bought them. I later added another woman whose story and personality were equally compelling.

I got to know these six women and their families better than I know many members of my own extended family. We talked about business, race, politics, intimate family matters, and more. A few of the insights about the people and realities of microfinance in the United States formed during these visits left a deep impression on me and would continue to crop up in my speeches for years to come. Indeed, in many ways these months were as revelatory for me as my time in rural Bangladesh. For example, I was struck by how the peer support and peer pressure that were crucial to the success of the Grameen lending model worked as well in inner-city Chicago as it did in Bangladesh. This insight helps to explain the spectacular success of Grameen America since its founding in 2008.

Also remarkable was the vibrancy of the so-called informal or black-market economy and its importance to many entrepreneurial families in struggling neighborhoods. There were street festivals (often including many arts and crafts vendors) but also house parties and trunk shows to sell all kinds of handmade and bulk-purchased products. Other informal businesses that played a huge role in the local economy included lemonade stands, vendor tables set up a night clubs, home-based day care centers, car detailing and lawn maintenance services, pushcart vending operations, food trucks (long before they became trendy on the East Coast), and much more. People who liked flexibility, or more often had family situations that required it, gravitated to these microbusinesses as a way to patch together enough monthly income to stay afloat and aid less fortunate or industrious family members. Not having college educations also played a role in limiting their options in the formal job market.

As in Bangladesh, the normal ways of thinking about economics and business did not apply to the inner-city microenterprises I studied in Chicago. When economists and the general public talk about people launching businesses, they tend to assume that their success should be measured by how much revenue and profit they generate, and by how long they remain in operation.

The reality is that people in the survival economy have multiple income-generating strategies that they switch among as the seasons change, or sometimes in the course of a single day. In this context, how long a business remains alive is meaningless, as it is simply one of many strategies that a poor person uses to patch together enough income to live on, and hopefully to slowly build surplus assets.

I was struck by how easy it was to develop trust and rapport with these African-American women, who were mostly a decade or two older than I was. Just showing up day after day, demonstrating sincere interest in their lives, and not putting my white male foot in my mouth too often, made it possible for them to come to trust and even, at times, embrace me.

The dramatic high point of the journey occurred when the leader of the women's group, Omiyale DuPart, got into trouble when she was cheated by a partner who was supposed to be importing some art work from Africa. Her ballooning debts endangered the loans for the others as the busy summer festival season approached in 1994. Omiyale went back to basics and began selling bags of homemade butter cookies and fruit on the on-ramp to the freeway that bisected Chicago's South Side. The money she raised in this way let her pay off her loan in the nick of time. Even today, Emily says she cannot read the scene in the book when Omiyale makes her final payment without crying. I was fortunate to choose women so open to my prying into their lives.

I learned some lessons about the politics of writing a book. When Omiyale was sent a copy of the galleys, which are basically the final proofs of the pages before they go to press, she became uncharacteristically enraged by some mildly critical comments about things like her often running behind schedule. She responded by faxing me photocopies of pages from the galleys with handwritten instructions about which sections she wanted deleted or changed.

When I shared this story with an author friend, he responded, "It's one thing to agree in principle to be written about in a book.

It's another thing to see that book on the verge of being published and your name being immortalized in it."

In the end, I gave all the women in Chicago the option of requesting that I substitute a fictionalized name for theirs. They all opted instead for me to use their real names, which was reassuring. When I was updating the book in 2007 to meet renewed demand after the Nobel Peace Prize was awarded jointly to Muhammad Yunus and Grameen Bank, I tried to track down all the women. The only one I could reach was Omiyale, who spent the better part of an afternoon that summer telling me about her life since 1996, and what she knew about the others in her group, which had disbanded in the late 1990s.

Writing *Give Us Credit* brought me many benefits. They included deeper insights about poverty in my own society, the enhanced credibility that came with being a published author prior to my thirtieth birthday, and the way I improved my writing skills with the help of the professionals at Random House. Most important, I learned much more about microcredit and the culture and society of Bangladesh, which would continue to play outsized roles in my life and work during the years to come.

The Years with CARE

WHEN I SPEAK ABOUT the early part of my career, I sometimes say that I lived in Bangladesh and worked with Grameen Bank for six years. This shorthand explanation is a bit misleading. It was actually more like five and a half years, and I spent the last two years working for CARE, one of the world's largest humanitarian organizations, while devoting my evenings and weekends preparing to launch the Grameen Foundation. Here's how it all came about.

At the end of 1994, Emily and I were at a crossroads. The manuscript for my book was complete, and Emily had experienced life with me in Bangladesh for a few months. I had proposed some ongoing work with Grameen Bank and Grameen Trust, but my ideas were politely rebuffed. Neither Yunus nor I was ready to start a Grameen-branded organization outside of Bangladesh, much less put me in charge, at the age of twenty-seven.

Another reality we faced was that Emily and I were broke. The $20,000 book advance from the publisher had been spent months ago, as had the small grants totaling $7,500 that I had cobbled together.

We returned home for Christmas, needing to figure out what was next. One possibility was to move to Kenya, where a friend from Bangladesh who was a senior official with UNICEF was willing to give Emily an eleven-month contract to use her skills as a nutritionist in battling the famine in Somalia. But then our friend was scapegoated and fired for some scandals that occurred on his watch.

Soon, three new opportunities for me emerged: to take a position with Opportunity International, a faith-based microfinance network, to open their Washington, D.C., office; to take over as the head of the Microcredit Summit, which Sam Daley-Harris was in the process of launching; or to work for CARE Bangladesh as a regional project manager overseeing their Integrated Food for Development program in one-third of the country.

As of mid-January, CARE was in last place in my calculations, a kind of backup plan. But when I interviewed with Opportunity, my youthful looks and demeanor (and perhaps a degree of overconfidence) led to the disappearance of that option. Then I got cold feet about the idea of working for Sam again. That left the CARE job. We moved back to Bangladesh in February.

In many ways, the two years I spent working for CARE was a forgettable part of my career. I worked hard at times, but put in nowhere near the hours I had before or would do later. I also became distracted, especially in 1996 as the Microcredit Summit loomed and Yunus began to warm to the idea of starting an international arm of Grameen and putting me in charge. I started spending my evenings and weekends, and sometimes (I am now ashamed to say) even my work days, volunteering for Grameen, helping to prepare for its delegation's participation in the summit and laying the groundwork for what would become Grameen Foundation.

In other ways, however, my twenty-four months at CARE were excellent preparation for the life Emily and I would soon begin back in the U.S. For example, I experienced what it was like to be in upper middle management. CARE had 1,600 local employees as well as about twenty foreigners, and I was among the most junior foreigners. Since I could speak their language, many of the Bangladeshi staff confided in me in ways they would be unlikely to do with other expats. Indeed, several of the Bangladeshi engineers I worked with at CARE remain friends of mine to this day. I was able to see a large organization working in a developing country through the eyes of the rank-and-file staff, observing how they experienced well-intended decisions that helped or harmed them in their work. I also got my first real opportunity to manage a large team, and to coordinate with other leaders and managers. I did neither particularly well, but I was at least able to start the process of becoming a solid manager and leader.

At the same time, I was able to put some energy into turning my manuscript into a published book and take the time off to do a twenty-one-day, low-budget book tour. Random House, which was surprised by the low number of preorders for my book, allocated just $1,000 for my tour and related expenses—barely enough for one event as traditionally budgeted. I was able to buy tickets on the cheap that allowed me to visit eleven cities on both coasts and the Midwest for $1,100, which surprised and pleased the publisher. I was put up by friends, in most cases RESULTS volunteers, in each city. Ultimately, Random House reimbursed me for the entire $1,100. (A few months later, *Give Us Credit* was also published in India, and I went there in August, 1996, for a short tour that included quite a bit of coverage in national newspapers. A post-Nobel Peace Prize edition of *Give Us Credit* came out in 2008 with a new title: *Small Loans, Big Dreams*.)

Those two years with CARE were also pivotal for Emily, though some aspects of living in Bangladesh were very hard on her. She never mastered the language, despite some determined efforts. As a six-foot-tall white woman, she was occasionally harassed on the street, especially if I was not around. In one case, it nearly turned violent and included stones being thrown at her by a group of male construction workers. The work Emily did during the first of these two years did little to leverage her skills as a newly minted holder of a masters of public health degree from the prestigious Johns Hopkins University. Mainly she edited the English-language annual reports for medium-size local nonprofits in exchange for payments roughly the equivalent of $500. It was not an easy time for our young marriage, as I was a clueless husband in many respects, unable to empathize with what she was going through. However, it did give us more time together than we had had or would have in the next phase of our lives.

I finally allowed myself to experience life as an expat, influenced in part by the fact that Emily never picked up Bengali, which made it awkward to spend social time around people who didn't speak English well. We became regulars at the American Club in Dhaka, where I played a lot of tennis and squash, and we were fixtures in the bar where we became favorites of the local staff, in part because I was one of the rare Americans who spoke their language. They allowed us to play the albums *Eagles Live* and Bob Seger's *Nine Tonight* each Thursday night from beginning to end, week after week, reflecting my tendency to assume that too much of a good thing is a good thing.

Most important, during her last year in the country, Emily was able to land a job with BRAC, the highly respected, Bangladesh-based nonprofit dedicated to social and economic development. She worked for a local salary of $300 per month with some incredibly talented women doctors who staffed BRAC's health division. They included the elegant Sadia Chowdhury, whose fluent English and poise were such that she often moonlighted as one of the broadcasters on the national English language newscast, and Zeba Mahmood, a highly competent physician with strong organizational skills and an easy, quirky wit that always made her a pleasure to be around. While Emily had access to other BRAC leaders, including Fazle Abed, the founder and chairman, Sadia and Zeba were her special mentors and friends. The work she was able to do with them propelled her into a demanding but mostly satisfying career at USAID starting in 1997.

It's unfortunate, in my view, that some people involved with Grameen and BRAC considered the two organizations to be rivals, even though there was grudging mutual admiration among many of the top people in both organizations. I joked at the time that since Emily was connected with BRAC and I was with Grameen, ours was a "mixed marriage," which usually got a laugh among Bangladeshis and knowledgeable outsiders.

As the time for our departure from Bangladesh approached, I resolved to see some of the sights of Bangladesh that I had never properly explored. Emily and I visited the tea gardens in Sylhet and the beach resorts and Buddhist temples in Cox's Bazar. I spent time in Old Dhaka, wandering around and getting on a small wooden boat to see the city from the big river that flowed by it. I intended to visit the Sundarbans mangrove forest, one of the world's largest, but got food poisoning one final time while in Jessore as I finished up some work for CARE, which scotched that plan.

Sometimes, when I talk about my years in Bangladesh, I gloss over the time spent working for CARE. I suppose I still see development in Bangladesh through the eyes of the local leaders who, to varying degrees, resent all the foreign people and organizations that drove major projects, allocated resources, and determined priorities, especially during the first thirty years after independence. Working for CARE, even briefly between long engagements with Grameen, felt a little like selling out. But international organizations based in rich counties, such as CARE, World Vision, Mercy Corps, and even Grameen Foundation, have played positive roles in Bangladesh and elsewhere. I am not proud of how I have occasionally minimized my involvement with CARE, and I hope to stop succumbing to that temptation once and for all.

6

Running My Own Show

Launching a nonprofit dedicated to realizing
my own vision—and beginning to master
the challenges of leading an organization

EMILY AND I ARRIVED in the Washington, D.C., area from Bangladesh in the final days of March, 1997. We didn't bring many possessions with us from Bangladesh—we didn't own very much at the time—but we did have a half-dozen large suitcases that we piled into the den and basement of our friends Geoff and Jacki Drucker, who agreed to put us up in their home in Arlington, Virginia, for a few weeks. Our stay ended up being extended to four months.

We were there in D.C. to launch my new nonprofit—the Grameen Foundation, the first organization outside of Bangladesh to use the Grameen brand.

I was just thirty years old and had less than $10,000 in start-up capital, $6,000 of it in the form of a seed money grant from Muhammad Yunus himself. That grant represented half the interest earned on the World Food Prize, which Yunus had won in 1994; it had been sitting in a bank account, awaiting permission from the Bangladeshi authorities to bring it into the country and be used for poverty alleviation projects there.

My other resources were equally meagre. I had few contacts and fewer qualifications. My main asset was my association with Yunus, along with my knowledge of how Grameen actually worked in Bangladesh and how it had been successfully adapted in Malaysia and the Philippines.

Yunus had initially suggested that I start Grameen Foundation. He also helped get it off the ground, not only by providing some seed money but more importantly by making it a priority to attend our board meetings and donor cultivation events for the first five years and sporadically thereafter. This encouraged others to join the board and then show up and contribute. Ultimately, Yunus loosened the reins and let me and my colleagues take GF in the directions we thought best without interfering, though he remained accessible when we needed him. Yunus was not always pleased with all the decisions I made, but he kept his occasional displeasure with us out of public view, which was generous of him.

In 1997, all of this was still in the future. The brand-new GF was housed in a small room within the RESULTS/ Microcredit Summit Campaign offices on Capitol Hill. Emily and I showed up on April first and surveyed the scene, feeling some dread mixed with a sense of history. Soon details filled up our time and minds, and the magnitude of the opportunity and risks receded into our subconscious.

I knew the limitations of this building well from my days working for RESULTS five years earlier. Cockroaches were known to crawl out of one's computer, and many other unexpected locations, at any time of day or night. Our little room was filled with leftover books and textile products from the Microcredit Summit, which had been held seven weeks earlier. Soon we would install a computer and take delivery of hundreds of copies of *Give Us Credit*, which we bought for around two dollars each from Random House.

Emily agreed to work for GF for two weeks until Geoff Davis arrived after a cross-country drive. I'd bumped into Geoff during the Microcredit Summit, and he'd agreed to become my first regular employee.

We got to work. Equipment needed to be unpacked and set up, phones connected, prospective donors and board members met with. If I'd been someone who easily got overwhelmed by details and tasks that I did not know how I was going to complete due to lack of time and expertise, I would have been frozen with paralysis during those early months. But I just pumped up the adrenaline, used a good night's sleep to recover when I got weighed down, and embraced the adventure of it all.

Geoff turned out to be a hard-working soulmate who shared my sense of adventure and agency. When he noticed how much work needed to be done, he made some phone calls to Utah, and within a couple of weeks three energetic Mormon students from Brigham Young University showed up, ready to work long hours all summer for no pay beyond the satisfaction of being part of an idealistic startup. Geoff went on to do terrific things for the humanitarian movement over the course of his career, and he became a lifelong friend.

On May 5, Jacki Lippman, whose house Emily and I were squatting in, organized a successful fundraiser for us at an Indian restaurant near the office. Within a few months, she became a full-time employee. Lynn McMullen, then the executive director of RESULTS and also a GF board member, provided sage counsel to me, pitched in on projects like this first fundraiser, and, even more important, was someone I could share some of my anxieties and insecurities with.

When some of the first donation checks cleared, we rented a tiny office on another floor of 236 Massachusetts Avenue, while retaining the one in the RESULTS suite for the time being. We began selling Grameen publications. It seemed that GF was up and running for real.

Making a Splash

WE SOON ENJOYED our first big media success. A friend of my younger brother happened to be the daughter of Walter Anderson, the publisher of *Parade* magazine, the weekly supplement that accompanies hundreds of Sunday editions of newspapers around the U.S. She suggested the idea of a story about Grameen to her father, and he bit. I had originally hoped that *Parade* would cover Grameen by serializing my book, *Give Us Credit*, which had been published the previous year. It turned out that Walter assigned Michael Ryan to write a story on Grameen, which included making a trip to Bangladesh. But Ryan was kind enough to agree to quote both me and my book, and to encourage readers to contact Grameen Foundation if they wanted to get involved.

By the time the article was due to appear, my former research assistant Mannan had come and gone for a two-week visit to the U.S. that I paid for personally despite GF's flimsy finances—it just seemed like the right thing to do. I cancelled a planned trip to a college reunion to spend a weekend freshening up our very basic website in anticipation of a possible flood of interest. After all, I knew that *Parade* reached sixteen million people, which meant the article would bring us publicity equivalent to $1.6 million in advertising.

Immediately after the article ran, a few phone calls came in to our offices. But more encouragingly, about 1,600 letters and emails arrived, some with checks or promises to send year-end donations. This helped us begin to build a mailing list, and showed the power of media coverage to help or, occasionally, harm us—a recurring theme in the years ahead.

Challenges Accepted

AS OUR FIRST TRUE STAFF MEETING approached in September, 1997, I felt a sense of anxiety out of proportion with the moment.

I had participated in and even led meetings in professional settings off and on during my first twenty years in the workforce. But I nearly froze up as I walked into the RESULTS conference room, which we occasionally used for meetings as an alternative to the Subway restaurant on the ground floor of our building. Somehow I slogged through the agenda, and perhaps the small staff did not pick up on my unease. Within minutes of that awkward milestone's passage, I was back at work trying to keep the organization afloat so that it could one day become a confident and respected player in the movement to end world poverty.

Our initial agenda was set in part by requests from Muhammad Yunus. We agreed to help raise $10.6 million for Grameen Bank to invest in the rapid expansion of GrameenPhone, the for-profit company that was providing millions of women with the opportunity to launch microbusinesses as "phone ladies" in their local villages. That led to some dramatic fundraising challenges that I'll detail a little later in this book.

We also responded to another of Yunus's priorities: revitalizing the handloom industry in Bangladesh. Thousands of handloom weavers were Grameen borrowers or their family members; many others were quite poor. At the time, Bangladesh had a significant ready-made garments industry that over the next twenty years would grow to be the second largest in the world, after China's. (This led to tragedies like the 2013 Rana Plaza disaster, in which more than 1,000 workers were killed when a shoddily constructed garment factory collapsed.) The growing Bangladeshi garment business was a boon to the economy, but Yunus was mortified that most of the fabric used to produce those garments was imported from India. That included Madras check, used for cotton shirts popular as summertime wear in the West.

Yunus became determined to organize Bangladesh's weavers so they could supply those factories with fabric, thereby increasing the local value in the garments and boosting their own incomes. It turned out that many weavers and the dye masters that lived and worked among them could match the quality standards of their competition coming out of India, mostly from automated power looms, and they were competitive on price, too. Supervision by Grameen officials could help them to manage quality control, parcel out big orders to individual weavers, aggregate their production, and deliver it on time. The result could help to energize the rural economy on a massive scale.

There were many obstacles to Yunus's vision, including the fact that quite a few of the owners of the garment factories were Indian and preferred to buy fabric from their own country. But within a couple of years, Yunus got some traction with the product he called Grameen Check, selling thirty million yards of it to local and international companies for use in making garments and home furnishings.

To advance this agenda further, Yunus established a company called Grameen Uddyog (Rural Initiatives) and hired a retired civil servant named M.L. Majid to run it. Majid offered Grameen Foundation some funding to try to drum up business with U.S. companies. Not knowing whether or how we could help, we jumped at the chance to generate some revenue and contribute to a Yunus priority while leveraging one of our few strengths at the time—our location in the world's largest economy. The grant enabled us to hire, at a very modest salary, a woman named Ruth Hoffman who had worked in the fashion industry at the retail level and had international development experience through the Peace Corps as well as relevant training gained through an innovative masters degree program in Vermont. Jacki Lippman served as our supremely dedicated development director and mother hen. Rounding out our staff that fall were Geoff Davis, Shomit Ali, who volunteered with us as a young technology expert, and Chitra Aiyer, an energetic and bright Indian American who came fully funded thanks to a John Gardner fellowship she had secured.

However, our Grameen Textile Project was doomed to fail. It turned out that, despite herculean efforts by Majid, Yunus, and Yunus's deputy Khalid Shams, Grameen Check could never supplant the power-loom-woven fabric from India and elsewhere. We also discovered that, even if Grameen Check could compete, the mostly likely buyers to sign new contracts were based in Dhaka, not in the United States. We did succeed in drawing some new attention to Grameen Check by distributing patchwork quilts made from the fabric at our foundation's first gala, held in June, 1998. A year later, we secured a commitment from *Skymall* magazine to sell products made with Grameen Check through its airline-based catalog business. This led to Robert Worsley, the CEO of Skymall, speaking at our second gala, held at the U.N. in November, 1999.

In the end, however, the money ran out. While we subsidized Ruth's salary for a while, Majid shifted his attention to a Seattle-based Internet start-up named World2Market that was focused on selling crafts from emerging market artisans. One day, I received a call from Majid and some staff members from World2Market saying that they were signing a contract to collaborate that did not involve GF. Around the same time, Ruth told me she was leaving GF to work for what I now saw as our competition. I was outraged at the time, but looking back, it was probably the right decision for Grameen Uddyog.

Unfortunately, World2Market never fulfilled their commitment to buy Grameen Check products, and the company folded in the dot-com bust of the early 2000s. The good news for GF was that we were freed up to focus on areas with more promise for success, such as the growing microfinance movement in Asia and Latin America. Ultimately, Grameen Uddyog repositioned itself to focus on the domestic market rather than overseas, which made more sense.

During these early months at GF, I was in perpetual motion. When nature called, I jogged rather than walked to and from the bathroom in order to shave off a few more seconds for work. I felt as if I was continually falling behind, but somehow I knew we were making progress. I was making some good decisions as well as many poor and mediocre ones. Above all, I was inspiring some idealistic and hard-working young people to do their personal best to make us into the organization we dreamed of becoming.

PART TWO: LEARNING TO LEAD

7

Fundraising as a Win/Win/Win Proposition

Understanding and dealing with the biggest financial challenge of running a nonprofit—the art of fundraising

WHETHER YOU ARE NEW to the nonprofit world or an experienced nonprofit leader, you already know that fundraising is one of the most time-consuming, emotionally challenging, and utterly crucial tasks you'll be called upon to handle. Because fundraising consumes so much of the psychic energy of nonprofit leaders—and contributes more than its share to the problems of stress, anxiety, and burnout that bedevil them—there's no better place to start my leadership lessons for young mission-driven leaders than by sharing what I've learned about this vital activity over the years.

I know how widely hated fundraising is. Like most people in the nonprofit world, I have heard some variation on the following statement hundreds of times from staff, volunteers, board members, and CEOs: "I love this organization's mission and I will do *anything* to support it—*except* fundraising. I hate fundraising and I am not good at it."

I shared this attitude when I founded Grameen Foundation by the seat of my pants in 1997. However, I later came to understand that this attitude is based on a highly disempowering paradigm. Adopting a different paradigm can make fundraising enjoyable and a fundraiser much more successful. No lesson that I have learned in my career, related to fundraising or any other aspect of social change, has proven more fundamental or valuable.

The disempowering paradigm that most people naturally adopt when thinking of fundraising is based on zero-sum thinking. The fundraiser has to ask a potential donor to give up something they have—money—in order to satisfy the needs, goals, and preferences of the fundraiser. If the gift is made, the donor ends up having less money at their disposal, and the fundraiser's cause has more in exactly the same amount. Soliciting for grants in this scenario is a negotiation with a clear winner and a loser—one party comes away with more and the other with less.

If someone thinks about fundraising like this, it's understandable that they would want to do as little of it as possible. Especially given all the hangups our society has around money and being indebted to others, it's a wonder anyone who thinks this way about fundraising can attract any money at all for the causes they believe in.

But when I began to learn the concepts and techniques of Cedric Richner, a brilliant fundraising consultant we met through our second board chairman, the late Jim Sams, I adopted a completely different paradigm or attitude towards fundraising.

What does this alternate universe look like? First of all, it acknowledges that the growing economic inequality that characterizes today's world leaves a lot of people with more money than they will ever need. Yet those same people are often keenly aware of their deficits, which are not financial, but more often related to meaning and their ability to bring their vision of a better society closer to reality.

When wealthy people are approached in the right way—with sophistication and thoughtfulness—many of them are more than happy to exchange their excess money for an opportunity to connect with and support people and organizations that can bring meaning to their lives through having a positive impact on society.

In this paradigm, the fundraiser is a broker to a transaction where everyone wins. The donor gains meaning, connections, and hoped-for impact; the recipient organization receives additional resources to carry out its mission and potentially, a motivated evangelist (the donor); the beneficiaries of the organization gain resources they need to positively change their lives or the society they belong to; and the fundraising professional (or volunteer) becomes the satisfied broker in this win/win/win transaction.

Putting Janet at the Head of the Line

WHAT FOLLOWS IS A REAL-LIFE EXAMPLE of how the win/win/win approach to fundraising can work.

One fall afternoon in 2003, I was in my office at GF, about to tackle the most important challenge of my day—a crucial fundraising appeal. But as I dialed the number of one of GF's top donors and activated the speaker phone so a colleague could listen in, I felt surprisingly calm. I had a good feeling about our chances. My goal: to get a new commitment for $350,000 to help GF launch a major new project.

"Hello, this is Janet," one of our top donors said when she picked up her phone. At the time, she was still running a multi-billion-dollar mutual fund, a job she would retire from in a few years.

I had met Janet through Susan Davis, a GF board member and friend who would become our third board chair. Susan invited Janet to one of our galas in the late 1990s, and she had contributed to a couple of one-off projects since then. Today, I was going to present another.

"Thanks for agreeing to talk, Janet," I began. "I have a project I would like to present to you. I think you will find it exciting. In fact, knowing how much this might be attractive to you, given your philanthropic priorities, I decided to bring it to you first, and give you right of first refusal."

Janet chuckled and invited me to outline my proposal. Through our partnership with the South Indian microfinance organization SHARE Microfin, we had an opportunity to provide what was essentially a $350,000 security deposit (or partial guarantee) so that SHARE could get $4.3 million in new loan capital through an innovative financing mechanism known as securitization, which had never been used in a philanthropic context before. (As it turned out, technically what we were enabling was a portfolio sale, not a securitization, but when that distinction became clear later on, it didn't seem to matter to Janet or to anyone else.)

Since SHARE's loans averaged $100, this infusion of funds would allow more than 40,000 loans to be made to its poor female clients with the intention of enabling them to start or grow tiny businesses and work their way out of poverty. Once those loans were repaid to SHARE, they could be lent out to other women who had credit needs for their business ventures.

SHARE was giving us an opportunity to multiply the impact of our philanthropic dollars by a factor of twelve to one. They didn't have $350,000 just lying around, but they probably had multiple ways to get it donated or lent. Because we had delivered for them in the past, GF had earned enough of their respect and trust to be the first organization they asked for the funds. I immediately sensed that this would be a great way to tickle Janet's desire to move the microfinance movement forward, thereby becoming what many call a strategic philanthropist.

"So, Janet, this is an opportunity to be the catalyst for a historic transaction, where your grant will be multiplied twelve times. Would you be willing to consider supporting this effort?"

"Well, Alex, I really like that you approached me first and how you framed the opportunity. This is attractive to me. I'd like to review a short proposal, but I am inclined to do it." I exchanged glances with my colleague, and we both broke out in big smiles. I could see that she was surprised at how bold I'd been, and at how receptive Janet was in turn.

A few weeks later we received the grant, wired the money to India, and got word that the transaction had been completed. ICICI Bank, the largest private bank in India, was the buyer of SHARE's portfolio, which helped this progressive financial institution to satisfy certain regulatory requirements in India when making loans to benefit disadvantaged populations. A few weeks later, *The Economist* ran an article on the transaction and on GF's role. Janet ultimately termed the entire project a "home run" for her and for us. (She was rigorous in her philanthropy, but she always made an effort to offer affirmations and compliments when things went well—one of the many ways I consider her the most perfect philanthropist I ever met.)

Let's analyze what happened in this successful fund-raising experience.

If we think of Janet's $350,000 grant as a transaction, she had given up something she had in abundance—money—in exchange for something she wanted more of: being a vital player in an innovative project to advance poverty reduction through making essential financial services available to the poor. She came out ahead, as did GF, SHARE, SHARE's women clients, and even the bank that provided the $4.3 million.

For me, this is how fundraising can be transformed from something to be fearful and ashamed of to something joyful, even slightly intoxicating. It's an opportunity to be at the center of making multiple parties feel fulfilled.

Now, what happens next?

Many inexperienced fundraisers would have the tendency to let Janet alone for a while after closing such a big gift. They might fear that communicating with her frequently might prompt a bright person like her to probe into the project more and perhaps become dissatisfied with some aspect of it. They might also choose to avoid her due to their feelings of gratitude for her having made the donation. But this is old-paradigm, zero-sum thinking. Essentially, the fundraiser who responds this way is stuck in thinking that Janet has come away with less rather than more; therefore, she deserves a "break" from being approached again with a proposition that would have her losing more. It is somewhat akin to beating someone in a competitive sport—a tennis match, for example—and then refraining from challenging them to a rematch because you feel sorry for them.

As I was learning at the time, that would have been exactly the *wrong* way to approach our relationship with Janet. If I keep top of mind the perspective that in good fundraising *everyone* comes out ahead, why on earth *wouldn't* I follow up that win (for us *and* for her) with something even bigger, bolder, and potentially more fulfilling?

In that spirit, during the year after securing Janet's $350,000 grant, I decided it was time to stop approaching her for one-off projects. We had proven our ability to do exciting, innovative things and to execute well. Janet had proven to be a generous, discerning, and trustworthy donor whose preferences we understood well. So now we went even bigger. Susan Davis, the board chair who had first involved Janet in GF, joined me in a $5 million pitch to Janet to make a pace-setting grant to support our new five-year strategy. She listened to our proposal with interest, and within a few days she and her husband George Miller agreed to donate the amount we had requested, only changing the term to six years.

Janet's decision in turn helped prompt Pierre Omidyar, the founder of eBay, to join with four partners at a major venture capital firm in Silicon Valley in effectively matching her donation. In fact, Janet enthusiastically accepted our request to talk to the staff who advised Pierre on philanthropy as they were considering making their own multi-million-dollar grant. Rather than seeing this request as an imposition, she took it as a welcome opportunity to help shape the philanthropy of someone even wealthier than herself. As a result of these efforts, we raised $10 million from three parties over the course of a few short weeks in late 2004.

Janet didn't end up with *less* when she donated $350,000 to us in late 2003 and $5 million one year later. In fact, she felt so well served by GF that she continued donating even after her $5 million grant was fulfilled in 2010. She did this despite the fact that by then she was more focused on other humanitarian causes and organizations.

The win/win/win paradigm also affects the amount of money you should request. My fundraising teachers and my own experience have taught me that most fundraisers, especially those who are not well trained and who do not come from wealthy backgrounds themselves, have a tendency to ask for significantly less than they should. So I always made it a point to ask Janet for stretch gifts, and she often agreed to give what I requested, though generally not a dollar more—which was one of her ways of reminding me that she was not infinitely wealthy or someone who just threw her money around without consideration.

There was one exception. When I approached Janet to support a gala to mark the end of my eighteen-year run as the CEO of GF, I considered what I knew of her priorities and her wealth and was about to ask her for $10,000. However, she preempted me by offering to pledge $25,000. This expression of gratitude for the opportunities for impact that I had brought her was, in a sense, her final gift to me.

Can all fundraising be done using the win/win/win paradigm? No. People—whether rich, middle-class, or poor—have a wide variety of perspectives and motivations around philanthropy, which continue to evolve over the course of their lives. Some people donate in a purely transactional way, grounded in zero-sum thinking. Their primary aim may not be to change society in a positive way but rather to assuage a personal sense of guilt, to assist them in social climbing, to earn public recognition, or to gain access to people who can help them in business. Others give for reasons such as encouraging a friend who is passionate about a particular cause. But even when the motivation for giving is not as noble as Janet's, they are gaining something in the transaction. Thus, their philanthropy is still not a one-way street.

I recommend withholding judgment about why someone gives and what they hope to receive in return. Instead, focus on providing them with the benefit they seek in an ethical and efficient way in order to secure the grant and advance your mission. Meet donors where they are, even as you try to gradually influence how they practice philanthropy. In my case, I always tried to subtly get them in touch with their inner Janet McKinley.

Some donors resist the win/win/win paradigm for other reasons. Those who experienced the Great Depression or other forms of economic hardship sometimes find it hard to accept that they have enough money or possessions, which leads to a tendency to hoard. It is difficult to get people who approach life this way to buy into my preferred paradigm for their role as donors.

At one point in my career, I worked for an organization that raised most of its money according to a transactional, zero-sum paradigm. Many of their donors were mainly interested in gaining access, influence, and stature for themselves. I raised as much as I could given this dynamic. But I found this culture of giving somewhat distasteful, and when I found it hard to dislodge, I left.

Don't get me wrong: I rarely turn down money given in any spirit. But the type of fundraising that I will always gravitate to, and that brings in the most money in the most satisfying ways for all concerned, is rooted in the alternative win/win/win paradigm.

The key lesson: Never, ever ask for money (or anything important) apologetically or hesitantly! Remember that what you are giving is worth at least as much as what you are receiving, and have the courage of your convictions and passions. Excitement about changing the world for the better can be contagious.

Hitting the Fundraising Curveball

NOW THAT I'VE PROVIDED YOU with a better fundraising paradigm than the one you probably started with, let me offer some

FUNDRAISING AS A WIN/WIN/WIN PROPOSITION

more specific guidance for making your fund-raising more effective. I'll start with the challenge of dealing with an unexpected question or surprising opportunity—what you might call a fundraising curveball. Here's an example from the earliest weeks of GF.

The story begins with a rather blunt question from an important potential donor—a question that many fund-raisers might find intimidating: "Well, how much do you need?"

Aryeh Neier, the head of the billionaire investor George Soros' foundation, posed that question as he peered at me over his notepad. We were sitting in a sterile meeting room in Manhattan in May, 1997.

The question seemed to hang in the air for a long time. However, I actually answered it within a few seconds.

Those few seconds—when I debated what to say and how to say it, five weeks after I had launched GF on barely a shoestring—would go a long way to shaping the organization's destiny in the years ahead. Two weeks earlier, Muhammad Yunus had asked me to organize a meeting to discuss an urgent matter related to his Grameen Telecom initiative. The goal was to bring cell phone service to villages in Bangladesh and turn thousands of poor women into "phone ladies" who would sell communication access to their neighbors. But Yunus was in desperate need of cash—$10.6 million of it, to be precise. He needed that much to ensure that his fledgling telecom start-up could leverage its first-mover advantage to grow quickly. While his Norwegian joint venture partner was willing to invest all the money required, if Grameen Telecom did not make its own investment now, its shareholder rights would be diluted, and Grameen Telecom would lose influence and future financial benefits. Without this infusion of cash, Yunus's plan to cut the women of Grameen Bank and other Grameen companies in on the windfall—which would ultimately amount to hundreds of millions of dollars—would fail.

When Yunus told me he needed my help to raise a large amount of money fast, I asked if he had any ideas who could help. I was too prideful to mention it, but at that moment, Grameen

Foundation was itself quickly running out of money. Making payroll in June, as small a sum as it was at the time, was far from assured.

All of this was the background behind the meeting I was having with Aryeh Neier—leading up to his blunt question, "How much do you need?"

The honest answer, $10.6 million, seemed like a ridiculous amount to ask for. It was a lot of money. I was running an organization about to run out of money. I did not yet understand Grameen Telecom's business model at a deep level, so if Neier were to probe into the details of the initiative, I would likely be unable to answer his challenging questions, and my credibility would be damaged.

I was sorely tempted to make the mistake that many inexperienced and unconfident fundraisers do when asked a direct question like this—to preface my response with a kind of stammering half-apology, something I would come to call "stepping on your ask" in the future. (As I was to learn, many nonprofit CEOs make this mistake repeatedly.) Doing so usually diminishes the person asking for money and the request itself in the eyes of the prospective donor; it conveys amateurism, lack of conviction, or both. I unconsciously sensed that stepping on my ask would be a big mistake. Still, I had never asked anyone for anything near this amount before, even in writing, much less in person. I did not want to offend him or in any way breach philanthropic etiquette that I barely understood. I was nervous as shit, but I was also desperate not to disappoint Yunus.

So I trusted my instinctive urge to project conviction and confidence over the equally powerful urge I felt to equivocate. In other words, I decided, in that moment, to be bold and direct—or least to fake it.

"Ten point six million dollars," I replied simply. I looked Neier in the eye when I said it, and tried to be as matter-of-fact as possible.

Then I held my breath, wondering whether he would laugh derisively or even walk out of the meeting.

"Okay," was all he said as he wrote the number down. I rejoiced inside. I had not offended Neier with my outrageous request. He took it—and me—seriously.

The conversation went on for a bit longer. At one point, Neier mentioned that his wife was interested in our organization, and he suggested that he put us in touch. That fall, Yvette Neier would be elected to our board of directors, where she would serve with distinction until 2010, acting as our vice-chair during the tumultuous early years and helping to keep the peace when needed. The Neiers would end up contributing personally to GF for the next decade, with Soros's foundation triple-matching every dollar they gave.

"Well, I don't think this is the kind of thing that George will want to do," Neier finally said about the $10.6 million loan. "But I will bring it to him." I left the stressful meeting relieved and exhausted, and with a feeling that something good would come of it.

About a week later, Neier sent me a message saying that Soros was interested, and that since his wife was likely to get involved in Grameen Foundation, he would put his deputy, Stewart Paperin, in charge of the negotiations in order to avoid any potential conflict of interest.

Over the next twenty months, with help from an advisor Yunus recommended and two pro bono lawyers he helped me find (one being the future GF board member Jennifer Drogula), I worked intensively with Soros's lawyers, Grameen Telecom's leadership, Paperin, his staff, and many others to pull the deal together. It closed in February, 1999. The intensely frugal Yunus unexpectedly paid GF a small commission on the transaction, and also sent us several letters of thanks. Ultimately, this initiative succeeded—commercially, financially, and from a social impact perspective—to an extent that no one except perhaps Yunus could have imagined. Arguably, its successful, then-novel business model went a long way to convincing business and technology leaders that cell phones were not meant to be just a tool for the elites but could be marketed to virtually anyone.

To have played a role in securing crucial financing for this deal was one of the most important early accomplishments of GF and a great learning experience for me. By the time it was completed, I was deep into discussions with Craig McCaw, the billionaire mobile phone entrepreneur, and his wife Susan about building a center of excellence for using the information revolution to accelerate poverty alleviation. When the time came to ask him for the start-up funding for this center, requesting the $2 million confidently and without apology came almost naturally to me—and the McCaws came through with the grant.

What's the big takeaway from my initial, challenging conversation with Aryeh Neier? First, never ask for anything important hesitantly or apologetically. And second, in major gift fundraising as in life, you should prepare meticulously for important meetings, calls, and events. But you should also be prepared for—and, in fact, expect—the unexpected. When you encounter something you did not anticipate, be willing to improvise, think on your feet, and be imperfect in the service of your purpose and mission rather than playing it safe and pulling back or pulling out.

If you don't couple your meticulous preparation with a readiness to improvise when the unexpected happens, then your preparation can change from a powerful tool into a dangerous trap.

On one occasion, the unexpected came to me in the form of a phone call in the dead of night. Once while on assignment for GF in Cairo, Egypt, I received a call from our terrific fundraiser Barb Weber. The ringing phone woke me from a deep sleep.

"Hey, Alex, I guess it is pretty late there," Barb said a bit sheepishly and in a hushed whisper. More than anything, I could hear urgency in her voice. It turned out that Barb was in Redwood City, California, in the offices of the philanthropic organization started by the billionaire founder of eBay, Pierre Omidyar.

"Listen, a few of us were having a meeting with the Omidyar Network staff when Pierre walked in a couple of minutes ago," Barb said. Pierre had begun asking some challenging questions. Barb wanted me to participate in the conversation remotely.

I stood up and looked at the clock. It was 1:45 a.m. I hate participating in meetings of any kind by speaker phone, especially when the others are face to face. You are at a disadvantage, unable to see who is taking part in the discussion and to read the nonverbal cues and the critical messages they send. And of course, to be dragged into a meeting out of a sound slumber, with no time to prepare mentally or emotionally, is far from ideal.

But I took a deep breath. There were only two alternatives: to let Barb integrate me into the meeting, or to tell her to just do the best she could with the people in the room. Both were bad, but I surmised that one was less bad than the other. I managed to say, "Okay, I'll give it my best." I was not thrilled by the circumstances, but I appreciated Barb's complete dedication to her job. She understood that when the principal, in this case Pierre Omidyar, is at the table, you need to be at your very best.

Within a few minutes of Barb's putting her cell phone down on the table, turning on the speaker-phone function, and announcing that I was going to take part in the call, I began to insert myself into the conversation.

Pierre Omidyar is very smart and sometimes quite opinionated, which is understandable, since his instincts made him a billionaire by the time he was forty years old. (In fact, as I was later to learn, Omidyar is almost exactly my age. He had graduated from Tufts University the same year I finished at Cornell.)

The crux of what they were discussing was whether GF's investment strategy amounted to "market distortion," which Omidyar wanted to avoid in his grant-making. I did my best to explain, despite the fog of just having woken up after three hours of sleep, that we were playing a positive role by correcting market failure rather than distorting markets. It took some effort, but eventually I was able to get Omidyar to grant that I had a valid point. After about twenty-five minutes, he left the discussion, satisfied, and let the staff continue the negotiations on our grant. I signed off and went back to sleep.

Over the years, Omidyar's philanthropic organizations gave us more than $6 million. Two-thirds of that came in a single, $4 million grant, restricted only by the requirement that we spend it on a five-year strategy we had devised the year before. While we would later receive grants as large as $9.9 million from the Bill and Melinda Gates Foundation, never has a single grant been so important to our future.

I believe that my willingness and ability to think on my feet, moments removed from being in a deep sleep, and to both listen to Omidyar and to tactfully challenge him, played a big role in our success with him and his team. Without that dialogue between the principals, albeit on terrain on which I felt deeply uncomfortable, the negotiations between our staffs might have bogged down.

You probably know the saying, "Don't let the perfect be the enemy of the good." It applies to fundraising in spades. If you are a perfectionist who can't proceed with a conversation or a meeting unless every detail of the situation is to your liking, you may never achieve as much in fundraising as the improviser who is willing to take a chance under less-than-perfect circumstances.

When Should You Ask?

ONE OF THE QUESTIONS many fundraisers agonize about is the *timing* of "the ask." Here's my advice about it.

If you are meeting with a donor to ask them for money, it usually makes sense to get the ask (including the specific dollar amount) out on the table in the first five minutes of the meeting. If the meeting is over a meal at a restaurant, make the ask within five minutes of placing your orders. (Typically, the time before orders are taken is time for chitchat that helps everyone ease into a conversation.) After you ask people for money in a solicitation meeting, just be quiet and let them speak, even if that results in an awkward silence at first.

Here's a story that illustrates why I offer this advice.

"So, given everything, Lucy, we would like you to consider making a commitment of five million dollars towards our new strategic plan."

By speaking those words, roughly five minutes into a meeting held in a bustling Dallas-area bakery during the fall of 2004, I asked a wealthy GF board member to match the commitment that Janet McKinley, another female supporter of ours who is profiled earlier in this chapter, had just made. After making the pitch, I looked Lucy Billingsley in the eye, sat back in my chair, and shut up. It was her turn to speak.

I have always considered fundraising seventy percent intuitive and thirty percent counterintuitive. (For people who grew up in wealthy households or are familiar with sales in a commercial context, perhaps only twenty percent is counterintuitive.) Until a fundraiser figures out what is counterintuitive *to them*, and then alters their approach accordingly, they are likely to keep tripping themselves up and raising less money than they could.

For me, making the ask with a specific dollar amount early in a solicitation meeting was definitely counterintuitive. My inclination would have been to build up to it over the course of an hour-long session and make the request towards the end after being able to put forward as many arguments in as much detail as possible. It took me quite a while to learn the opposite approach and to apply it consistently. I'm glad I did, because this rather counterintuitive method has served me well.

After a few moments, Lucy smiled, looked at my colleague Randi Nordeen, then returned her gaze in my direction. "Well, I am pleased Janet is stepping up. But I don't think I can do that, Alex. But I can do one million. I'd like to think about how to structure this commitment so it helps you raise even more."

We spent the rest of our visit talking through the details of her gift. Ultimately, those discussions led to an agreement whereby two-thirds of her donation ($130,000 per year) would go towards hiring a Dallas-area fundraiser. That individual, a wonderfully talented woman named Tricia Bridges, ended up generating about $400,000 each year in collaboration with a dynamic network of volunteers, most of whom were friends, business associates, and admirers of Lucy.

This was a major development. It was especially surprising when you consider that, early in our relationship, Lucy had tried to lower my expectations by telling me, without prompting, that we could count on her for just $10,000 per year, or perhaps as much as $20,000 if there was some special project or need. (This points to another related lesson: Always take a donor's statements about the maximum amount they will be able to give in the future with at least a grain of salt.)

The key elements of this successful solicitation were that I struck while the iron was hot, in terms of travelling to Dallas soon after securing a $5 million commitment from someone we knew Lucy admired; asking Lucy for a stretch amount early in our meeting with her; and then quietly letting her respond to my request. Earlier in my career as a fundraiser, I would have been reluctant to take advantage of any momentum I had (fearing that I would squander it or discover it was a mirage); I would have asked for less than I should; and I would have filled the silence following my ask with some kind of inane verbiage in hopes of staving off awkwardness or an unambiguous no from the donor.

As we left the bakery, my colleague Randi Nordeen, our top fundraiser at the time, took me aside and said, "Alex, you played that exactly the way fundraising experts would advise." I nodded, appreciating that my bold approach had earned me some additional respect from a senior colleague with more formal fundraising training than I had.

I was beginning to get the hang of fundraising.

Within a few weeks, Lucy would be sitting in the living room of the legendary venture capitalist John Doerr, grateful to be rubbing shoulders with some of Silicon Valley's best and brightest and watching me, on the sidelines, wrap up negotiations for Janet's $5 million gift, a $4 million grant from Pierre Omidyar (who was sitting a few feet away from her at the time), and another $1 million from John and his partners. She would describe that weekend as one of the most exciting of her life, and within a short time her own grant agreement was signed.

There are people and cultures where a specific funding request made early in a conversation would come across as abrupt. If access to the donor has not allowed for as much prior cultivation as would be ideal, then addressing that gap in the first half of the meeting could make sense. If an unexpected guest invited by the donor joins the meeting, reviewing some of what has been discussed in earlier meetings may be appropriate. However, under other, more normal circumstances, asking early is better than waiting. In any case, if at all possible, try to avoid leaving the ask until the end of the meeting.

The tendency to put off directly asking the donor for money during a solicitation meeting is caused, in part, by people living in the zero-sum paradigm discussed earlier in this chapter. If asking someone for money is risky, distasteful, and likely to leave the other person with less, then putting it off as long as you can and leaving as much time as possible to effectively convince or manipulate them into doing something against their interests makes perfect sense. Furthermore, if the person says no, the meeting is basically over anyway—they won, you lost—so there is no awkwardness about what to do with the rest of the time.

However, in the alternative win/win/win paradigm, asking early is usually the best approach. It's the most important and exciting part of the meeting, so why not lead with it? If the donor is interested, putting the request on the table early allows for more time to negotiate the details and potentially to get closure before the meeting ends. It also shows conviction on the part of the fundraiser. Last, if the donor is not inclined to grant the request, it leaves time to demonstrate that you acknowledge and accept their decision, to reaffirm the importance of your relationship with them, and to discuss alternative projects for the future.

The Beautiful Sound of Silence

THE POWER OF THE PREGNANT PAUSE in the fundraising context was driven home to me by several of my mentors, but by no one as memorably as by Michael Pascucci, an Italian-American businessman and philanthropist whose family had been major benefactors to our work in Latin America during the 2000s.

Early in our relationship with the Pascuccis, Michael agreed to chair our November, 2000 fundraising gala at Lincoln Center. This was our third New York gala. Despite our growing confidence in our ability to run such events, we were wise enough to follow his lead in many respects as we planned for what we hoped would be our best event ever. This included hosting a luncheon at the United Nations for potential sponsors a few months before the gala, most of whom were friends and business partners of the Pascucci family.

Midway through the lunch, Michael, with me seated next to him, asked people in the group what they were willing to commit to the event in terms of buying tables at prices that ranged from $5,000 to $25,000 each. After presenting the opportunity, he paused. For a moment, no one said anything. Feeling terribly uncomfortable and embarrassed for my sponsor and patron, I began to speak in a fruitless attempt to distract people from how flat our request had apparently fallen.

Somehow, perhaps through observing Michael's body language, I figured out that I should shut up. After another minute of silence, people began to hold up their hands, pledging to buy tables. We walked out of the luncheon with more than half of the gala filled.

A few weeks later, Michael and I were talking on the phone about the gala. In a gentle way, he explained my error. "When I made the pitch," he said, "what we needed to do was just be quiet. The pressure was on them. When you began talking, it made it seem like we weren't serious about selling the tables. The only way to break the tension in the room at that moment is for them to make commitments—which they did."

I got it, and I appreciated Michael's taking the time to educate me. It was a lesson I would apply hundreds of times in the years to come.

8

Managing Up

Nonprofit organizations are usually dependent on support from the wealthy and powerful. Here's how I learned to deal with them

WE LIVE IN A WORLD where wealth and power translate into status and respect. It's a reality that impacts even those of us who are deeply aware that people with money are not necessarily superior to anyone else in terms of intellect, wisdom, or moral worth. The first time you meet with a multimillionaire or a billionaire—perhaps an industrialist whose picture you've seen on the cover of *Fortune* magazine or a philanthropist you've seen interviewed on CNN—it's natural to feel a bit awestruck. And a trace of that feeling often persists even to the tenth or the fiftieth time you take part in such a meeting.

It doesn't help matters that most of us who work in the nonprofit world come from a very different economic and social stratum than the wealthy people whose support we often rely upon. Many of us know we'll never earn in a year as much as one of our donors might spend on a car or a summer vacation. Superficial? Of course. But still, for many of us, emotionally resonant.

It takes time, practice, and reflection to learn how to overcome the feeling of being intimidated and awestruck when dealing with the wealthy and powerful. And it's important to do so. The more comfortable and effective you can become in dealing with the high-level business, financial, and philanthropic leaders your work depends upon, the more those leaders will come to trust, respect, and communicate openly with you.

Developing that sense of comfort begins with remembering the better fundraising paradigm that I shared with you in the previous chapter. Never forget that you have something to offer the rich and powerful that can be just as valuable to them as their money may be to you and your organization—namely, the opportunity to support an organization, solution, campaign, or cause that brings meaning, happiness, and fulfillment into their lives. In that sense, you and your donors are equals and partners, working together to forge relationships from which all sides will benefit, along with society as a whole.

Once you internalize and learn to live by that core truth, then developing strong, positive connections with your most important donors and supporters will be much easier.

In this chapter, I'll share some of the ways I've discovered over the years to help create and maintain those sorts of connections.

Wooing and Winning Supporters

IF YOU ARE NEW to the world of nonprofit leadership—or if you are a veteran leader working with a nonprofit organization that is relatively small or little-known—you may feel a bit overwhelmed by the thought of competing for philanthropic dollars with bigger, older, and more famous organizations. "The rich people I need to approach are inundated with requests from every charity under the sun," you may think. "How can I stand a chance of getting their attention?"

One advisor helped me find a fresh way of thinking that enabled me to overcome that discouraging mindset. It began with a simple, seemingly daunting observation—the fact that Stanford University (the alma mater of many of the top executives and entrepreneurs in Silicon Valley) had no fewer than 297 full-time employees working on fundraising as of the late 1990s (and probably more today).

What's the point of this comparison? A small organization like Grameen Foundation couldn't possibly compete with Stanford when it came to the *volume* of relationships we could manage. But when it came to any *single* relationship, we could compete with them and compete successfully. We had some strengths that Stanford didn't have, and vice versa. In many ways, the playing field was not absurdly tilted but was actually quite level.

So how do you compete with the philanthropic titans like Stanford University if you are a nonprofit with under, say, $5 million in revenue? It takes a full-court press. Working well with a wealthy individual donor who shows both capacity and inclination to provide significant support to your organization is similar to how you treat someone you are madly in love with.

People in love—especially those in the first crazy flush of infatuation—tend to spend an inordinate amount of time thinking about what they can do for the other person to make them feel special, appreciated, understood, and not taken for granted. The more I practiced working with major donors, the more I realized that cultivating them effectively has many of the same qualities.

For example, when talking to a major donor, I listen intently to everything they say so I can learn more about their desires, preferences, and pet peeves. Then I work to make it clear to them that I have heard them, which in itself is noteworthy in a culture where so many people barely track what the person across from them is saying. Here are some of the tactics that I have had success with as a part of a relationship-building approach:

- Repeating back what I have heard a donor saying, even (or especially) if it was difficult to digest, such as a time they were displeased with something one of my staff or I did, or failed to do
- Reinforcing that I have heard them by sending a follow-up letter or email that reflects what they said, and perhaps also referring to it years later
- Customizing reports on grant implementation drafted by my colleagues to address the donor's specific interest areas
- Providing links to articles or to people that I think would interest them
- Telling them about an event (such as a concert or play) not connected with my organization that I think they might enjoy
- Tastefully expressing empathy after a business or personal setback
- Inquiring about how I could help their children (whose names I try to memorize early in the relationship) get internships or other opportunities
- Showing interest in another nonprofit or an artist that they care about—and letting them know that they turned me on to them
- Inviting them to lunch with another donor whose values and interests are similar to theirs
- Getting them an autographed copy of a book by an author they admire

The "madly-in-love" approach takes a lot of time and mental energy, because it can't be done in a generic way but must be highly customized. The trick is to not only get good at the work of delighting people while bearing in mind their individual quirks, but to learn to enjoy the challenge of doing it well.

Another essential part of this approach is to realize that it doesn't scale to dozens, much less hundreds of people, especially if your organization has just a few full-time staff members focused on fundraising. Thus, it's essential to focus this kind of premium engagement on your most financially capable donors and prospects, rather than the ones you find most agreeable and available—which is another common mistake among inexperienced fundraisers.

I have come to not only savor the big checks that come at the end of such courtships, but also the satisfaction of making someone else feel special. It's a skill that I have adapted and extended to my friendships, my extended family, and even my marriage.

Over time, I learned to use the advantages that GF enjoyed as a small (and later medium-sized) nonprofit to help us compete successfully against the Stanford-sized charities. We not only had a compelling mission, but we also were small enough that a donor with giving capacity as little as $100,000 could get a fair amount of attention from the CEO and board chair—attention that a major university would probably be unable to consistently deliver.

Most wealthy people with a philanthropic orientation make, during the final decade or two of their lives, a donation that in the fundraising industry is called a lifetime gift. It often amounts to as much as five percent of their net worth, and represents the apex of a relationship with a nonprofit that has been building for many years. Nonprofits of any size can compete for gifts of this magnitude if they give highly customized attention to their most capable donors over a sustained period. Doing so takes discipline, consistency, resilience in the face of setbacks, and not a little application of the desire to delight another human being that we all experience when we are in love.

Written by Hand

ONE OF MY FAVORITE relationship-nurturing techniques traces back to an incident from the summer of 1993. I was travelling with a wealthy acquaintance named "Stan" who served on the board of Oxfam America, the respected international humanitarian organization. I was living in Bangladesh at the time, but my travelling companion had offered to pay my way to travel with him in Central America to teach some activists there about how microcredit worked.

One day, Stan reached into his bag and carefully pulled out something he wanted to show me. It was a handwritten note from Oxfam's president, John Hammock. Stan let me look at the message, written on the inside of a card with some kind of elegant design on the front. The handwriting was small and the message clearly personal—this was no generic cut-and-paste job.

I enjoyed the trip a lot and met some great people. But what stuck most in my mind from that trip was how meaningful that handwritten note had been to Stan. Even then I had the ambition to one day run my own humanitarian organization. So I made a mental note that this was one thing even I could do that required no special training, just thoughtfulness, discipline, and willingness to devote the time and effort required to write something that made another person feel special and, above all, not taken for granted.

Having Stan remind me of the power of a written message cast my mind back to an experience from my childhood.

In fifth grade, I ended up sitting next to Ilene Haber, a short girl who wore her hair in pigtails. I immediately liked her, most of all because of her quick wit. (It was no illusion: Ilene made her living as a stand-up comedian for a few years after college.) Towards the end of the school year, Ilene got sick with mononucleosis, and our teacher, Mrs. Padilla, required us all to write her get well cards. She then read some of the notes out loud before sending them.

Most of the boys wrote perfunctory if not slightly rude notes. Not knowing any better, I wrote from the heart, telling Ilene how much I missed her cheerfulness and her jokes, and that I hoped she would soon come back to school. The boys began to laugh at and mock my words even as they were read aloud, approvingly, by Mrs. Padilla. In one of those mini-moments-of-truth opportunities that life presents, I stood by my words. "Everything I wrote is true," I declared, "and if you don't like, you can screw off!"

The life lesson I learned in Mrs. Padilla's class has stood me in good stead as a nonprofit leader whose job includes making strong, lasting personal connections with people.

Early in my career, inspired by the card Stan (the Oxfam board member) had showed me, I developed the habit of sending handwritten notecards to donors while travelling abroad to see GF's work at the field level. I always wrote about what I had seen during the last few days and how it made me think of that donor's generosity and unique contributions to me and our organization. I made sure to mail the cards from whatever exotic location I wrote it in, so there would be a foreign postmark on the envelope, adding to the you-are-there immediacy of my message.

Could I have written an email with some of the same sentiments? Yes. On occasion, I did that if I was pressed for time or if I suspected the person on the receiving end would appreciate it more. But the thoughtfulness of writing to someone in longhand while on assignment overseas, when most people limit what they do to what *must* be done before they return home, made a deep impression on many donors. In addition, for years I wrote handwritten cards to someone anytime they contributed $500 or more to GF. When the volume became too much, I raised the threshold to $1,000. I might fall behind for a time, but I would always use slack periods or even vacations to catch up.

The impact of such messages is difficult to measure, but it comes out from time to time in the remarks people make or the things that they do.

One woman who headed the philanthropic arm of a global financial services company remarked on multiple occasions how unique and meaningful those notes were to her. While the grants from the foundation she ran, which totaled around $500,000, were not solely the result of those signature gestures, they clearly didn't hurt and very likely helped. Notably, those donations stopped when she retired and someone else took over this corporate foundation.

On another occasion, Steve Rockefeller, an incredibly dedicated GF board member, ended a conversation with me by commenting, "I want you to know how much your letters mean to me."

I had written him a two-page, single-spaced letter a few weeks back thanking him in great detail for all his fundraising help to me and to GF. I had composed another such letter on a slow day a few months earlier.

"You know, I save all of your letters," Steve said. "I keep them in a special drawer in my desk. Whenever I feel a little down or depressed, I take them out and reread them. I have read each of them many, many times. They never fail to cheer me up."

What went unsaid, but was abundantly clear, was that highly personalized gestures like these letters deepened Steve's commitment to our organization and to me. They clearly played a role in how often he went the extra mile for us and also in how willing he was to overlook my inevitable errors and omissions as a friend and as a philanthropic partner.

I came to call these longer, typed expressions my "love letters." They allowed for longer reflections on what someone meant to me (compared to a handwritten note card, which allows for only a few sentences). Most often I would write them out of the blue, for no reason except that I had some time on my hands (or because I was procrastinating about something else) and felt indebted to someone I relied on as a colleague, donor, volunteer, or board member.

When I decided to write one of these letters, I would usually sit quietly at my desk, visualizing the person I was writing about at their very best in terms of how they uniquely made contributions to GF and to me. I would put myself in their shoes and reflect on what words, coming from me, would be most meaningful to them. Then I would start to compose the letter.

It would usually take me about an hour to get a good first draft. I would tweak it over the next day or so, and perhaps get some input from a colleague or two. I sought their input mainly in terms of clarity and grammar, rather than content, as I didn't want the letter to sound like anyone other than me or to reflect anyone else's experience. Eventually, I would put it in the mail.

These letters became one of my signature gestures as a CEO. Over time, I came to write them when someone reached a milestone in their lives or with my organization (such as joining or leaving our board of directors). A related technique was giving a heartfelt tribute to someone in a moment of transition and then reconstructing my remarks in a letter I would send them or, if they approved, as a post to some appropriate blog. By taking this additional step, I was giving them a document they could reread and refer to for the rest of their lives.

It's easy for you to practice this same method of forging strong connections with those who support your work. As often as possible, write old-fashioned letters to your donors and your volunteer fundraisers to tell them what you appreciate most about them. Handwritten notes are particularly effective. So are typed letters spanning two or three single-spaced pages, either in response to some milestone of theirs or sometimes for no particular reason at all. Letters mailed from an unexpected location, such as an assignment overseas or from one's vacation, stand out even more. Extend this practice into your personal life and how you relate to your colleagues: When they do something helpful for you or accomplish something meaningful for themselves, write them a thoughtful note that reflects as best you can that you understand and appreciate them on a deep level. It is one of the most effective ways to communicate with a donor, colleague, or friend.

In my mind, there are two central lessons here. First, letters expressing thoughtful and highly personalized gratitude can deepen virtually any relationship. More than anything, they show that you don't treat people as generic moneybags. Wealthy people who donate to nonprofits often feel taken for granted, especially after they send in big checks. I believe that the problem of donor churn often results from these feelings.

Wealthy people aren't the only ones who resent being taken for granted. I recall a moment during my first year in Bangladesh where I was living in a rural area where everything was cheap and I had plenty of money to meet my living expenses. One day, the people at the Grameen branch where I was posted said they wanted to go see a movie. As we made our way to the rickety theatre, I gradually realized that they wanted me to pay for everyone's tickets. I could have easily done so, but the fact that they didn't ask but just assumed I would do that as the person with the most wealth offended me. So I rather petulantly refused. No one likes to be thought of as a piggy bank first, and as a friend, colleague, or human being second.

The second lesson is that nonprofit leaders should work to find their own signature ways of expressing appreciation and gratitude to their donors, employees, and board members. The methods you devise will impress and they will build loyalty. Over time, they can and should be tweaked and adapted, which helps keep them fresh.

Engaging Minds and Hearts—Not Just Pocketbooks

ANOTHER POWERFUL WAY to "manage upward" is to organize in-person gatherings that give your donors and other supporters a way to get deeply engaged with the issues your organization faces and the successes it is achieving, as well as to connect with other people who care about the things that they do.

Every so often, an opportunity presents itself to pull together your most capable donors and let them grapple with the opportunities that your organization and your field face. If you bring together the right group of people and curate a simple and thoughtful agenda, it can be incredibly powerful and reverberate for years to come.

One time, on the advice of a consultant, GF called together our top donors and donor prospects for a weekend retreat at the home of the legendary venture capitalist John Doerr. My talented and energetic colleague Barb Weber had taken the idea and run with it. It allowed her to focus her energies, and she worked wonders with the concept.

As the weekend for the retreat approached, I worried that all or most of the big names we'd invited would drop out at the last moment, as so often happens. (For our New York gala in 2000, we had heard that the chairman of one of the world's leading insurance companies was coming, but instead he was a no-show.) We got a scare when Doerr's staff informed Barb a few days beforehand that he had a scheduling conflict and might have to cancel the entire weekend. Barb didn't have the heart to tell me. My own father had died just a few days earlier, so she quietly headed off the near-disaster on her own.

The weekend went off as planned. It began with a Friday evening dinner at which Muhammad Yunus spoke. And all the key attendees showed up. The people in the room when the retreat started the next morning were a who's who of Silicon Valley and West Coast technology wealth—not just Doerr but Vinod Khosla, the founder of Sun Microsystems, both co-founders of Google, the founder of eBay and the head of his foundation, and others near that caliber. All told, there were twenty-four donors and donor prospects, their spouses, and a few GF staff and board members.

Now that everyone was present, shoehorned a bit uncomfortably into the living room of John's San Francisco home, I had two new worries concerning the retreat. A consultant who'd helped us design the session had recommended that we not pitch anything specific for the donors to fund. Since several of those coming had recently committed to giving us a combined $10 million—in fact, one of them, Janet McKinley, brought the signed agreement for her $5 million pledge that very day—I knew we would not come away empty-handed. But there were others who were newer to GF, and I worried that they, or our board members present, would feel that we'd frittered away our opportunity to hit them up for donations, in a context where peer pressure could work in our favor.

My other worry was about the morning exercise we'd planned. It started with an announcement from Henry Wendt, our co-host and former CEO of the pharmaceutical company Smith Kline Beecham, who had agreed to serve as the master of ceremonies for the weekend. Henry called out the words, "Okay, now break into groups and spend forty-five minutes coming up with an answer to the question, 'What will it take to defeat world poverty?'" I felt sure that the entire gathering, planned so meticulously for so many months, would fall apart soon after he uttered them. I feared that asking our guests—people with huge pocketbooks and presumably egos to match—to go off and solve a major global problem with their entrepreneur/CEO rivals, in all of forty-five minutes, would feel contrived and manipulative. Would one or more of them walk out in protest at that point?

So I sat there with bated breath when Henry stopped talking and directed everyone to go to their assigned groups. If I hadn't been so emotionally depleted by my father's recent death, I probably would have been even more anxious. There was an element of passive resignation to my mood at that moment.

And then something incredible happened. These titans of industry played ball. They dove into the assignment with energy and seriousness. As I commented in a *New Yorker* article about this historic retreat two years later, to their credit the most high-profile participants "got in touch with their inner graduate student" and started working with one another on grand plans to defeat poverty. Peer pressure and a desire to do good things on a big scale trumped ego and caution.

I joined the group with Pierre Omidyar and Larry Page of Google, and within minutes the discussion was going terrifically. Occasionally they would ask me for a fact or a statistic, and I would answer as best I could, estimating or even guessing if I needed to, in order to keep their creative juices flowing and not slow down their momentum. (I was learning that showing more confidence in your command of facts than you actually have is sometimes the best decision to make on the fly.) At some point,

Barb stuck her head in the room and said that the other two groups, upstairs, were going at the task with similar gusto.

A short time later, all three groups reported to their peers. Their plans for eliminating poverty were bold, at times brilliant, but rather simplistic and grandiose as well. Susan Davis leaned over and whispered in my ear, "Don't challenge the details of these plans. This is how these people think—bold! They have other people to work out the details. In this case, it's *us*!"

Fortunately, my years working under Yunus—another man with a fondness for big, bold ideas—had softened my resistance to plans that initially lacked nuance. In any case, I was in no state to speak up. But as I looked over the agenda, I saw that once this reporting-out session was complete, there was a break, and then I was supposed to present Grameen Foundation's five-year plan.

The idea was to see if the group would buy into the idea that our plan contained the details needed to make their poverty-ending dreams a reality. I was going to spend the break writing up a guide to our plan on a flip chart to help guide me and the audience. It would also allow me to mentally prepare myself for the one time during the weekend when I would be the sole presenter.

Barb conferred with Henry Wendt. I wondered what she was saying to him. Then, after the final report was complete, Henry announced that we were cancelling the break and would be going straight into my presentation. I was aghast. Where was my time to collect my thoughts and write up some notes on the flip chart? Gone!

I stood up and began with a few words of appreciation to the group, as I was still a bit overwhelmed by the energy they had brought to the morning's exercise. I then went on to describe the key elements of our strategic plan: adding five million microcredit borrowers, ensuring half got out of poverty within five years of taking their first loan, and spawning three industry-changing innovations. Barb prompted me with a question to explain the difference between "high-growth" and "seedbed" partners. I wrote HG and SB on the flip chart, and I said a few words about our differentiated products for larger and smaller microfinance institutions (MFIs). These were things I could explain in my sleep, and in some sense I was sleepwalking through this presentation, weighed down by the magnitude of the moment as well as my personal loss and the emptiness it created in me. Still, I did not embarrass myself.

Over the lunch that followed, Janet McKinley presented the case for using the capital markets to finance the growth of microfinance, and faced some tough questions that she dealt with deftly.

And then something amazing happened. Three of those present—John Doerr, Vinod, and Bob Eichfeld—began conferring in the hallway between the dining room and living room. I heard John saying that the group wanted to have some sense of collective accomplishment before leaving that afternoon. What could we pitch? Thinking fast, Bob said that just giving them something to donate to, like our strategic plan or some element of it, might fall flat and feel unimaginative and even manipulative. So he proposed that we dust off an idea that he had pitched, to no avail, to some banks on Wall Street eighteen months earlier—a loan guarantee program backed by the assets of wealthy supporters of GF.

In short order, the agenda was changed yet again to allow for Bob to present his idea. Before long, John Doerr was asking people whether they were willing to commit 0.1 percent of their net worth to this idea, if we could pull such a vehicle together.

At one point, someone in the room voiced some doubt about it, and urged us to go for a more market-oriented approach. Deeply aware of the high stakes, I summoned all the strength I could muster, despite the recent loss of my father weighing heavily on me. I said, "Well, what you are asking for is exactly what this guarantee program can be. It is practical and market oriented, and it will correct a market failure that is keeping millions of poor people stuck in place."

I exhaled, wondering whether I had overstepped my role.

It turned out that I'd succeeded. In a few minutes, John asked people to hold up their hands if they were willing to commit 0.1

percent of their net worth. A few hands went up. It was clear that a critical mass of the room was on board.

Now it came time for Susan Davis to give some closing remarks for the day. She used the time to have the group generate its own summary of what they had discussed and agreed to. It was brilliant—putting the focus on *their* ideas rather than on hers, and on what they had accomplished together and what came next for them.

At one point, as Susan was filling up a flip chart page with points, Pierre Omidyar stood up and demanded that she add the following words in capital letters: END POVERTY NOW.

Mission accomplished.

That memorable weekend taught me an invaluable lesson about nonprofit leadership. Sometimes the most powerful, impactful engagement can arise when you simply bring your best donors and supporters together and invite them to share their ideas, passions, insights, and dreams. Remember, you are in the business of giving people opportunities to find meaning in their lives. A gathering like the one GF held that weekend filled the bill in unforgettable fashion.

Quality, Not Quantity

ANOTHER POINT ABOUT GATHERINGS is that a *small* event can be highly successful. The trick is to make sure that the people involved don't feel as if they are at a failed gathering due to the low attendance. Rather, create the impression that the intimacy was intended.

One method is to make sure there are as few empty seats as possible. For example, if twenty-five people have confirmed their plans to attend a meeting or presentation, I often set out as few as ten to fifteen chairs, since it often happens that only about half of the people who plan on coming to an event actually show up. That way, almost every chair is filled. If more than that number show up, I pull from a stash of spare chairs to accommodate everyone. While I lose a few minutes in scrambling to seat the attendees, I create a sense that this ticket was in high demand.

Sometimes, it is obvious that fewer people have showed up than the organizers hoped for or expected. But even those situations can turn out to be quite successful, as the following story illustrates.

Around 2002, a woman named Sandy Cohen agreed to invite people to hear me talk about GF in her Dallas home. About two hours before we were supposed to start, it began raining. As I was to learn, when it rains in Dallas, people tend to cancel nonessential travel.

The calls began pouring in as the start time approached. In the end, exactly two people came to hear me give my speech—a graduate student from India in search of a job, and a woman who stopped in on her way to her yoga class. However, being a professional, I spoke as if a hundred people were there.

As it happened, I did not seem to satisfy either attendee: The graduate student didn't get the job he hoped for, and the woman en route to yoga didn't seem particularly taken with my presentation or the answers I gave to her questions. Nonetheless, it ended up being one of the most productive events in the history of GF. The woman en route to her yoga class was Lucy Billingsley, the wealthy real estate developer whom you met in chapter seven. She got my attention by sending a $5,000 check the next week, asking me to channel it to one of two programs featured in our recent newsletter, which she obviously had read closely. In time, Lucy would go on to become a major donor, a prolific fundraiser, and a productive GF board member.

The lesson here is that the success of a gathering is determined more by the quality of the people who show up than the quantity. In fact, I've often told this story when the turnout for a meeting is small. It seems to help people relax and stop thinking that they are at an unsuccessful event.

Document Your Relationships

ANOTHER KEY TO BUILDING close, productive, long-lasting relationships with your supporters is to thoroughly document what happens in every meeting, phone call, or substantive email exchange with them. Share that information with people who can help you advance the relationship. Don't just provide a summary of what was discussed, but also describe the mood of the meeting, what you learned about the donor from small talk, family members dropping in, or the photos and decorations on the wall. Details like these can help you understand more about a donor's philanthropic preferences, financial capabilities, and biases. Writing reports like these makes you not just a fundraiser but also a detective and even, at times, a psychologist and confidant.

Like so many other tactics that I use, I initially learned about this technique by studying and learning from people who knew fundraising better than I did. At first, I was skeptical about it, but over time, I became borderline obsessive about documenting each call and meeting. Eventually, GF adopted the software program Salesforce as our information and knowledge management platform, which made logging data about our donors much simpler. I am sure some people thought I went overboard, and on occasion I probably did. But the alternative is to have a trove of valuable institutional knowledge residing solely in the minds of people who may leave the organization at any time or even turn against it. Unless donor contacts are documented, seamless fundraising staff transitions are almost impossible. Furthermore, documenting things properly promotes transparency and trust in one's colleagues. It's true that knowledge is power, but in a well-run nonprofit, insights about donors are important assets that should be shared openly with colleagues to help advance the organization's mission.

In addition, donors and other supporters really appreciate it when you and your team members make the effort to keep track of facts and details about them and about your relationship. In a world where people want to feel heard and understood, and where this feeling is unfortunately all too rare, this is a critically important way a nonprofit organization of any size can distinguish itself—especially among small to medium-sized groups, where turnover in fundraising teams is often very high.

Yes, there can be a downside to thorough reporting on supporter relationships. Documenting contacts and sharing them with your team can lead to abuses. Staff members may share the information inappropriately with the people written about in the reports, their friends, future employers, and the media. A hacker could steal the files and publish the information, leading to embarrassment for everyone involved and perhaps ruined relationships with donors. Sometimes people add extraneous information or opinions to their reports, driven by the desire to show off or to deliver a message to internal stakeholders.

For all these reasons, you'll want to establish clear rules about your reporting practices and enforce them rigorously. But the positives of documenting your relationships far outweigh the potential negatives. Develop this habit and take advantage of the benefits it offers.

Making Lemonade

SO FAR, ALL THE ADVICE I've given focuses on the positive aspects of "managing up"—ways you can build strong, happy, rewarding relationships with your powerful supporters. But inevitably, managing up brings with it challenges, disappointments, and stresses. Learning how to deal effectively with these is a crucial skill every nonprofit leader must master.

When a serious mistake is made with a major donor, or for some other reason they become unhappy with your organization, realize that this is no time to give up or stick your head in the sand. Rather, use the moment of crisis as an opportunity to distinguish yourself as an organization that responds to problems in creative, proactive, and pragmatic ways. By making lemons into lemonade, you may be able to turn a negative into a positive.

In November, 2000, GF held a gala fundraising event in New York City. As I mentioned earlier, the Italian-American philanthropist Michael Pascucci agreed to chair the event. Unfortunately, despite being quite successful in certain ways, in others it turned into something of a fiasco. The evening was poorly planned, it ran much longer than intended, and it brought in somewhat less money than we'd hoped. The Pascucci family members in attendance were visibly, and justifiably, disappointed. It was all I could do to conduct a rather perfunctory staff-level debriefing, emphasizing what had gone well—after all, we had raised $450,000—while also touching on the many things that could have been improved. By then, I was hoping simply to keep my head down and move on to the next challenge. Once the dust settled, I was tempted to do what many nonprofit leaders would have done—to write off the Pascuccis as future allies and financial supporters.

Imagine my surprise when, a few days later, a letter from Michael Pascucci arrived containing a generous check for $50,000. It reminded me that we had never settled on his family's sponsorship amount, which was yet another mistake I'd made. In a short note that came with the check, Pascucci said he looked forward to getting a post-mortem about the gala.

I wasn't sure how to respond to this request until after I'd had a helpful call with one of my mentors. The advice he gave has stuck with me ever since. His key point was that, while we were unlikely to receive much future support from all the Pascucci friends who'd attended our poorly run gala, we had a great opportunity to turn the event into a positive with the Pascuccis themselves. This mentor guided me through the process of writing a thoughtful, detailed and succinct post-mortem memo to Michael Pascucci that lauded his role, emphasized how we and he had been successful, and acknowledged what we had done wrong and what we had learned.

It worked. Before long, the Pascucci family resumed its tradition of making a $1 million donation in support of our work in Latin America every few years, and Michael's son Chris joined our board of directors, where he added immense value, especially by helping me become a more discerning judge of talent. Behaving in a professional fashion after a major blunder, and thus distinguishing ourselves from other nonprofits that tend to run and hide in such circumstances, made all the difference.

Using Leverage Wisely

SOMETIMES IT'S NECESSARY to play hardball with a donor, usually in order to ensure the fulfillment of a prior pledge of financial support that they are signaling may not be forthcoming. When this happens, do it ethically and professionally—but don't do it halfway.

I learned a lot about the art of negotiating with potential donors by observing Muhammad Yunus at work and listening to his advice. Some of the things I learned from him I later decided did not fit me well. But many of his tactics remain part of my repertoire.

Yunus had a shrewd sense of when it would pay to be tough and uncompromising. He and I were once deep in negotiations with a U.S. government agency that we hoped would lead to a $2 million grant for one of Yunus's poverty-fighting organizations. Only a single sticking point remained. I urged Yunus to give in on that point, because the grant would have been a powerful tool for spreading the Grameen model internationally (as well as a feather in my personal cap). Yunus, who was directing me from 8,000 miles away, insisted we stand firm; in fact, he urged me to raise the issue early in our next meeting and say that if they were unable to accept our position, the meeting was over. Then I should begin to walk out of the room.

I don't know what Yunus saw that I didn't; perhaps he sensed that the agency was very eager to make a deal. But whatever the reason, I was amazed to find that my counterparts in the negotiations implored me to stay and agreed to meet our requirements. Within a week, the documents for a $2 million grant, on terms highly favorable to us, were being drafted.

Yunus somehow realized that we were the ones with the leverage in that situation—and if you have leverage and know how to use it, you can usually win the battle. The biggest insight I took away from this episode was that, when in a negotiation, you sometimes have much *more* or much *less* leverage than you think you have. As a result, it is important to remain alert and curious in order to figure out whether your assumptions are correct or way off the mark.

One of the first times when I got a chance to use leverage to extract something from an important potential ally came in the early 1990s when I worked for RESULTS. A key contact for us was the policy director of a humanitarian group that we belonged to. He was never very helpful to us, though he tried to appear open to our requests, since we were an institutional member of the association that employed him. Like many in Washington at the time, he thought RESULTS was too pushy, too aggressive, and too certain about the rightness of its priorities. But I thought the problem went further than that: I suspected that the policy director underestimated and even looked down on Sam Daley-Harris because he lacked polish and the right kind of pedigree—that is, the Ivy League degree followed by Peace Corps service that many international development professionals boast on their resumes.

One day, my suspicions were confirmed. The policy director had written a letter to Sam explaining why he did not support a bill that we had helped draft. However, rather than send it to us, he forwarded the unsent letter to a consultant and added a handwritten note describing his disdain for us.

Unbeknownst to the policy director, the consultant was a friend of a RESULTS activist, and he sent the letter to her. When it ended up in my hands, I was furious.

I photocopied the unsent letter and sent it to the policy director with a letter of my own, saying that we deserved better treatment than to have him sniping at us behind our backs.

About a week later, the policy director came to our office and, without referencing the letter directly, apologized for not being as responsive and open as he should have been. He promised to serve us better in the future, and he proved to be as good as his word. Sam never asked me what prompted his changed behavior, but as an intuitive person, he probably suspected that I had gotten some leverage over him and used it.

On another occasion, I came into possession of an email related to promised support for an organization on whose board of directors I served. It showed that an intermediary organization had made a clear commitment to us, but was now backing off of based on a change of heart by the donor involved. As I knew the donor, I shared this evidence of a firm commitment having been made on their behalf. That led to a grant of $250,000 coming through, and, unfortunately, the staff member at the intermediary organization losing his job.

Twice during my years leading nonprofit organizations, I applied pressure to donors who had made verbal pledges of funding for GF and were not intending on honoring them.

In one case, a technology executive had stated his intention, at a moment when he wanted something from GF, to make a future donation to us in the range of $20,000 to $25,000. Especially back then, that was a lot of money for us. After some time passed, I brought up his commitment and asked the executive how he would like to deliver on it. He demurred. I could have let the matter drop, and if I'd expected further donations from this individual, I might have done so. But I figured this was my one and only chance to get any money from him, so I hatched a plan. Knowing that this man deeply admired Professor Yunus (as so many people do), I told him that I intended on sharing with Yunus a list of all unpaid pledges, and I added, "I'd rather not have your name on that list." Within a few weeks, a check for $20,000 arrived.

In another case, a woman had pledged $35,000. When no check arrived, I began calling her every few weeks, mentioning that if the delay went on much longer, I would need to alert some respected philanthropists in her community that we had an unexpected revenue shortfall due to the fact that she was not following through on her commitment. It took a few months, but we ultimately received the $35,000.

It's often better *not* to press donors to make good on financial pledges. Letting them off the hook so as to preserve the long-term relationship is frequently the best course—though when this happens it can be surprisingly satisfying to vent in private about the hardball tactics you'd like to use, even if you have no intention of doing so.

In another case, a major donor's staff member informed us, somewhat sheepishly, that her employer might not be able to deliver on the remainder of a large pledge due to financial setbacks they had experienced. At that very time, the family was appearing in news stories describing their conspicuous consumption. Maybe the consumption was part of the reason for the financial difficulties, or perhaps these donors were spreading those tales to keep up appearances among their well-heeled friends.

Whatever the explanation, I was very upset. I bent the ear of my board chair about it, and we even talked about the possibility of leaking their potential default to the press in order to embarrass them into fulfilling the pledge. But we ultimately decided not to do that, and I am very glad we didn't. Perhaps because we had taken the high road and chosen not to embarrass them, the same donors soon introduced us to several of their wealthiest friends. And when their business recovered, they gradually made donations that ultimately exceeded their original unpaid pledge, and one of the family members even became deeply involved as a volunteer.

Using leverage—social, political, or moral—to push a supporter into living up to a promised commitment can be a gratifying strategy, and sometimes a rewarding one. But in most cases, effective leadership lies in the art of knowing when *not* to use the leverage you have over someone, instead remaining patient in the belief that, in the long run, most people will prefer to do the right thing.

9

When Leadership Is a Struggle

How to manage a nonprofit team through the inevitable times of conflict, frustration, and stress

MY LONG LABOR DAY WEEKEND a few years back was turning out great—or so I thought.

On the train coming back home from a business trip to New York City on Friday evening, I'd come up with a plan. I'd spend Saturday on a mix of personal projects, including some related to my board service with an organization combating climate change. I'd spend Sunday doing work for my employer at the time. Then I'd spend Monday, Labor Day, working on this book. In between these activities, I'd intersperse cooking, listening to live music, ample sleep, practicing new habits I was trying to develop, reading, exercising (including a ten-mile run on Sunday), and watching as much of the U.S. Open tennis tournament as time permitted.

By the time I woke up on Monday morning, my plan was working well. I'd made some modest progress on a few thorny issues I was dealing with at work, and I'd enjoyed a conversation with my friend Karen O'Malley, which included making plans to go out dancing with her in New York a few weeks later.

But one particular issue hung over me. If I could get it resolved by Monday morning, it would make my weekend nearly perfect. For the last three weeks, I'd been conducting difficult negotiations about extending the contract of a colleague whom I'll call Vikram. He was our India country head. I'd offered him a generous package on Thursday morning, and he'd asked for some time to think it over. I felt as though we were just hours away from an agreement.

As I prepared my Monday morning tea, I turned on my computer to check my emails. I figured that a message from Vikram accepting my offer, or at worst making a reasonable counteroffer, might well be waiting for me.

Sure enough, there was a message from Vikram. It was a resignation—followed shortly by a second message from Vikram saying that one of his top deputies, a talented man whom I saw as a possible successor to him, had also resigned. "The timing isn't great," Vikram remarked. I'll say!

What to do next? How to deal with these two unexpected body blows? My heart raced, and I began pacing around my home anxiously.

I tried to steady myself. The night before, an article in the *New York Times* had caught my attention. A pull quote describing it read, "The tech world has branded workaholism as a desirable lifestyle choice." In its first paragraph, the article announced, "An entire cottage industry has sprung up [in Silicon Valley], selling an internet-centric prosperity gospel that says that there is no higher calling than to start your own company, and that to succeed you must be willing to give up everything." Later, a social worker whose patients included many stressed-out tech workers, quoted one of her clients as having told her, "The expectation is not that you should work smart, it's that you should work hard. It's do, do, do, until you can't do anymore."

Every line in the article reminded me of myself when I fell back into old habits that had ruled me earlier in my career—except that I was a nonprofit leader, not a high-tech executive. Like virtually every area of human endeavor, the higher reaches of the do-good professions are highly competitive, filled with achievement-oriented people who push themselves and their colleagues hard. However, unlike technology leaders or their counterparts in finance, consulting, and similar fields, humanitarian leaders get neither bonuses nor stock options. Instead, they're generally expected to live rather austerely in order to show donors that their money is "going to the cause." At the same time, they are also supposed to be entirely comfortable around people with unimaginable wealth.

In place of comparable material benefits, leaders like me are supposed to derive some kind of spiritual benefit from working to right the world's wrongs. However, for more than a few leaders, that promise rings increasingly hollow as their careers progress. They see too many projects bog down, too much talent flee to greener pastures, and too many supposedly successful initiatives turn out, after the passage of time, to look more like houses of cards. All the while, these leaders are supposed to project optimism and self-confidence in their ability to achieve rapid progress on vexing societal problems in order to keep their jobs, satisfy and motivate colleagues, secure positive media coverage, and make progress in their careers.

Over the decade or so leading up to my Labor Day surprise, I had figured out, to a degree that I found surprising and encouraging, how to avoid the trap of being a stressed-out, workaholic humanitarian professional. But it was not always that way.

Earlier in my career, getting the resignation letter of two people I relied on and whom I had trusted to stick it out with me would have likely pushed an already stressed-out Alex Counts into the dysfunction of panic, blame, anger, and a massive overreaction.

Of course, those reactions could—and often did—make the problems I was grappling with worse. But through a painstaking process I undertook in my thirties, I had learned how to destress myself, lead a more balanced life, and deal with setbacks in a much more constructive way.

After reading Vikram's email, I decided *not* to obsess about my lack of a plan to deal with my sudden workplace crisis. Channeling the wisdom of Alcoholics Anonymous, a fellowship to which I do not belong but still admire, I focused instead on simply doing "the next right thing," with the confidence that a comprehensive response would emerge over time. I informed my board leaders, which had the effect of causing some smart people to partially own what until that moment had felt like *my* problem—and with that ownership came the responsibility help me solve it. (By contrast, earlier in my career, I would have been tempted to hide the problem for as long as possible in order to retain my autonomy in trying to fix it—a risky and usually ineffective approach.)

I thought about whether there was anything else I had to do immediately, and realized that there was not. That meant it would be best not to do anything rash that could make things worse, such as writing a caustic email. I told my wife, Emily, so she could be aware of my state of mind and commiserate with me a bit about this unhappy development. I put off for a few hours deciding whether I was going to work on my book, then ended up writing the first draft of this section. As a way of centering and distracting myself, I did a few things to reinforce habits I was trying to develop to improve my physical and mental health: I ate a piece of fruit, wrote in my journal about ten things I was grateful for, and flossed. I wrote a note to a friend who was facing a personal crisis, mentioning that I had come across the birthday card she had written me earlier in the year and telling her how it had touched me. I sent a section of my book manuscript to a professional colleague now running a large humanitarian organization who had expressed interest in reading it. I ran a few errands, which gave me a small sense of accomplishment during the early part of the day. While in the grocery store, I surveyed the people working the checkout counters, whom I had developed some affection for over the years, and reminded myself how fortunate I was to do work that I loved most of the time while being reasonably well paid for it.

Most important, I took a deep breath and reminded myself of one of the most important things I had learned over three decades as a professional and as a human being: that bad news or setbacks often end up being much less severe than they initially appear, and sometimes they end up being unexpected blessings.

Within a few hours, I'd steadied myself and was moving forward with a plan to deal with Vikram's departure as well as all my other work priorities. I felt a sense of accomplishment, momentum, and inner calm. Rather than allowing this surprising setback to destabilize or even paralyze me for a day or more, or prompt me to lash out and burn bridges, my approach that weekend allowed for a solution to emerge. Within a few weeks, the board and I figured out how to keep Vikram in the organization in a position he was happy with, and that worked well for me, too.

As a nonprofit leader, you'll inevitably face moments of unexpected difficulty, setbacks, even crisis. These moments will test your judgment, your strategic instincts, and your decision-making skills. But the first challenge they'll pose will be to your sense of equanimity, purpose, and self-discipline. If you can remain calm when unpleasant surprises hit, resisting the temptation to let powerful emotions shape your response and dictate your behavior, the chances that you will make smart decisions that will enable you to weather the storm—and perhaps even turn it into an opportunity for positive change—will be far greater.

In this chapter, I'll recount some of the times when I've faced conflict and turmoil in my work, and share some of the lessons I've learned about how to keep such moments from driving me, and the organizations I have led and governed, seriously off course.

How to Admit Your Mistakes—and Learn from Them

MY HEART SANK. Soon after the start of a morning meeting with my chief financial officer, she'd delivered some devastating news: The decision that I had made a few weeks earlier to send some promised funding to a partner organization in India—before the grants we needed to pay for the funding had materialized—had backfired, big time.

The spreadsheet showed that we were down to $200,000 in the bank. That was way too low, for many reasons. It was 2001 and we were no longer a scrappy nonprofit startup; Grameen Foundation had now grown into a midsized organization with around fifteen full-time employees and a board populated by influential business leaders. Now I was facing the real possibility of being fired in disgrace and having GF collapse a few months later. That night, I sat in our tiny basement apartment with Emily and did something I do about once every five years: I cried. In fact, I sobbed.

Over the next few days, I tried to maintain a semblance of calm while at times I was nearly immobilized with fear. The first thing I had to do was make sure we had the facts straight. I asked the treasurer of GF and my friend, Paul Kane, to help by poring over our financial statements and confirm the predicament we were in.

On his second full day in the office, Paul made an important discovery: he realized that our CFO had wrongly booked a transfer of $200,000, showing it as a debit when it should have been a credit. In reality, we had $600,000 in the bank.

This didn't get us all the way out of the woods—we were still short of the funds we should have had on hand. But it gave us a fighting chance to turn our finances around.

I called our small staff together. I described the financial problems we were facing, emphasizing that our situation was not ideal but far from dire. I told the staff that we had had a scare in terms of our finances, but that things were going to be fine.

I also went on to say that I was making some fundamental changes in how I led the organization, effective immediately. A near-death experience can sometimes prompt you to examine your life. Having faced the prospect of career death, I had found myself questioning my behavior as a leader and the ways I had been treating people. I realized that my strengths—decisiveness, intelligence, candor, an intense work ethic, and high expectations for myself and for those around me—all had dark sides when I indulged them too much or in the wrong way. Decisiveness sometimes became impulsiveness; candor morphed into belittling criticism; intellect came across as arrogance.

In the staff meeting that day, I listed some of my behaviors that I knew people resented at times, and said that I had decided to stop them all from that moment forward. I am not sure whether people were relieved or incredulous, as I was not yet good at reading a room, but it didn't matter.

In the months that followed, I became a bolder and more aggressive fundraiser. I also fired the CFO and brought in a new, more skilled financial officer. By the end of 2003, our finances were healthy again, and we were poised for rapid growth in 2004 and beyond.

As for my vow to reform my leadership style, that proved to be much more of a mixed bag. The truth was that, within a few months, I was back to most of my old habits. For example, I resumed being decisive, while occasionally veering into impulsiveness. That was who I was.

Over many years, that strength and its associated dark side would evolve in a positive way. But it took time—a lot of time.

That moment of financial crisis, and its aftermath, taught me a number of valuable lessons for leading an organization through times of turmoil.

One was that learning from your mistakes and making an effort to continually improve as a manager is both absolutely essential and far more difficult than I'd originally realized. It's rarely possible to switch off a bad leadership habit and instantly substitute a better pattern of behavior—and making rash promises to do so is likely to backfire. Instead, self-examination, reflection, learning, and growth are gradual processes that demand constant attention and thought, as well as patience and self-acceptance.

Here's the approach that I've developed in the years since my near-death experience in 2001.

If you are the leader of an organization, regularly set aside time to share with your senior team and board members the worst mistakes you've recently made and the lessons you feel you learned from them. Encourage the managers who work with you to do the same with their direct reports. If you feel comfortable doing so, you can also share your mistakes with a broader group of organizational stakeholders. Admitting your errors, studying them for the lessons they can teach, and sharing your insights with the members of your team is probably the best way to minimize the chance that you'll repeat them. It also enhances the sense of team cohesiveness that can play a huge role in helping you survive the next time you face a shared crisis.

Board members and donors also pay attention to the how nonprofit organizations deal with their setbacks and shortfalls. As Susan Davis once said to me, sophisticated philanthropists realize that there are two types of organizations: ones that regularly shoot themselves in the foot and have honest conversations about those missteps, and those that do the same thing but put their head in the sand and never admit it, even to themselves.

In the early days of GF, I facilitated periodic staff retreats myself. (In later years, we often enjoyed the luxury of offsites organized and led by outside professionals, but for financial and other reasons this wasn't possible earlier.) I would set aside time to summarize what I felt were my biggest and most costly mistakes over the previous few months. The first time I did this, I went through a laundry list of a dozen or so blunders, some relatively minor, others more substantial. Perhaps the worst was a case in which I'd decided not to review and give input into a draft grant proposal that had been prepared by Chitra Aiyar, a smart young staff member, in collaboration with a partner in Bangladesh. I later concluded that if I'd spent even two hours on Chitra's draft, we would have won the grant. My mistake probably cost us a million dollars—a lot of money for GF, especially at that time. (Today Chitra continues to do a world of good as the executive director of the Sadie Nash Leadership Project.)

It felt purifying to come clean about what I had done wrong; no longer did I bear the burden of being the only one to know about my mistake. As I went through my list of mistakes in a rather matter-of-fact yet unsparing way, I watched the staff listen in silence. They exchanged intense and excited glances with each other and occasionally looked at me, rather dumbfounded by my unexpected candor.

The session had a much more positive and lasting impact than I'd expected. It turned out that my openness impressed them—indeed, team members talked about it for weeks, even years afterward. Encouraged by this response, I continued the practice of being open about my mistakes with colleagues and others, such as board members, donors, and even peers in competitor organizations. I've tried to ingrain such openness into the DNA of organizations that I have led, helped, governed, or advised. Rather than trying to cover up or minimize errors, I've tried to make admission of mistakes and their impacts feel normal and healthy, even habitual. I find that it breeds openness and recognition of the fact that in order to make progress, risks are necessary, and that errors, even serious ones, are to be expected.

I sometimes half-joke that one of my management mantras is that everyone knows that you reward success, but it takes a truly wise manager to reward failure—because failure can be a great educator, searing lessons into people's consciousness more effectively than simply reading or hearing about them can ever do.

Our willingness to admit and learn from mistakes was further deepened when we hired several retired senior executives from Microsoft and other tech giants to help us start a Seattle-based operation that would focus on using technological tools to help combat global poverty. Led by Peter Bladin, a smart and conscientious "Microsoft millionaire" originally from Sweden, this group had been steeped in a corporate culture that included using product launch post-mortems as a way of guarding against complacency. One of the stories they liked to tell was about releasing six products at the same time in the late 1990s, five of which ended up being rated best in class. CEO Bill Gates responded by criticizing his team for the one "failure" and demanding that they get to the bottom of why that sixth product did not place first in its category. I appreciated this example of Microsoft's cultural rigor, though I tried to soften its application within GF.

One of the most memorable examples of GF's openness about our mistakes emerged organically from our first big public health program—Mobile Technology for Community Health (MOTECH). This Ghana-based project had two components: mobile midwife, which sent alerts to pregnant mothers suggesting safe motherhood practices such as eating vegetables and going for regular check-ups, and a nurses' application that allowed frontline health workers to digitize the medical records of their patients that could be done even on the very basic mobile phones (like the ones many Americans used fifteen years ago) that they already had.

As you might expect, we made all kinds of mistakes over the course of our first major health project. Rather than cover up our blunders, the team working on the project, led by Microsoft alumnus Tim Wood, decided to publish a brutally candid report on what they learned during MOTECH's first two years. In fact, by this time, the culture of honesty was so embedded in GF that no one even asked for my permission before the report was released. Two more documents about lessons learned were published by the MOTECH team over the years, each more than a hundred pages in length.

After Bill Gates visited the MOTECH program in 2013, he wrote on his personal blog that ours was the best health program of its type he had seen, which he ascribed mainly to our strong learning culture.

Openly discussing mistakes is particularly important for nonprofits. Our tax-advantaged status means we owe it to society to openly share most, if not all, of our insights and lessons learned, including what doesn't work, since nonprofits exist to help the community and advance the common good. I believe that we have an ethical responsibility to help other nonprofits not repeat our mistakes, even if that means embarrassing ourselves occasionally.

Empathy as a Tool for Controlling Anger

IN TIMES OF ORGANIZATIONAL TURMOIL, one of the emotional pitfalls that can lead you astray is the sense of defensiveness and pride that makes it hard to acknowledge, admit, and learn from your mistakes. Another is anger, which for many people is the instinctive or habitual response in a situation that involves danger or threat. Rather than taking the easy path of expressing the anger you may feel when you believe you're under attack, pause and take a deep breath. There are other, more constructive responses that may lead to a positive solution without intensifying the conflict.

One of the ways I've learned to control my anger instinct is by trying to see every situation through someone else's eyes—specifically, through the eyes of a person I might be inclined to view as an adversary, an opponent, or even an enemy. In one case, this approach may have saved my life. Two colleagues and I had to visit a remote area of Indonesia to negotiate with the leaders of a wayward partner organization. My colleagues were justifiably upset about the problems we'd experienced with the partner group, including apparent misuse of funds, and during the discussions they wanted me to get tough. Instead, I bent over backward to let the organization's leader know that we understood her position on matters like the importance of local knowledge and practices, while still insisting that the problems we'd observed needed to be addressed honestly. This approach helped to keep the disagreement from escalating into unchecked hostility—even when, mid-meeting, a dozen strongmen in bulging jackets that appeared to conceal weapons silently entered the room and surrounded us. This act of intimidation made me and my colleagues very nervous, but I stuck to my conciliatory style. We emerged unscathed a few hours later.

By contrast, letting anger shape the assumptions I make about another person shapes my response in unhelpful ways. At the most basic level, it allows my contempt for the other person to come through, further irking them. And since anger makes me assume that they will continue their behavior, I end up essentially dehumanizing them in a way that can fuel a self-fulfilling prophecy.

Over time, I developed a different approach. Instead of assuming that the person I am struggling with is being difficult because of spite, cruelty, narcissism, or greed, I try to imagine how they could be taking their position based on a principle or value that is important to them, and that I myself would respect in some situations. Thinking this way tends to lead to more constructive responses, ones not shaped by the blind rage that anger generates.

Some years ago, a gifted employee I'll call Joanne was creating a lot of dissension in GF. Among her problematic behaviors were criticizing me and other leaders behind our backs, not meeting with her direct reports, making unreasonable demands for a promotion, missing or being late to meetings, and being angry and sarcastic during the meetings she did show up for. In one case, I had a senior colleague phone in for a senior staff meeting from his office down the hall, since he found being in the same room with Joanne so distasteful.

I struggled to make sense of her behavior until Susan Davis, chair of the GF board, did something unusual and helpful. She started thinking out loud about how the situation looked to Joanne. "Alex, we know that she likes to give speeches and represent us in coalitions and working groups. She goes out and spends a few hours at a conference, gives a speech, gives advice, and what does she get? She gets praise, applause, kudos, right?" I nodded in agreement, not quite knowing where Susan was going.

"That probably relaxes her and makes her feel good," Susan continued. "She then moves on to another conference or meeting before they see any other side to her. To them, she is a rock star.

And then she comes back to our organization, where she has been for more than a year, and people don't treat her as a rock star. They have demands and criticisms. And so she has one context where she is almost universally praised and admired, and another where it is more mixed. She assumes, perhaps unconsciously, that the problem is *ours*. And this justifies her behavior that to us seems obnoxious and disruptive. She sees it as an effort to wake us up so that we appreciate her talents more."

In that moment, Joanne was suddenly humanized for me; she became someone I could extend empathy to. Once I had this insight, I was able to think through my approach to her in an entirely different and more effective way.

Ever since then, I have tried my best to understand any conflict through my antagonist's eyes before figuring out how to resolve the conflict.

The Get-Out-of-Jail-Free Card

ABOUT A DECADE into GF's existence, in the middle of some kind of argument, a colleague said something that offended me. I can scarcely remember what it is now. A few weeks later, after the underlying issue had been resolved, I wondered whether I should confront my colleague about what he'd said. Up until then, I believed that, when done in the right spirit, talking directly with people about how their words and actions had impacted me was always the best approach, and the sooner the better. But in this case, I wondered whether it was really necessary, since the underlying problem was now past.

I shared my dilemma with an advisor, who asked me a simple question: "Has this person ever offended you in this way previously?"

I thought about it for a minute. "No," I answered.

"Well," she replied, "sometimes it's better to let a single episode go. If they repeat it, then talking to them about it makes sense.

But maybe this is an anomaly, based on something that was going on with them that day."

After thinking about it for a few days, I decided this made sense. I formulated a new rule that referred to the board game Monopoly, which I loved playing as a child: "Everyone gets one get-out-of-jail-free card."

I have practiced the rule as much as I can ever since. But during my final year at GF, I faced my biggest test in applying it.

That test involved a fundraising event we were organizing. After initial agreement about the program was reached, I left on a summer vacation, during which, unbeknownst to me, there were vigorous debates among senior staff and board members about changing the theme of the event. When I returned, the consensus was that we should change the focus, and a leader on the board explained it to me. I said that I did not agree with the new approach, and I explained that the way that I and others had been promoting the event—and how we had secured financial commitments from donors—was not consistent with the new focus. There was a danger that we would confuse people, or worse.

After a number of heated exchanges about this issue, I arranged to discuss it with the board leader and a facilitator we both trusted. But the board leader called me the day before our planned meeting, and I unwisely took his call.

This particular board leader was one of the most humble, empathetic, and helpful volunteers we'd ever had. So I was unprepared for the conversation that would unfold over the next thirty minutes.

"I think I know how you are feeling about this, Alex," he began. "But I want to tell you how *I* am feeling." He went on to say how much stress he was experiencing in regard to his Grameen responsibilities, and the growing ambivalence he felt about his long record of service and his generous donations. What he left unsaid, but made abundantly clear, was that *I* was the person mainly responsible for his stress and unhappiness.

He went on to say that if the gala was organized along the lines I favored, I would risk "embarrassing the organization and myself." He suggested that the conflict we were having was my fault. And while he acknowledged that he could not impose his preferred solution on me, he urged me to capitulate.

This conversation left me feeling terribly upset. The idea that this board member would blame me for his unhappiness was deeply offensive to me. I found it manipulative and unworthy of a person I greatly admired.

Later that day, I enlisted another board member to serve as an effective mediator. Fairly quickly, we resolved the issues surrounding the event, with both of us making some reasonable concessions. In the weeks that followed, most of the board members involved came to see the wisdom of my original approach, and said so to me. Somehow, that only made me angrier. Why had the board leader needlessly elevated this issue and then caused so much stress and conflict over it? I was sorely tempted to vent my frustration and give him a piece of my mind.

I never did. I reminded myself that the board leader had never behaved this way before, and that he had truly been under a lot of stress at the time. I silently issued him his get-out-of-jail-free card. If anyone in the history of GF deserved one, he did.

In the months that followed, the two of us enjoyed a series of increasingly warm conversations that evoked our decade-plus of working well together. We now have both retired from active roles in GF, but we remain in regular contact. He actually called me out of the blue while I was finalizing this chapter just to ask about how I was doing, reminisce a bit, and invite me to join him for a baseball game.

This was a case in which living up to a sound leadership principle was very difficult for me to do—but I'm glad I did.

Responding to the Unasked Question

SOMETIMES, AN INTERPERSONAL CONFLICT can take a very subtle form. Rather than an explicit attack or even a harsh criticism, a colleague or team member may say something (including asking a question) that *implies* their disapproval. My advice in such circumstances is to avoid escalating the potential conflict. Though it may be difficult to do, resist the temptation to respond to the unstated or implied challenge. Otherwise, you will convey defensiveness and insecurity—and perhaps provoke a battle that never really needed to happen.

As I outlined earlier in this book, Sam Daley-Harris was a longtime mentor and inspiration for me. During my early days running GF, I found myself talking to him about my leadership journey from time to time. Sam's advice was often helpful, but he had some strong views about how GF should be run that I didn't always agree with.

One day, I mentioned to Sam that GF had a board meeting coming up that Muhammad Yunus would be unable to attend because of a change to his travel schedule. I felt that we should go ahead with the meeting, partly out of respect for the others on the board who had made travel plans to be in attendance. But I had other, bigger reasons for the decision. I was trying to build a board that took its governance role seriously, and that meant demonstrating that they weren't simply window dressing meant to make us look like a well-governed organization while all the decisions were in fact made by Yunus and me.

Sam clearly didn't agree with this philosophy. When I made it clear that I still intended to go forward, he asked, "So, are you going to have Yunus call in to your board meeting?" I sensed that Sam felt that it would be unwise for us to meet and certainly to make any decisions without Yunus's participation and consent. For my part, I have never been a fan of having people participate in meetings remotely when everyone else has showed up in person; and in this case, Yunus's travel schedule would have made a remote connection very difficult to arrange.

For all these reasons, I responded to Sam's question with a simple "No"—and then I almost fell into a trap. I felt strongly compelled to explain *why* I'd made that decision. From our past conversation patterns, I sensed that Sam wanted to know why I was not including Yunus, and would likely challenge my decision and reasoning.

But in reality, Sam lacked any real standing to ask me about that; he had no official role in GF. Therefore, I restrained myself from answering his unasked question. I thought to myself, why answer the question Sam has not even asked? It will just make me defensive and resentful. I'll signal that Sam has some power over me, and I'll shine a light on my insecurity as a leader. So, in an instant, I simply decided to leave it at a simple "No."

Afterward, I felt unexpectedly elated that I had stood my ground. I was outgrowing the relationship of mentor and mentee that Sam and I had so long maintained. When Sam didn't explicitly ask his implied question, but let the conversation move on, it felt like a sign of respect, whether conscious or not.

Ever since, when I feel that people are interrogating or questioning me in a way that feels inappropriate, I listen carefully and try to respond only to the questions they actually ask and the suggestions they actually offer. I avoid getting caught up in trying to convince them or win their approval—and, in particular, I avoid anticipating lines of questions or suggestions and responding to them in an attempt to justify myself when doing so is not necessary.

When an Employee Must Be Fired

YOU CAN SEE that I have a personal preference for avoiding conflict when possible. Being empathetic to people whose behavior bothers you, providing them with one get-out-of-jail-free card, and resisting the temptation to respond to an unasked question—all of these are ways to prevent a potential conflict from escalating unnecessarily.

But there are times when conflict is unavoidable. When this happens, it's best for a leader to deal with it forthrightly and with self-confidence. It takes time to learn how to do this, but it's an important weapon in your leadership arsenal.

One circumstance when conflict simply must be faced involves the employee who absolutely needs to be fired. It's an unpleasant, often painful duty—but it's one that an organizational leader must learn to handle.

One time, I arranged one-on-one mentoring sessions with four major donors to GF, all experienced and very successful managers from the for-profit business sphere. One of the issues I asked each of them about was when and how to terminate an underperforming employee. I posed the question this way: "How often in your career as a corporate leader have you let someone go and later regretted doing so? Conversely, how often have you let someone go and later regretted not doing it sooner?"

All of these highly successful business leaders said basically the same thing: "I have never regretted letting someone go after having done so. On the other hand, there have been many times when I regretted waiting too long to fire someone."

I was surprised by this unanimity. But the longer I've served as a nonprofit leader, the more I understand it. Firing someone is inherently unpleasant; most people instinctively shy away from it. So by the time you find yourself seriously contemplating firing someone, it is probably long past time for you to do it. Get it over with. It is unlikely you will regret easing them out of the organization sooner rather than later. Your colleagues will probably appreciate your decisive action, especially because some of them may well have been covering for their colleague who is not succeeding.

Of course, you should make an honest effort to handle a necessary dismissal with humanity and dignity. Pay a fair severance package and provide outplacement assistance to help them land on their feet. And make symbolic gestures that show you care about their feelings. I remember the first time I had to fire an employee of GF. Although "James" didn't report directly to me, I invited him to lunch in a relatively nice restaurant so I could break the news to him personally. We gave him a couple of weeks' advance notice to cushion the blow. As his final day approached, he asked permission to take part in a staff retreat. We gave that permission, and he actually contributed good ideas to our discussions.

Before leaving, James thanked me for handling his dismissal in a humane and sensitive way. And years later, when he joined a consulting firm that was in a position to help GF, he made sure that happened.

Don't be dissuaded from firing someone by fears that you will be sued, even if risk-averse human resource professionals and legal advisors raise this possibility. Yes, it's good practice to document their performance problems in the event you need to justify your action in court. But the vast majority of working people are more interested in moving on to their next job and succeeding in it than in spending time and money on litigation. If you fire someone in a way that respects their dignity, it is likely that they will not only forgo legal action but they may also speak well of and assist your organization in the future.

10

Turning Points

A leader must learn to identify and deal with crucial moments in the life of an organization, when major strategic choices must be made and implemented

AS I LOOK BACK ON MY CAREER, I have concluded that successful transformations like the one Grameen Foundation was destined to undergo are forged in a small number of moments of truth and how leaders respond to them. One such moment occurred in April, 2002, when I realized that GF had arrived at a crossroads—one that demanded a thoughtful strategic response.

As GF's board of directors gathered in Los Angeles that month, we were celebrating our fifth anniversary as well as a year of remarkable progress. Our team in Seattle had soft-launched a promising technology initiative the previous year, for which expectations were building. Yunus was starting to disengage from GF and focus on newer organizations that he had helped get off the ground—indeed, this would be one of the last GF board meetings in which he would participate from start to finish.

We were attracting new allies, such as an Iranian-American businessman based in Los Angeles who came with his family to a dinner we organized after our board meeting. He ended up generously supporting our work in Pakistan over the next several years, and later, the organization as a whole. These and other developments were signs that GF was about to enter a new era of growth.

I realized that we needed some clear direction and shared goals as we headed into this period of change. So I announced at the board meeting that the staff was about to start a strategic planning process. I hoped that our plan could be presented to the board for its approval in the fall of 2002 or, at the latest, in the spring of 2003. I solicited the board members' input up front. The focus of the plan would be, first, on our support and advocacy of microfinance, and, second, on the niche we were creating for ourselves in using information technology to supercharge poverty reduction initiatives. I felt a strong sense of responsibility to ensure that we measured our success not just by the number of microloans we generated or the number of handheld devices we distributed, but by how lives were changed as a result.

Convincing a critical mass of people in an organization to support a defined multiyear strategy is both an art and a science. It's not easy. Problems can crop up at every stage in the process. It is dangerous for the leader to control the plan creation too tightly, but it is even more dangerous to outsource strategy development too much to deputies, board members, or consultants. There is often a need to buckle down at some point and pull it all together in order to get closure, so as to ensure that the planning process does not get put on hold, kicked down the road, or shelved. Once you finalize the strategy, there will be naysayers who feel they did not have enough input. Don't worry about them too much. Rather, rise to meet the opportunity of bringing in new financial supporters and building momentum, which, if successful, will help convince most if not all of the holdouts.

Pushing a Decision When Momentum Is on Your Side

AFTER WE RETURNED from our board meeting in Los Angeles, I contacted Heidi Craig, a longtime RESULTS volunteer, to see whether her son Nick, who had done some organizational development consulting for RESULTS in the early 1990s, could help us with our strategic plan. Nick agreed and ended up designing and facilitating several memorable planning retreats for GF. During the later stages, he involved an associate of his named John Anderson, who would take an increasingly important role in our planning work and go on to become our chief operating officer—a job he did exceptionally well, serving as a stabilizing force during an exciting but turbulent era of fast growth, big impact, and major mistakes. (Later I'll share something profound he taught me that reoriented how I thought about managing people in the workplace.)

During one particularly dramatic moment in a planning retreat, we were debating whether our goal should be to help our microfinance partners expand outreach by three million or five million over the next five years, from a baseline at the time of around 900,000 clients. Nick sensed the importance of letting people have their say rather than leaving it to me or the board to decide. So he asked people who supported three million as our goal to line up on one side of the conference room, while those who supported five million should go to the opposite side. Then he encouraged people to try to recruit people from the opposite group, which led to conversations that were both fun and substantive. Ultimately, the vast majority joined the five million group, after which the few cautious staff who'd remained on the three million side of the room abandoned their position and joined the rest of the team in a show of solidarity. The entire exercise was a deft display of participatory planning.

We added a second major goal—a benchmark based on the percentage of borrowers who would emerge from poverty within five years of taking their first loan. We did not have much to go on in defining an aggressive but realistic goal. I thought about one study of Grameen Bank that said that five percent of its clients were emerging from poverty every year. While the research was later challenged, at the time it was considered valid. I did some back-of-the-envelope calculations of what this would mean over a five-year period, and then stretched the goal, since I thought many countries would be more favorable to rapid poverty reduction than Bangladesh. Quickly, we adopted a goal of having half of the clients crossing the poverty line within five years of taking their first loan.

The members of our tech innovation team in Seattle were supportive of these two goals, but thought they were incomplete. Most important from their perspective, these targets did not explicitly encompass our efforts to harness the information technology revolution to benefit microfinance and the broader movement to reduce and end global poverty. They pointed, for example, to projects such as Village Phone Uganda (VPU) championed by my exceptionally diligent colleague David Keogh, which was in the process of setting up 80,000 African women in profitable microfranchise payphone businesses in partnership with MTN, the country's largest mobile phone provider, and more than a dozen Ugandan microfinance institutions. I argued that, if successful, most of these technology projects would result in microfinance clients coming out of poverty faster, thus contributing to the second goal. In other cases, our technology consulting work would help microfinance institutions scale up faster, and in the process contribute to the first goal. But the Seattle team was not satisfied with these indirect measures. I was frustrated by what I felt was their intransigence.

We had some contentious planning sessions and staff meetings, and initially I dug in my heels. The tendency to do so is not one of my better leadership qualities. The Seattle team dug in their heels as well. Then, in a moment of inspired and inclusive compromise, I figured out a way to resolve the issue. We all felt that the Seattle technology center was fundamentally about innovation, whereas the rest of GF was mainly focused on scaling up known solutions (most of which had originated with Yunus and his team in Bangladesh). Clearly the two priorities could be complementary and synergistic, if we thought about them the right way. This pivotal insight led to the solution: Rather than create a goal solely around information technology, we would set one for innovation. It took only a few moments after I had that insight for me to propose what became our third goal: to champion three innovations to benefit the poor that would be transformative at either the national, regional, or global level.

Everyone got on board with this three-goal approach, and the planning process picked up steam. We costed out what it would take to reach our goals and estimated that we needed an up-front investment of several million dollars in staff and systems to have a chance at delivering on these goals.

We decided to present the plan at our next board meeting, which would be held at the Rockefeller estate in Westchester County, New York. However, a screw-up in transporting people from downtown Manhattan to Westchester ate into the time we had to discuss the plan, and made everyone anxious—especially me. Underwhelmed by what they heard, the board members gently but firmly sent us back to the drawing board to revamp the plan and make it more compelling and realistic. I was initially crestfallen, and fumed, somewhat implausibly, that the delay in starting the meeting had doomed us—when in fact, we probably would have encountered resistance even if we had started on time.

Then I started to focus on how to get the plan passed at our next opportunity. Susan, our board chair, suggested that we expand and reinvigorate our board committee structure in order to get more buy-in to and better understanding of our proposed approach. We followed her suggestion, which worked very well. Dialogue between the board and our staff on the plan, and on our work generally, reached higher levels than ever before.

But as we approached the October, 2003, deadline to ship the plan along with our other meeting materials, a lot of loose ends remained. A few people proposed that we delay the strategy discussion until the following spring, six months hence. I rejected that, fearing that we might never get closure, since staff and board members would feel that all their efforts related to planning were yielding nothing tangible. I could see that our most talented and trusted staff and volunteers, who'd been largely driving the strategy process, wanted the satisfaction of having something to show for their efforts before too much more time passed.

With the time for completing the plan days away, I holed myself up in a Dallas-area guest house owned by Lucy Billingsley, the real estate developer mentioned earlier, who was by then a member of our board, and wrote feverishly over the course of a three-day weekend. The resulting 185-page document contained some clunky writing, but it held together reasonably well, and the six-page executive summary was excellent. One colleague at the time described this as the time when I "went to the mountaintop alone and came down" not with two tablets but with a spiral-bound document. The departure from our highly participatory process unfortunately caused a few of our team members to lose their sense of ownership of the plan. But that was what was necessary to get something adopted by the board rather than pushing off a decision for another six months.

We shipped a three-ring binder with our regular meeting materials to each board member, and a few days later followed up with the voluminous strategic plan. The sheer weight of materials overwhelmed some of our directors, but the most influential board members, seeing that the plan was essentially sound and that the staff needed the endorsement and affirmation after all the hard work following our fiasco in the spring, pushed for adoption of the plan. They seemed to appreciate that we did not sulk or abandon the planning effort after having been rebuffed, but rather redoubled our efforts under the guidance of our board chair. The fact that we had set a goal of increasing our revenue in 2003 from $4 million to $6 million, and that we were already on course for meeting that aggressive growth goal, clearly influenced some directors, giving us an important credibility boost at a critical time. A resolution to adopt the strategic plan passed unanimously.

I was exhausted and elated. I hoped that the plan would be the basis of fundraising and programmatic successes far beyond anything we had achieved up to that point. Despite the flaws in the plan and the process that led to it, it would become the basis for rapid, even unimaginable growth over the coming twelve months and beyond. In fact, we busted through our goal of five million new clients in five years, exceeding it by more than forty percent by the time 2008 rolled around.

Most people associated with GF were thrilled that we finally had a clearly defined, multiyear strategy to guide our programmatic and fundraising work. By the spring of 2004, we were getting good at pitching the plan to major philanthropists. I caught a break when a meeting with the head of Pierre Omidyar's philanthropic organization was booked with a few hours' notice during a hastily planned trip to northern California, shortly before I was scheduled to go on a three-month sabbatical. With diligent follow-up by my colleague Barb Weber on the Omidyar Network contact and a few other promising leads, by the fall we had raised three grants totaling $10 million in support of the plan, with few restrictions on any of those donations.

A new era in the story of GF had dawned.

By this time, we were raising $1 million per month to advance social change, and within a few years we would double that rate. I was becoming comfortable negotiating and collaborating with people like Bill Gates, eBay founder Pierre Omidyar, Google co-founder Larry Page, and the famed venture capitalist John Doerr, as well as my charismatic mentor, Muhammad Yunus. The journey had turned into a wild ride—thanks, in large part, to our persistence and determination in pushing the strategic planning process to a successful conclusion, despite the problems and setbacks we encountered along the way.

Recognizing When the Moment for Decision Isn't Ripe

AS A LEADER, I believe that decisiveness is a strength. In many circumstances, a good decision made quickly is more valuable than a great decision made after a long delay—an approach I saw modeled very effectively by MasterCard CEO Ajay Banga when I worked with him while at the American India Foundation. But it's also important to realize that sometimes the time to make a decision simply *hasn't* arrived—in which case kicking an issue down the road may be the best course of action.

Beginning in 1999, I was involved in fundraising for the Fonkoze organizations, which provide microcredit and other social services to the poorest people in Haiti. I later joined the board of directors of one of these organizations, which I was elected to chair a few weeks before the massive earthquake of 2011. I spent a great deal of my personal time supporting this organization because I believed in its mission and people so strongly. As much as any institution I encountered over the years, they internalized and tried to apply Yunus's vision and values, and did so in a harsh and unforgiving environment. I am pleased to say that, as of 2019, Fonkoze continues to innovate and achieve new heights, led by dynamic women including Mabel Valdivia, Carine Roenen, and Dominique Boyer.

Several years before Mabel joined Fonkoze USA and Dominique took over its for-profit arm, I was involved in a daylong retreat for Fonkoze leaders. Matt Balitsaris, then vice-chair of Fonkoze USA, advanced a creative solution to gradually resolve a vexing intercompany debt issue. As the person chairing the meeting, I let Matt lay out his idea, which had been debated a bit in earlier meetings. I then told the group that I thought it made sense. However, the head of the for-profit arm of Fonkoze at that time objected. This was predictable, since Matt's plan appeared to have negative financial implications for that already struggling group. Others in the room weighed in with alternative approaches, all of which were equally problematic, if not more so. The discussion was becoming increasingly complicated.

Julian Schroeder, a board member, donor, and volunteer who'd worked creatively and tirelessly for all the Fonkoze organizations and had earned the respect of everyone in the room, remained silent for a long time as the discussion progressed. Finally, Julian spoke. As was usually the case, the group hung on his every word.

"Folks, on difficult issues there is a time for being decisive," Julian said. "But sometimes, it is better to muddle through and pick the issue up at a future date. My strong sense is that the intercompany debt issue is not ripe for resolution now. The best course is to muddle through and to defer it until other issues are resolved."

I had never thought that "muddling through" could be seen in a positive light. Rather, I saw it as a sign of weakness or indecision. So I was initially disappointed by Julian's statement. But I came to see the validity of his point in this instance. Deferring a decision would prevent the meeting from devolving into chaos and ill will, which would have made my job as moderator nearly impossible. Everyone quickly voiced support for "muddling through," and we moved on to productive discussions of other agenda items during the remainder of the day. Happily, our group cohesion was not undone by that divisive issue, mainly because no proposal had been pushed through in the absence of agreement.

Julian didn't simply let the issue drop. Over the next two years, he worked to cobble together a consensus for an approach to the intercompany debt problem that was radically different from the one that Matt Balitsaris and I had proposed, but which accomplished the same objectives. At one point, all that stood in the way of implementing his solution was one holdout on the board. Had I been in Julian's shoes, I might have lost patience and succumbed to the temptation of criticizing this individual, which would have likely resulted in his position hardening. Instead, Julian courted him and ultimately won his consent. In short order, this thorny issue was resolved, once and for all.

Since that fateful day when Julian humbly implored us to kick the debt issue down the road, I have learned to recognize other instances when pushing for quick resolution of an issue is not the best approach. More often than we recognize, problems solve themselves or even turn out not to be problems at all. But even when this doesn't happen, timing is everything. Sometimes a group is simply not ready to rally behind a painful solution, even if it is necessary. You may be able to steamroll or defeat a few holdouts, but doing so may result in a victory that proves futile, since your embittered opponents may end up undermining the agreement. What's more, the political capital you've lost in the process may imperil other priorities.

Of course, muddling through isn't always the best choice. Some issues are so urgent, or so linked to others, that they need to be resolved, even imperfectly, sooner rather than later—even if it makes the people driving for that solution enemies in the process. Recognizing the difference takes judgment, insight, and experience. And leading your team to the right decision also requires an individual with an appropriate supply of social capital. Among the members of the Fonkoze team, Julian was probably the only person who could have gotten us to accept a muddle-through decision on the debt issue. If that option had been advocated by someone with a reputation as a weak or indecisive leader, the team's reaction would probably have been highly negative, perhaps turning the meeting into an angry exchange of accusations and complaints.

It's a great example of why effective leadership is more art than science—a collection of skills that must be learned and then wielded with enormous sensitivity, thoughtfulness, and care.

11

Coping with Success

How to deal with the different—but equally challenging—issues that arise when a nonprofit enjoys a sudden wave of recognition and support

HAVING TOO LITTLE MONEY can create tensions in a nonprofit or mission-driven organization—that's obvious. Yet having a large influx of money, as well as other outward signs of success, can also create unexpected tensions.

When unprecedented sums of money flooded GF at the end of 2004, I dimly realized that it would change a lot for us. Having operated on a shoestring budget for so long, I didn't know what changes it would bring, so I was unable to prepare myself and the organization very effectively.

The new financial realities brought many benefits, of course. Long-delayed programs, hires, and raises could be approved. Some tradeoffs that created tensions disappeared; no longer did we always have to rob Peter to pay Paul. Our past approach to budgeting, based on a bottom-up process, where leaders were allowed to spend only what they had raised in the current or previous fiscal year, had created lots of frustration. Now that we were relatively flush with cash and assured of a secure pipeline of resources for the next five years, we could plan and act in new ways.

For example, at one point in early 2005, Peter Bladin, one of the former Microsoft executives who'd joined our organization in 2001, suggested that we carve out a portion of the $4 million we'd received as a grant from the Omidyar Network and use it to launch a capital markets team. To run this new operation, we would hire Jennifer Meehan, a top finance professional with terrific emotional intelligence and an unmatched work ethic who'd been working for us as a consultant. According to Peter's plan, we would allow and even encourage Jennifer to hire two or three good people as fast as she could find them. One of those hires, Camilla Nestor, turned out to be one of our best staff members ever. Launching this team was a big bet for us, one that would have been impossible just six months earlier, but we decided to do it—and it worked out very well. I am glad that I overcame my urge to hoard the money and backed Peter's bold idea instead.

There was a pent-up desire among many staff to hire more people who already had outstanding reputations in the fields of microfinance and information technology for development. The allure of patiently growing our own talent in the spirit of gung-ho amateurism had faded, especially since it was not our only option anymore. Our organizational structure, which had always been considered unusually lean, would soon begin to be criticized as too top-heavy.

But there were pitfalls to the new normal. Some team members became less cost-conscious when spending GF resources, which rankled those who remained penny pinchers. The people who felt they'd done the most to secure our big new grants felt that they deserved outsized influence in decision making. Thus, our new wealth didn't eliminate organizational tensions, as I'd hoped it would, but simply created new ones that displaced some of those that had become familiar.

When Stresses Mount, Don't Be Shy About Asking for Help

DURING MOMENTS OF ORGANIZATIONAL CONFLICT, invest heavily in talking one on one with people who can help you navigate the turbulence. Tell them why you are leading the organization the way you are, and ask for their advice. These are the moments when seeking help can pay enormous dividends.

Here's a story that illustrates how this can work for you.

The influx of cash we enjoyed in late 2004 drove some major personnel changes at GF. Feeling flush and filled with self-confidence, we hired more and more senior people, including one person who was a genuine superstar of the nonprofit world, a woman I'll call Judy. This hiring would turn into a double-edged sword.

Judy approached her job with enormous energy and had great ideas. She recruited outstanding people onto the staff and our board committees, and leveraged her reputation and relationships for GF in other ways. She worked well with me, at least at first, and was reassuringly respectful of my role as founder and CEO. A senior staff member, who was initially deflated by no longer reporting to me but to Judy, dealt with it professionally and grew to like her active and supportive management style. For a time, I basked in the glory of having hired Judy.

However, as the months passed, the honeymoon began to fade. A series of unfortunate personal tendencies in Judy's behavior started to surface. She seemed to create hierarchies where none were needed; she felt slighted without cause; she engaged in gossip about her colleagues (including me); and she spent more time playing office politics than nurturing her staff. These and other problems made people throughout the organization increasingly tense. Judy's relationship with our chief operating officer deteriorated, until one day he resigned suddenly.

As her integration into our organization unfolded, I made two critical mistakes. First, I somewhat passive-aggressively averted my gaze from Judy's problematic behaviors, perhaps in part because I hoped that her approach would lead people to appreciate my management style more by comparison. Second, I passed up some opportunities to feed her ego with praise and other subtle signals of her unique status, which probably exacerbated her need to "self-stroke" through political gamesmanship.

However, as time passed and the problem continued to fester, I realized I couldn't ignore it any longer. I also decided that I needed help in dealing with it. Accordingly, I scheduled private meetings with ten senior or influential staff members to discuss the situation. I told each of them that I was moving toward the conclusion that we would have to let Judy go, and I asked for their feedback and advice.

As I spoke privately to these selected colleagues, including a few whom Judy had recruited into GF, I noticed some things that raised my spirits. I'd been worried that people would judge me harshly, believing that Judy's problems were due to my deficient leadership abilities. That didn't seem to be the case. As it turned out, most of them had a fairly balanced view of her awesome talent as well as her increasingly disruptive behaviors.

I was also pleased by the feedback these team members offered. They asked clarifying questions, expressed their own doubts about Judy's behavior, and offered advice about how to navigate the next few weeks. Almost all of them responded positively to my conviction that letting Judy go was the right thing to do, and they offered me their empathy and support. It turned out to be much easier to navigate these choppy waters than I had imagined. I sensed that taking people into my confidence and seeking their advice and support in a private setting changed the dynamic significantly. (Bob Eichfeld stepped in help convince the one colleague who doubted my approach that it was in the organization's best interest—just the kind of essential intervention that he would make time and again over the course of his sixteen years on our board.)

When the time came, Judy and I had what became our final conflict. I struggled very hard to maintain my composure and control my emotions during our final one-on-one meeting, but somehow I held it together. I offered Judy an expanded role at GF and a promotion that she had coveted, but only if she agreed to receive and take on board some anonymous feedback from her colleagues in a few specific behavioral areas—something I knew she would refuse to do. For a moment, she accepted my offer—then quickly changed her mind. By the time the meeting ended, Judy had agreed to leave.

There was one additional step in terms of closing ranks and moving on that our chairman at the time took on his own initiative. He sought out Judy and met her for a cup of tea soon after her decision to leave. He tactfully allowed Judy to express her feelings about the situation, wished her well, and then rather pointedly asked her to confirm that she intended to do nothing to harm the organization or me in the months and years ahead. She said that was her intention—and, to her credit, she carried out that promise faithfully.

Our chairman was the perfect person to play this role. He was probably the wealthiest and most influential person on our board, and he was someone Judy respected and wanted to stay in the good graces of. His well-timed gesture in orchestrating a professional and mutually respectful parting probably helped to shape her behavior. When he later reported the essence of this conversation to the board, it helped them digest the episode and somehow raised the level of loyalty, support, and dedication that everyone gave to the organization from that point onward.

For my part, I made sure to attend Judy's farewell gathering at GF and to speak up, sincerely thanking her for her many contributions and for her gestures of friendship to me personally.

The biggest takeaway for me is that, in moments of organizational turbulence, it's important to invest a lot of time in talking privately with your most trusted and influential employees, team members, donors, and volunteers. Explain what is happening, what you are doing to address the situation, and why. Be clear about what has been decided and about what you are open to revisiting or changing. Ask for their advice and listen to it, and reaffirm how much you value their dedication to the organization.

If you do all these things when your organization is struggling to cope with change, your chances of surviving to lead the team to bigger and better achievements in the future will go way up.

The Nobel Prize: Microfinance Becomes a Target

"ALEX, YOU HAVE A PHONE CALL," my wife Emily shouted into the bathroom as I showered.

I was not used to getting calls like this. It was 5:05 a.m. Who would be calling so early?

"Something about Professor Yunus," Emily added. I was momentarily alarmed. Had my mentor suddenly died? He was only sixty-seven years old.

I gulped, quickly toweled off, and grabbed the phone.

"This is CBS News," a voice announced. "Muhammad Yunus and Grameen Bank have just been awarded the Nobel Peace Prize. Would you be willing to be interviewed about this in five minutes?"

"Uh, yes," was all I could manage.

Could it be? After years of Yunus's team and his friends around the world wondering whether either the Nobel Peace or Economics Prize would be conferred on him—bringing with it recognition, resources, attention, and hopefully insulation from any future efforts by the government of Bangladesh to persecute him—our prayers had been answered. Or were they?

I checked the Internet through my maddeningly slow dial-up connection. Sure enough, there were other reports that the announcement had just been made in Oslo.

When the CBS reporter called, I proceeded to answer a handful of obvious questions over the course of three or four minutes. After I hung up, Emily and I just stared at each other in disbelief. A few hours later, I was on a live radio program where the other interviewee was the Indian Nobel-Prize-winning economist, Amartya Sen.

I had no idea how to prepare for all the emotions, activities, demands, and celebrations of the days that were to follow, though I had enough sense to put on a jacket and tie, as I did not always dress formally for work in those days.

The hours that ensued were a blur, though at times it was strangely calm. Occasionally I sat at my desk, wondering what to do. Anyone connected to Grameen and Yunus was swept up in all the hoopla. Congratulatory flowers arrived, courtesy of Lauren Hendricks, a senior executive at CARE whom I barely knew at the time, but whom I would come to admire in the years ahead. (She became an important ally and ultimately was appointed second in command at GF in 2016.) Emails from friends and professional colleagues flashed on my computer screen, with words of congratulations and assumptions that I would be too busy to respond. I wrote back immediately, in part to reinforce that this unexpected development was not going to insulate me from anyone. I fielded countless calls, including one from Jennifer Robey, a former romantic interest who admired Grameen and was studying Mandarin in a remote part of China at the time. I did media interviews and conferred with my board chair, Susan Davis.

I felt unprepared for this whirlwind, but at least I had the presence of mind, in the early afternoon, to call together the staff who worked at the headquarters of GF. Twenty-five of us gathered, standing in a circle. I invited people to share their thoughts, emotions, and ideas. Many were too stunned to do so. There were a lot of smiles.

Towards the end of the session, I searched for words that would give my staff something to think about while also motivating them. I came up with this: "The announcement today is going to bring everyone associated with Grameen new resources, new friends, and new capacity to get things done. We need to be ready to take advantage of this. At the same time, it will bring new scrutiny, new critics, and new hostility. We need to be ready for this, too. For now, let's just get back to work."

The group dispersed, slowly. Everyone was excited. Little did I know how prescient my comment would be—especially its second half.

I wondered how Yunus himself was doing. That evening, I called his unflappable chief secretary, Mir Akhtar Hossain. It was morning in Dhaka. Akhtar told me to call Yunus at home, which I did. The man who had become known as the father of microcredit picked up the phone. We exchanged a few words in Bengali about this unbelievable development, and then he hurriedly said that he had to go, because the latest of what was clearly a long stream of well-wishers had just barged into his modest apartment.

A few weeks later, the conclusion of a decade-long campaign to reach one hundred million of the world's poorest families with microcredit and related services was marked by a huge conference in Halifax, Nova Scotia. Buoyed further by the Nobel Prize announcement, the conference took on the air of a celebration.

In the aftermath of 2006, everything seemed possible for the microcredit movement—continued growth fueled by capital provided by savers, donors, and investors; adding new products while reducing the borrowing cost to loan clients; and building on growing credibility with support from governments throughout the world. The years that followed did indeed usher in rapid growth for microfinance.

They also brought inflated expectations of what was possible. Among some practitioners, ethical and operational standards fell and—perhaps inevitably—opponents and critics began to prepare blistering and bewildering attacks.

Then, in 2010, I watched as the frenzied growth of microfinance in India reached its logical conclusion with a huge influx of money from banks at the end of the fiscal year (March 31) and the long-anticipated initial public stock offering (IPO) of the rapidly growing microcredit company SKS. The IPO had been shrouded in secrecy for months as the necessary paperwork was filed with the regulators. Now India had its first publicly traded microfinance institution, whose mostly overseas investors reaped windfalls as the share price was quickly bid up and senior managers became millionaires overnight. No direct benefits accrued to SKS's women borrowers, something I had argued for on many occasions, including during a public debate with the CEO of SKS at the Asia Society.

Other Indian microfinance institutions (MFIs) began preparing to follow SKS's lead and go public even as a hornet's nest of opposition to microfinance in the state of Andhra Pradesh was bubbling over. It would lead, that fall, to the passage of long-threatened legislation that would effectively outlaw microfinance except when provided by the government. Microfinance opponents in the state parliament, the state and federal bureaucracy, and the media piled on, accusing MFIs of all manner of sins against the poor—a few of which were plausible and probably true, most of which were exaggerated, and some of which were outright lies.

As 2010 came to a close, worldwide supporters of microfinance were knocked off balance by the dramatic events in India. Then Grameen Bank itself was drawn into the narrative. A television documentary attacking microfinance and especially Muhammad Yunus was aired in Norway. Grasping at straws, the documentary insinuated that Yunus was involved in corruption based on a minor controversy between Grameen Bank and the government of Norway about a transfer of funds from the balance sheet of one Grameen company to another. The money never actually changed bank accounts, much less benefitting Yunus or anyone else personally. Despite the flimsiness of the charges, Sheikh Hasina, the prime minister of Bangladesh, seized on the documentary to let loose a tirade of criticisms aimed at Yunus and Grameen Bank. She called for an investigation, and her political allies and the media began a drumbeat of hostile actions and statements that continues to this day.

In 2011, the Central Bank governor wrote to Professor Yunus to say that he should leave his position as managing director because he had stayed beyond the 60-year mandatory retirement age. At this point, Yunus was 71 years old, which means that, according to the letter, he had over-stayed in the position for more than a decade. Yet the Central Bank had never questioned this appointment at any time during the previous 11 years. Furthermore, Yunus had been appointed by the board of an enterprise which was 97 percent owned by private individuals, namely the borrowers of the bank. His service term was decided by the board, and, as managing director of Grameen Bank, he was not subject to government service rules.

Under the circumstances, it was commonly understood in Bangladesh that the Central Bank governor had taken this unusual action under direct order from the highest authority in the country. Professor Yunus went to the high court of Bangladesh to argue that the statutory age limit did not apply to him. But the court's verdict was that he had no *locus standi*—in other words, he had no legal scope for seeking redress. He then went to the Supreme Court, which upheld the verdict of the high court. In accordance with the court verdict, Yunus resigned.

Potshots from the Sidelines

MEANWHILE, MICROCREDIT WAS UNDER ASSAULT on another front. Researchers, economists, and academics—some apparently with various kinds of axes to grind—had begun publishing articles and reports that they spun so as to convince many people that microcredit had failed.

At first, I was optimistic that researchers could play a valuable role in helping microfinance practitioners to test, analyze, and improve their methodologies—and, at times, they have indeed played this function. But by the mid 2010s, communication and trust had broken down between microfinance researchers and practitioners. The two groups hardly acknowledged one another's existence or their relevance in shaping the future of financial inclusion efforts. They should have found common cause in answering the most extreme critics and, much more menacingly, the populist governments that were causing havoc to the sector.

Imperfectly, I tried to keep the dialogue going through my blog posts, speeches, and direct discussions with people involved in these matters. But my patience boiled over in early 2015 when I attended a meeting of the program committee of GF board in Seattle. That session was joined by Dean Karlan, a professor of economics at Northwestern University who is also the founder of Innovations for Poverty Action (IPA), a New Haven-based think tank. It was a long tradition of GF to invite experts onto our board committees in order to make our discussions more robust, and Karlan, despite my differences with him, was a noted thought leader. Therefore, I did not block his appointment to this committee, which had been recommended by my colleague David Edelstein.

Karlan was contributing to the 2015 committee meeting as well as he normally does, which is to say, as long as the topic was not financial services for the poor, his added value to the dialogue was significant. Then, during a break in the meeting, I took Karlan aside to tell him that I had a serious bone to pick with him. I told him that a press release that had been issued by IPA to accompany a scholarly article summarizing six recent studies on microfinance had been irresponsible and dishonest. The headline, I said, was particularly unfair. It read, "Microcredit does not live up to promise of transforming lives of the poor, six studies show." Karlan immediately became defensive, saying he was unaware of the headline and thought that the press release itself was balanced. (Of course, with all such documents, many people only read and remember the words in large font at the top.)

I had read the full thirty-page article while preparing for an upcoming speech I was to give—a speech, ironically enough, that was the result of Dean Karlan laudably attempting to reach out to me and those who agreed with my views about the role of research in shaping microfinance policy and practice. The article was rather nuanced in most respects, and its main conclusions were fairly encouraging: the typical microcredit client benefits modestly; roughly ten percent of clients benefit significantly; and there is no pattern of harm being done to clients (as the most vocal critics of microcredit contended was the norm). If you take into account that the six organizations studied were far from the best regarded MFIs in operation, the news was even better. And once you considered that microfinance had grown large enough to reach close to 200 million families, and that modest and at times substantial benefits were accruing to such a large number of people on a financially sustainable basis, this was, to my mind, *really good news*.

However, the article had an odd tic that gave IPA the opening to stir controversy. In almost every case when the authors described some modest benefit accruing to typical microloan clients, they wrote that while these were real, the programs had *failed to deliver* the "transformational" benefits promised. Success was thus recast as failure. Two of many examples: "Summarizing and interpreting results across studies, we note a consistent pattern of modestly positive, but not transformative, effects." "Other results on the composition of consumption, as with income, suggest some potentially important if not transformative effects." (Neither did microfinance cure the common cold, but the authors felt no need to call attention to *that* shortfall!)

Why denigrate the positive impact a couple of microloans could have over a one- to two-year period by comparing it to the unrealistic benchmark of providing "transformational" benefits to the typical client? The only answer I could think of was that, consciously or not, the researchers were trying to draw attention to their work by distorting their findings to convey that they had proved the opposite of what people expected. (Understandably, the researchers I have shared this hypothesis with have denied it.) But, in fact, their research found that microloans provided by these six programs *were* helping—just not as dramatically as some of the earlier studies had concluded and that the most passionate advocates of microfinance had hoped for.

As mentioned above, the IPA press release summarizing the report made matters worse by emphasizing this distorted point even further, particularly in its one-sided headline. Even now I can't think of a more tendentious way of summarizing what was essentially good news, thereby making it sound like bad news.

When I confronted Karlan on this matter in Seattle, he responded by saying that microcredit practitioners and advocates had overpromised and thereby set a trap for themselves. I'd heard this argument before. Typically, some overheated rhetoric from the past was produced to make this case; ironically, a speech given at the original Microcredit Summit by Sheikh Hasina, then (and now) the prime minister of Bangladesh, was often used for this purpose, despite the fact that she later became one of the most vocal and hostile critics of microfinance. Of course, these and other examples of people lauding microfinance were not representative of what people in the field said, and, in any case, many of those claims had been at least somewhat justified by what the most thoroughly vetted research had been telling us for many years.

But as my tense conversation with Karlan progressed, I saw an opening for a useful dialogue, given the fact that both of us were scheduled to appear at a World Bank seminar just one week later. I pressed Karlan to use that event as an opportunity to clear the air. "Dean, like any industry, we aggressively promote our product and our approach," I said. "But remember that, for years, our claims were backed up by the most authoritative research available at the time, the Pitt/Khandker studies that were so positive." These were peer-reviewed papers, which meant they had supposedly withstood the highest level of academic scrutiny before publication. "Later," I continued, "the research community turned against those studies, and once we heard the critiques and saw new research showing less dramatic impact, we modulated our rhetoric. Why blame us now? The real problem is that the researchers have been sending out mixed and contradictory signals. We've simply used them as anyone in our position would."

Karlan constructively acknowledged the validity of my point and agreed to highlight this historical fact during his presentation at the World Bank seminar. "That will go a long way to healing this rift," I told him.

The next week, when I watched Karlan's talk at the World Bank seminar, I got excited when he put up a slide that included mention of the Pitt/Khandker studies and how they had emboldened practitioners, financiers, and advocates to expand the reach of microcredit—while also prompting skeptical researchers to try to validate and replicate their very promising findings. Unfortunately, Karlan never actually referred to this slide in his spoken remarks, which I ascribed to him being a little sloppy or nervous on stage, rather than due to an effort to downplay them. In any case, the omission was unfortunate.

During the last panel of the morning, I was invited up with a moderator and two other presenters. I made two basic points. First, I said that people should focus on what microcredit has accomplished rather than what it has not, and stop comparing it to the unrealistic standard of being rapidly transformative in the life of the typical or average client. I compared microcredit to modern medicine in its earliest decades, when the benefits it produced were modest. Aren't we all glad, I asked rhetorically, that people didn't give up and throw the baby out with the bathwater in frustration, and that they instead kept refining and improving medical interventions?

I then summarized what microfinance had already accomplished. Most important, it had demonstrated the ability of organizations providing microloans to cover their costs from fees paid for by the poor themselves—a unique achievement in the world of anti-poverty work. This economic sustainability led to a second accomplishment: the creation of a network of providers that had scaled up massively in a decentralized way. Third, this solution, which had proven to be both sustainable and scalable, was bringing consistent, though perhaps modest, benefits to the typical client within the first twelve to twenty-four months of their first loan, and much more significant benefits to a minority of them. "One can argue," I said, "that tens of millions of modestly positive impacts is anything but 'modest.'" I published my short speech online the day after the conference ended.

The response to my remarks from microfinance CEOs, practitioners, and advocates was very positive. Even competitors like Accion, the global nonprofit that had popularized microcredit in Latin America, published it on their blogs and sent it to top supporters and board members. The media picked up it, and I was interviewed and quoted in several stories that appeared in the weeks after the seminar, often being used as a counterpoint to Karlan and his allies. In general, the journalists reported neutrally or slightly favorably on my position.

But the research community greeted my challenge to their public accusations of failure with silence. While there were some good presentations during the afternoon sessions of the World Bank seminar, including a few who asked whether the research questions being asked were fundamentally the wrong ones, not a single speaker mentioned, referenced, affirmed, or even challenged what I had said. This silence continued in the online commentary on the subject in the weeks to follow, after which the debate died out or at least moved on.

In my final days working at GF, Beth Rhyne, the managing director of the Center for Financial Inclusion, made some striking observations in a very nice tribute to me and my years in the field:

> Alex has worked harder than anyone else in microfinance to reconcile the field with the assault launched on it several years ago by the "randomistas" of the Jameel Poverty Action Lab (JPAL) and Innovations for Poverty Action (IPA) who subjected microfinance to randomized studies and found it less impactful than previously hoped. Alex has repeatedly—almost obsessively—attempted to understand and process the results, to caution the academics against over-hyping the negative, and most important, to take up the challenge the academics are offering: that randomized studies could help test and improve product innovations. With his encouragement,

Grameen Foundation has worked with IPA and others on randomized studies.

Beth noted, further, that, "it is characteristic of Alex's approach to life that he debates Dean Karlan of IPA publicly, even while asking Dean to formally serve as an advisor to the Foundation, as a member of its program committee." Such nuanced and thoughtful praise was very meaningful given Beth's stature as one of the great thought leaders in the history of microfinance and financial inclusion—a stature that convinced me to become a founding member of her center's advisory council in 2009, which I served on until 2020.

And her praise was also unexpected, since I had assumed that she and many others in our field saw my efforts to debate and engage some in the research community as heavy-handed and unproductive. In reality, she understood my intentions even better than I did—perhaps another reminder that it's usually best to do what you think is right and not worry too much about what other people think, since you might not realize how much they appreciate your efforts.

As you can imagine, it has been frustrating for me and for other microcredit advocates to struggle against ill-defined and often unfair attacks in recent years. But there are lessons to be gleaned from our experiences.

Perhaps the most important of those lessons is that many of us who were advocating for microfinance were operating under some false assumptions. Let me share a few of my own.

Some fifteen years before these crises burst on the scene, a small group of Yunus's supporters had brainstormed about what we could do to get Yunus a Nobel Prize. (We did this with no encouragement from Yunus himself.) We were motivated mainly by the belief that becoming a Nobel laureate would create a kind of protective force field around him that would dissuade any future government from trying to inappropriately interfere with or take over Grameen Bank. It turned out we were totally wrong about how the world's most prestigious prize would impact his, and the bank's, vulnerability. We figured the prize would protect Yunus and Grameen. In reality, it made them more vulnerable.

Second, my faith in the judgment, management prowess, and (I am sad to say) ethics of some early microfinance leaders was misplaced. A few of them strayed far from Yunus's ideals. This was especially true as they grew rapidly and came face to face with their limitations and a variety of temptations—such as fame, wealth, nepotism—and struggled to confront them while often resisting the assistance of people outside their inner circle of advisors and family members. I also underestimated the extent to which the microfinance brand could be coopted by people whose objectives and ethics were less pure, and in some cases diametrically opposed to those of the modern microfinance movement's original leaders—people like Muhammad Yunus and Ela Bhatt, who founded the Self-Employed Women's Association of India in 1971.

Third, I figured that, when microfinance got sufficiently big, in terms of the number of people and amount of money involved in a given country, its size would protect it from people and institutions that were, or at least felt, threatened by microfinance. In fact, once it got big, microfinance became a bigger and more vulnerable target. Ironically and unexpectedly, the countries where interest rates on microloans were the *lowest* were typically the ones where they were most often accused of exploiting the poor. The reason: Though the MFIs were most affordable in those countries, they were also big players in those markets, which made them appear threatening to powerful vested interests, which were broader and more powerful than I had imagined.

The message for other leaders in the nonprofit arena: While growth, fame, acclaim, and the resources they bring can be powerful tools for enhancing the good that you and your organization can do, they can also create serious challenges that are difficult to anticipate and prepare for. Bigness can make you a target. So can the perception of wealth and power, especially if it appears to be used for personal gain or benefit. (And don't forget that many people have unrealistic standards for how much nonprofit staff should be paid—one reason why I unilaterally froze my GF salary at a point well below the market level for an organization of our size.) When you become well known, all of your actions and even the language you use to describe your work will be subject to intense scrutiny—much of which may seem, and be, unfair.

Thus, there's no moment to look forward to when you can pronounce yourself, or the organization you lead, a success and rest on your laurels. The best you can hope for is to encounter a new array of challenges, risks, and perhaps attacks—even as you continue to strive to help as many people in as many ways as you possibly can.

Responding to a Crisis

WHAT HAVE MY EXPERIENCES in dealing with the attacks on Grameen Bank and on microcredit taught me about crisis management and high-pressure situations in general? My overriding approach is a simple one: When you feel as if you are under assault, strive to act as normal as possible, be willing to apply common sense, and improvise solutions to the unfamiliar challenges you're likely to face.

Many people, in times of crisis, tension, and heightened emotions adopt a radically different persona—a distortion of who they really are. The most common distortions are to become more aggressive, loud and blustery, to panic, or to become passive if not completely paralyzed, unable to make decisions about what to do next. None of these are helpful, and they impede the use of the most valuable tools in such situations: calm, common sense, empathy, and humor.

When a crisis strikes, I consciously take a deep breath and ask the question, "What is the most obvious thing to do next?" A detailed plan is not necessary. Often a helpful agenda is to ask people how they are feeling (and really listen to what they say); to propose a modest step to improve or clarify the situation; and to attempt to learn more about the crisis and to define your options for resolving it.

Then, I try to start taking these simple steps without second-guessing myself too much or asking too many people for input or consent. I also try to be confident, while watching to see whether my first responses are working. If they aren't, I try something else. Usually, this sort of deliberate response causes the people around me to calm down and follow my lead, while momentum for resolution slowly builds.

At the same time, it is important to act quickly and decisively if there is something that can be done immediately that you are reasonably sure will save lives or prevent the situation from deteriorating. Use common sense to determine which issues require expert advice—from a lawyer, for example—and then seek it out and quickly act on it. This might involve turning over certain functions to outside professionals, even if for a short time or on a particular aspect of the crisis.

These approaches are not rocket science, but it's striking to me how few people behave this way when a crisis hits.

I can't count the number of times when I have seen people make a crisis much worse by acting or behaving unusually aggressively or passively, or by ignoring common sense or the emotions of others. At the same time, I've been surprised by the success I've generally achieved at resolving crises, and the degree to which people look to me for leadership, simply as a result of my remaining calm and taking modest steps informed by common sense and strategic consultation with others involved, and, where necessary, an expert.

12

Building a Great Board

How to create and work with a highly effective board of directors and advisors

IF YOU'RE A NONPROFIT LEADER, the board of directors that governs your organization will be one of the major factors in determining your success or failure. Early in your leadership journey, you'll need to make peace with the fact that there are few if any shortcuts to building a great board. They are built one good member, one good meeting, and even one good agenda item at a time.

I learned this truth, in part, from John C. Whitehead, a renowned and beloved New York-based businessman and philanthropic leader who also served as a deputy secretary of state during Ronald Reagan's second term as president. I met Whitehead through Steve Rockefeller when Steve and I were raising money for our India programs in June, 2000. Whitehead, who was an advisor to the Rockefeller family, committed $50,000 to our effort.

He went on to meet with me dozens of times, committing hundreds of thousands of dollars without any restrictions as to their use, and giving me advice on many matters. On one occasion, he agreed to schedule a call with me during his vacation. On another, he decided not to take a call from the governor of New York so as to avoid interrupting one of our mentoring sessions.

As you can imagine, I took everything he said seriously. Still, I felt deflated early in our relationship when Whitehead told me, "Building a high-performing board takes time. You bring on someone better than your average board member and put them in a position to raise everyone's level of effort and performance. And then a year later, you do it again, and then again, after another year. Great boards are built one brick at a time."

I was impatient, and I realized that our early board at Grameen Foundation was far from ideal. But Whitehead's wisdom mirrored that of my most trusted and experienced advisors, including Susan Davis, our board chair from 2000 to 2006.

I once drafted a seven-page memo about changes I wanted to make in our board, and I shared it with Susan and a few others. None of them liked it, which helped punch another hole in my pipe dream of building a great board overnight. Everyone thought that the memo was too long, detailed, and prescriptive. If we were to change the board, the plan needed the input of the key members currently serving. Furthermore, Susan said that my idea of bringing in a lot of new members at once could be destabilizing to the board, even if they were good potential members.

Susan also thought that my memo sent the message that the people now serving on the board were failing—a message they were unlikely to receive happily. For example, I'd written that we needed to replace my pal, Paul Kane, with a more qualified treasurer. Susan read that and said, "Well, since you are friends, I guess you can say that . . ." Her voice trailed off. She helped me understand that in a professional setting, saying and especially writing such words would be insulting.

It dawned on me that I still had much to learn about being a leader, or even a competent professional.

These messages from some of my most trusted advisors finally got through to me. I gradually mastered my tendency to be impatient and started working methodically with my entire team to build a high-performing board. Here are some of the techniques we used to make that happen.

First, we tried to make every contact a board member had with our organization be a quality contact—one that would let them add value, enjoy the experience, and feel appreciated. This applied to one-on-one meetings and phone calls, committee meetings, board meetings, and ad hoc brainstorming sessions we had sometimes with a handful of board and staff members. It required careful preparation, focused effort, thorough documentation of what happened and what we learned, and rigorous and timely follow-up.

We worked hard to treat our board members as individuals with unique preferences, sensitivities, and perspectives. We spared no effort to make them understand that we customized our approach to them, rather than offering generic, paint-by-numbers engagement activities. When I or another staff member made a mistake in our engagement with a board member, we took responsibility, apologized, and did our best never to repeat the mistake.

We also provided regular feedback to our board members. We developed a system in which the board chair, the vice-chairs, the governance committee chair, our supremely dedicated general counsel Julia Soyars, and I would sit down together twice a year to evaluate each board member's performance. We used this meeting to figure out how to give board members recognition and feedback—including, sometimes, a gentle push to do better. Most important, we developed plans to set them up to be and feel even more successful than they had been previously. With one notable exception (for which we paid dearly), we never tried to force fit anyone into a role they didn't like—including board membership itself. Instead, we let people who did not want to join our board to serve in other ways, sometimes allowing them to enjoy the positive aspects of being a board member while avoiding whatever they disliked. (However, it is important to mention that there were certain things that every board member needed to do regardless of their preferences, such as contributing to the fundraising effort and learning about all aspects of the organization, not just those they gravitated to.)

Our efforts to optimize and customize the engagement experience for individual board members enabled us to gradually recruit a great mix of wealthy, smart, well-connected, wise, and collaborative people who worked together very collegially most of the time. Time and again, they stepped up in ways that impressed and delighted me.

The Life Cycle of a Board Member

MOST BOARD MEMBERS go through three phases: orientation, high engagement and contribution, and coasting. As a nonprofit leader, your goal should be for them to get through orientation fairly quickly (taking into account people's varying learning and work styles), to make the second period as long, productive, and enjoyable as possible, and then to ease them off the board when they hit the third phase, while making some modest effort to keep them involved as board alumni. It may sound simple enough, but managing these life cycle transitions can be tricky.

Most experts on organizational governance will tell you that limits to board members' length of service—generally to two three-year terms—are essential. The idea is that ensuring that people can't serve for an unlimited period encourages members to maximize their efforts so as to leave a positive legacy by the time their period of service is up.

I'm in the minority that disagrees with this approach. The weakness of term limits is that they assume that all board members progress through the three phases at the same rate. That's simply not true. I have seen some board members spend up to two years getting oriented and confident in their roles before they began significantly contributing their time, money, expertise, ideas, contacts, and reputations. I've seen others move through the orientation process in a matter of weeks, even hours. Some are highly engaged for a year or two, then get bored or distracted, while others continue contributing at a high level for ten or even fifteen years. Applying, say, a six-year limit to all these varied individuals would needlessly truncate the service of some while dragging out the ineffective tenures of others.

Far better, in my opinion, for the CEO and his or her team to work to get the most out of each board member for as long as possible after making their orientation as thorough and brief as possible. This requires the CEO and board leaders to monitor each board member's performance throughout their term to assess, among other things, whether they are beginning to coast. Whenever a member's term, usually lasting two or three years, is nearing its end, meet with them to gauge their interest in re-upping. If they are coasting, they are likely to volunteer to step down, particularly if board meetings are structured to visibly draw attention to the achievements of those who are performing well (and the shortcomings of those who are not). While some people will stay on board for years even though they are coasting, perhaps to maintain relationships with other serving members or to track the status of projects they helped get off the ground in an earlier era, it is possible to create a culture on a board where doing so is frowned upon and, in practice, rarely happens.

I've only seen this approach to board tenures backfire twice. Once, I told a board member who was performing at a lower level than in the past (and in fact needed to get bailed out of a commitment he couldn't keep by another board member) that the chairman and I thought he should step down. As he told me later, he was initially "mad as hell" at me, though he accepted our verdict. However, years later, he admitted it was the right thing for the organization.

In another case, the board chair and I decided to have a private meeting with a board member who was not performing to the level she had in the past. We outlined our expectations, listened to her comments, and said we would support her reelection if she made a good faith effort to improve. She agreed, but in the end her level of effort only increased marginally.

Other than these two cases, we experienced no problems with our flexible approach to board tenures. I also believe that term limits for board chairs are needless. I particularly oppose rotating the chairmanship annually, since most board chairs need at least a year in office to find their footing. But, in practice, informally rotating board chairs every four to six years makes good sense in most cases. Having active and engaged vice-chairs and committee chairs also helps ensure a steady stream of fresh leaders.

One small additional point: I don't think it is necessary to have the vice-chair also be the chair-elect, and in some cases it can even be counterproductive. Better to let the vice-chair, through his or her diligent work, earn the support of the board to emerge as the next chair.

Board Member as Change Agent

THERE ARE PEOPLE WHO SAY it's essential to ensure that the people you recruit to your board fit into the existing organizational culture. I see things a little differently. I prefer to talk about the evolving culture of an organization I associate with, and I look for people who will not simply assimilate but also help the culture become even better.

Sometimes even the best boards need change agents—people who will push the group out of their comfort zones and into their next phase of development. This can be a tricky role to fill. I was once recruited onto a board specifically to help transform how it functioned, only to find that the resistance to my ideas was so fierce that I was forced to resign.

At GF, I recruited one such change agent, but it wasn't easy.

During the mid-2000s, I tracked down a potential donor who had come onto our organizational radar during my 2004 sabbatical. A few different people, including me, had made half-hearted efforts to go to see him in his home in the Southeast where he had semi-retired after making a lot of money with a New York-based software company. When I finally met up with him, I learned that he had joined the board of a smaller competitor about a decade earlier, because GF did not yet exist. The thing that had inspired him was the *60 Minutes* segment on Grameen Bank that Susan Davis had starred in and that I had helped produce.

As I got to know "Gary" across a few meetings, I came to understand him as a serious, generous, straight-talking businessman who was somewhat lacking in diplomacy. At one point, I asked him for a big donation, and Gary countered with a request that we consider electing him to the GF board as part of the deal. I sensed that linking a donation to board membership in this way might be a little controversial among some on the GF board. Yet I wanted the donation—and I also suspected that Gary's approach to philanthropy and governance might help our board evolve to its next level of excellence.

After talking it over with a number of people, I became increasingly convinced that Gary would make a good board member. But since I felt that others might have doubts about his ability to fit in, I put it on the agenda for discussion at one meeting. I was prepared to argue the case for electing Gary and to encourage others to make their own cases against, living up to my growing conviction that boards shouldn't paper over disagreements but rather openly air them. I was coming to believe that open disagreements and non-unanimous votes are healthy and evidence that a board is doing its job well. But our board wasn't quite there yet.

On this occasion, after making my opening comments in favor of Gary's candidacy, I invited others to speak their minds on this important matter. No one spoke up. When it came time to vote, the resolution to elect Gary passed unanimously. I think this was driven in part by the fact that most members trusted my judgment and in part by their discomfort with openly challenging me.

I am pleased to report that Gary turned out to be a good, and at times excellent board member. He certainly had his own unique style. But he always came prepared, gave a lot of money, and often praised staff and board colleagues in well-informed and frankly touching ways. He later emerged as a strong and important ally of my colleague David Edelstein, who had the challenging job of running GF while my successor was being recruited. At one point, the universally respected Paul Maritz told me that, while Gary had an unusual style, at the end of the day, he was an outstanding board member. I passed the essence of that message on to Gary, and he was touched.

One of the things that Gary and I worked on together was changing the culture around how dissent was handled by the board. Previously, if a few board members were uncomfortable with a pending decision, they would talk informally to people in the lead-up to a meeting. If they did not sway enough people to their side, they would not make the case for their minority view during the meeting; instead, they would vote for the motion they opposed. The group valued collegiality so highly that robust debates on certain topics were sometimes minimized and unanimous votes were expected.

On two occasions, when Gary's view differed from that of the other board members, I actively encouraged him to speak his mind and to vote his conscience, so as to demonstrate how I thought healthy boards should operate. Both times, Gary cast a lone dissenting vote. I think that, with the benefit of hindsight, many others would now vote with Gary on at least one of those issues.

The role Gary played in helping us develop a new culture around dissent was one of his more important contributions. I have come to advocate open dissent on every board I serve on or advise, because I think it's an important practice for any board that wants to add maximum value to the organization it governs.

The Care and Feeding of Board Members

"THAT WAS ONE THING ABOUT YOU, ALEX," Eleanor Wagner said. "You always made me feel like I had an important role to play. You put me to work, and you always followed up." She and I were having a cup of tea several years after my departure from GF. Wagner had served as the board treasurer during my final months as CEO, and her words meant a lot to me. Nurturing the engagement of leaders like Wagner was one of my most important jobs at GF.

It took me some years of encouragement by advisors—and recovery from my early mistakes with our founding board—for me to resolve to devote significant time into cultivating our board members properly. Rather than wait for them to step up and preemptively justify my expenditure of time on them, I reversed the logic. I committed to investing far more time in them than many of my CEO peers would spend on their board members (except perhaps those who were major donors). In return, I felt they gave me their very best—often far more than I ever could have asked for or expected.

How did I give them my time? I scheduled calls and meetings with each board member on a regular basis according to their convenience; I prepared meticulously to ensure that the conversations would be valuable and successful from their perspective (and mine); I gave them my full attention when I was with them; and I followed up on the topics we discussed quickly and with high attention to detail and to their personal preferences.

Furthermore, I ensured that whatever committees they served on were staffed effectively so they could expect a satisfying and meaningful experience. I made sure that the value they brought to the organization was communicated to the other board members they most respected. I made it a priority for our staff members—including me—to follow up on every volunteer or donor they introduced to the organization, and I kept them apprised of how those relationships unfolded. I paid attention to which employees, volunteers, and board members they seemed to most enjoy being around, and figured out ways to maximize their time with them.

That wasn't all. Whenever possible, I tried to position each board member so that they could have a unique project or responsibility tailored to their interests that they could tackle for a number of years, ultimately yielding a sense of accomplishment unlike anything they had ever experienced. Finally, I showed interest in their hobbies, their other nonprofit commitments, their families, and anything else they cared about. For example, if I knew they liked tennis, I might try to figure out a way to get them some free tickets to a professional tournament.

Many CEOs see board engagement, like fundraising, as a necessary evil. This leads them to make some basic errors in relating to board members. For instance, they may be overly solicitous of the wealthiest people on their board while basically ignoring the others, allowing the board to develop an invisible but very real caste system. The result is often an understandable degree of resentment and disengagement on the part of board members.

Instead, I sought to create the ideal board experience for each member, regardless of their wealth and giving history. Even before inviting someone to join the board, I would try to engage them as volunteers; then, after they became board members, I would invest in them even more and expect them to push themselves in response. This treatment generally worked well. The majority of our board members attended almost every meeting (including committee meetings), contributed as much money as their means allowed, provided staff with encouragement and support, and often gave of themselves beyond the call of duty—for example, by covering for a fellow board member who was unable to meet a financial commitment due to Bernie Madoff's thievery.

So my advice to any nonprofit CEO who seeks guidance regarding board management is simple: Invest, invest and then invest some more. Make each interaction high quality and satisfying to the board member, and train your staff to follow your lead. In short, make creative and positive board member engagement an organizational habit. It will pay dividends far beyond what you imagine.

The Greatest Gift a Board Can Give—Making You Better

AS 2004 CAME TO AN END, I was exhilarated but also exhausted—more even than I knew.

Grameen Foundation had just completed its breakthrough year, growing our revenue to more than $11 million. It took everything I had to lead our team through the strategic planning process and then to hit the road to raise an unprecedented amount of money to support our strategic plan. I had pushed everyone, including myself, very hard. Perhaps too hard. After all, I had promised hundreds of people that we were going to achieve some world-changing things over the four years ahead—and, I am happy to say, we ended up meeting or exceeding many of those goals. But the journey was far from easy.

Along the way, my many weaknesses, insecurities, and gaps as a professional had begun to show. My state of mind included not just excitement and determination but also elements of bewilderment (I never expected success to come so quickly) and arrogance (I must be pretty amazing if all these people have rallied around my vision, my leadership!).

Thankfully, I was blessed with a wise and insightful board. They knew that, after such a successful and turbulent year, my annual evaluation—something many boards do as an afterthought or not at all—would be particularly crucial. Susan Davis and Yvette Neier realized that they had to figure out what to do with the complaints my team had about me. They had to figure out how to tell me, in response to my desire to go full speed ahead, "Yes, but not quite so fast." And they had to manage these challenges without discouraging me or breaking my spirit—while still making sure I heard their concerns and took them seriously.

When the day for my evaluation arrived, Susan and Yvette struck just the right balance. They sat down with me and started by praising me generously about the good things that had happened under my leadership. Then they pivoted. "We want you to be well equipped to steer the larger and more powerful ship that GF is now becoming," they said. "To make that happen, we want to invest in you as a leader." They insisted that I allocate the surprisingly large sum of $30,000 for my professional development, mainly to pay for a management coach that I would choose in consultation with the board leaders. (In retrospect, I suppose it *was* a reasonable amount when one considers how much money I had brought in the previous year and how much lower my salary was compared to leaders of similar-sized organizations.)

In that moment, I felt both appreciated and known—appreciated for how much I had achieved, and known for my many inadequacies and weaknesses. Part of me had hoped my foibles were invisible, while another part of me had hoped they would be seen so I could get the help I needed to improve. The board members showed me that they recognized the areas where I needed growth, understood them, and were determined not to condemn me for them but rather to support me in overcoming them. This gesture from the board was in some ways the greatest gift of the entire breakthrough year.

Every nonprofit CEO should seek to have an ongoing dialogue with their board about their professional development needs. That dialogue should be informed by input from colleagues, friends, peers in CEO roles, and others who know you well—your spouse, for example. The changing fortunes, assets, risks, and opportunities facing the organization should also shape the conversation. As for the educational and developmental tools you employ to enhance your current skills and create new ones, those should be tailored to your unique personality and learning style. My preference, shaped by GF's great human resources director Norm Tonina, is for customized advisory services, sabbaticals, study breaks, and stretch assignments.

Some version of this same approach should cascade down to all of your staff. People at every level ought to be treated as the most important resource of your organization—which, of course, they are.

Ending the Accountability Shell Game— By Learning to Trust

"ALEX, WE ARE NOT SETTING THESE GOALS to hit you over the head with them if you fall short on some."

They were just a few words spoken in one of hundreds of conversations I had with my board chair, Susan Davis. But they changed my approach to leading organizations forever.

Like many nonprofit leaders, when it came to target setting, I had engaged in a certain degree of deception and obfuscation during my early years leading GF. I had a set of ambitious, inspiring goals that, for the most part, I kept to myself. They encapsulated the impact I hoped to have on global poverty. But because I was unsure about whether I could reach those objectives, there were few people I felt I could trust with them. So I generally kept them to myself.

When my board of directors asked for annual or multiyear goals, rather than sharing my *real* goals, I would propose rather modest targets. This would protect me from being caught underperforming, which might lead to criticism and to new constraints on my autonomy—which I imagined would make it even more difficult to reach my private goals.

On the other hand, modest goals don't have much power to inspire. So I also became adept at presenting more ambitious targets to donors and the public in order to inspire them to take us seriously and to donate as much money and time as they could. Those goals tended to be somewhat vague and long-range—a kind of hybrid between my ambitious private targets and the modest ones I reluctantly allowed my board to hold me accountable for.

Everyone inside the organization seemed to understand that these public goals were more for marketing purposes than for planning.

When it came time to report on our progress, I adopted yet another stance. Rather than compare what we'd achieved in the last year to the goals we'd set, I focused on the most impressive-sounding activities and outcomes, mostly described anecdotally, and then pivoted to talking about hoped-for progress in the months ahead. If this presentation met the smell test of being at least adequate, typically no one would ask challenging questions or go back to the original targets and ask me to compare how we had performed against them.

This accountability shell game, in which nonprofit CEOs and boards are often complicit, came to an end during my life-changing conversation with Susan Davis. Her message was that it was safe for me to drop the obfuscation, because she would make sure that I was dealt with fairly if we fell short of the goals I proposed to the board. Susan had been a nonprofit CEO herself, and she had informally mentored me from the age of twenty-two when she worked for the Ford Foundation in Bangladesh and I was a Fulbright scholar there. If there was anyone I could trust, it was Susan.

So I decided to take the leap. I shared with Susan my hope that GF might increase its revenue from $4 million in 2002 to $6 million in 2003. As it happened, we met that goal almost exactly. As I'd hoped we might, we became thought leaders in the growing field of using information technology to advance poverty reduction, and we helped some well-chosen and strategically supported microfinance institutions (MFIs) in India grow significantly while seeding six new MFIs in Mexico and Central America.

At the same time that I began trusting the board with my goals, I took another leap of faith by letting colleagues and volunteers take the lead on implementing my ideas, and their own, without close supervision or direct involvement by me. In other words, I finally developed the courage to delegate. The results often exceeded my grandest ambitions. As mentioned earlier, our revenue hit nearly $12 million in 2004, driven mainly by major donor buy-in to our five-year strategic plan, itself developed through the participatory process described earlier—buy-in that was nurtured by a fundraising staff that worked overtime during the summer of 2004 while I took a three-month sabbatical. That long break represented perhaps the most significant and risky act of self-care in my entire career. It wouldn't have been possible if I hadn't been learning to trust the people I worked with.

In the years to come, similar breakthroughs occurred. In early 2005, we closed an historic transaction in India, where our $350,000 loan guarantee leveraged $4.2 million in capital to fund microloans averaging $100 in southern India (as described in chapter seven). The impetus for that achievement, which received positive coverage in the *Economist*, came from a mid-level member of my team—another dividend from my growing willingness to empower and to trust colleagues. We then built on that transaction later in 2005 by launching a global loan guarantee facility that had been conceptualized by board member Bob Eichfeld, who would later become chairman. Susan Davis and our exceptionally talented development officer Barb Weber closed a $10 million commitment to the facility from one wealthy supporter without my even being present; then they turned around and got another Silicon Valley titan to match it. Presto, $20 million! We added $11 million more within a few weeks and announced the milestone at the first Clinton Global Initiative.

Years later, around the time her six-and-a-half-year term as board chair was coming to a close, Susan made a comment that stuck with me almost as much as her original request that I trust her while goal-setting. Standing before around 150 people at the Harvard Club at a luncheon to celebrate our first ten years of existence and her tenure as chair, she commented:

> One of the things that Alex, and perhaps all social entrepreneurs, do is to ask people to do far beyond what would normally be considered reasonable to advance their organization's mission. Over time, the unreasonable becomes reasonable, and people devote more time and money than they

ever could have imagined in the beginning. And that's how organizations like Grameen Foundation grow and have big impact.

Later board chairs benefited from and built on the way Susan and I worked together. Like Susan, Paul Maritz, a technology entrepreneur and corporate executive, helped to educate me about the true purpose of goals. On one occasion, when he saw that we had fallen short on some of our goals in the wake of the global financial crisis, he said, with characteristic brevity and empathy, "Well, if we had met all of our targets, it probably would have meant that they weren't ambitious enough." On another occasion, Paul advised me that during the remainder of my career, most of what I would accomplish would be through others rather than mainly on my own.

In my subsequent roles as CEO, board chair, and consultant to other nonprofit organizations, I tried to recreate that kind of magical trust between the leader and the other stakeholders, where goals are clear and shared with everyone, where real responsibility is delegated, and where the best ideas bubble up and are developed no matter where they come from. I ensured that annual goals were explicit and that the extent to which they'd been reached was transparent to everyone in the organization. I have had both successes and failures along the way. But my willingness to trust a board with goals, and to trust my colleagues with implementing them, are two things that have endured and become major factors in all I've accomplished.

13

Forging Partnerships

Connecting effectively with outside individuals
and organizations to accomplish things
you could never achieve alone

NONPROFITS LIKE GRAMEEN FOUNDATION can bring tangible benefits not only to the poor, but also to the privileged. I realized this most clearly during a dinner I had with a lawyer in Houston who had contributed hundreds of hours of his time to help advise and shape complex and innovative GF programs. When I thanked Mitch Blakely for his help, he turned it around and thanked me!

When I asked him why, he explained how volunteering with GF had changed his life. In the course of his career, Mitch had gotten very good at one specialized aspect of the law—in fact, he was one of the best in the country at it. As a result, working on this one kind of transaction was often the only thing he was asked to do. He became significantly more financially secure than when he grew up, but also terrifically bored. He felt as if he was living the life of a lawyer starring in a remake of *Groundhog Day*.

Against this backdrop, Mitch often sought work outside his legal specialty, but at his billing rate, such work was rare. When Mitch began working for GF, he felt he gained a new lease on life. It allowed him to branch out, try new things, gain new skills, and rediscover the joy of learning. He wasn't being paid in cash, but the intangible benefits he was receiving were invaluable to him. And they were paying off in other ways as well. His work with GF made his days more interesting and enjoyable, and became a seed for his current adventures. And of course he was pleased with the positive social impact these programs were having, in part due to his pro bono support.

That dinner conversation was a revelation to me—another example of the win/win/win possibilities in philanthropy. It also illustrates one of the big truths of nonprofit work—the fact that we can often accomplish much more when we create partnerships with other people and organizations, from donors and volunteers to the people who create and run programs dedicated to goals that complement our own. In a sense, Yunus had applied the same insight by activating the poor women of Bangladesh to be his partners in reducing poverty there through his empowerment-oriented approach. Forging such partnerships takes work, trust, and openness—but when planned and executed with care, they can pay huge dividends for everyone involved.

Giving Volunteers the Power to Lead

MANY NONPROFITS HAVE PROJECTS and programs that could benefit enormously from an infusion of new energy and ideas. Yet when volunteers approach nonprofits to offer their time and expertise, they often get a tepid response. The reasons are understandable. Nonprofit leaders tend to prefer getting things done by employees that they hire and can direct (and even fire), rather than volunteers who often think they know better (sometimes correctly!) and are occasionally resistant to being managed. When volunteers are also donors, or people we hope will become donors, it can be awkward and difficult to tell them when we believe their ideas are off-base. As a result, they are often merely tolerated or humored rather than treated as serious partners with value to add and who can be held accountable. The unspoken message sent is, "Please, just give us your money and leave the work to the professionals." Volunteers end up disillusioned, feeling that the nonprofits they care about view them as piggy banks with little to contribute beyond their dollars. Staff come to see volunteer involvement as meddling by amateurs that just makes their jobs more complicated.

Awkward attitudes toward volunteering are widespread in the nonprofit world. Let me give you an example. A friend of mine heads a think tank that I am involved in. She once told me she hated asking people to serve on her advisory council because she felt she was imposing on them.

"I see it differently," I said. I told her that I viewed our twice-a-year meetings as terrific networking opportunities and a form of free continuing education, since they allowed us to catch up on the best ideas and papers in our field. "I think most of the other council members agree," I told her. "If anything, we feel that we owe you our thanks for the privilege of serving." I sensed that they wanted to be asked to do more, and the only thing that stood in the way was my friend's mindset that doing so was an imposition rather than an opportunity for those volunteers.

Sadly, I don't think my friend got the message. To this day, she struggles with asking people to join the council, and once they're on board, she hesitates to ask them to do much beyond attending meetings. Yet as I was completing this book, a leading council member told me he would like to be asked to do more.

I have been guilty of similar behavior at times. But my years at GF taught me that, sometimes, working with volunteers can solve multiple problems and create a positive chain reaction, leading to more donations, added value without any financial costs, and the emergence of fresh, creative ideas that can energize the entire organization.

One example centers on Jim Greenberg, an American businessman who was based for many years in Saudi Arabia. We met Jim as a result of a partnership with the wonderfully quirky financial advisory company Motley Fool in the fall of 1999. GF had sent Motley Fool a proposal describing how we would use donations from their clients if we were chosen to be one of their featured philanthropies during the holiday giving season. Our proposal specified that eighty-five percent of those donations would go towards capitalizing the loan funds of grassroots microlending organizations, and the remaining fifteen percent would cover our administrative costs. It was an elegant and compelling proposition. Our proposal was accepted, leading to more than $300,000 in donations and a vast expansion of our mailing list.

Among those donations was $10,000 from Jim and his lovely wife Lisa. Then, early one morning a few months after their initial donation, they sent me a fax saying they wanted to do more. Jim and Lisa had just had a good run of business and investment successes, and now viewed their first grant as a down payment in advance of a much larger one, for $500,000. However, this larger gift would have two conditions, which Jim spelled out in his fax.

First, he asked that we use his gift to support microfinance in southern India, where he conducted business from his base in the Middle East. Second, he put forward an idea that his wife Lisa had come up with: that we consider it a matching grant to catalyze an additional $500,000 from others. Jim offered to support us in attracting new donors, but it was clear he wanted us to take the lead in securing the matching funds.

My initial reaction was mixed. A grant that big would be huge for us, especially in those early days, and using it in southern India would not be a problem at all. But having to match it through a campaign that we had not contemplated as part of our still rather modest fundraising efforts that year seemed like a daunting, unnecessary, and even annoying condition. Why couldn't Jim just give us the money and leave us alone?

Still, I sensed a big opportunity. Within a few hours, I faxed Jim an encouraging response.

As I awaited his reply, I thought about how Jim's and Lisa's desire to volunteer with us, rather than being passive donors, could be turned into a positive. A few weeks earlier, I'd met Steve Rockefeller, the grandson of Vice President Nelson Rockefeller, at an event organized by his employer, Banker's Trust (which today is part of Deutsche Bank). He worked in the private banking unit and seemed to have an interest in microfinance and philanthropy. Perhaps Steve could take the lead in mobilizing the $500,000 in matching funds that Jim was challenging us to raise.

I also recalled that, a few months earlier, three microfinance leaders in India had told me that they could use $1 million as a grant or low-interest loan to attract $8 million in local funding, thereby expanding their services from 46,000 women to 165,000 within thirty months (a project I've described earlier in this book). Once matched, Greenberg's grant would get us all the way to the $1 million target. I began to get excited about the possibilities.

Within a few days, Steve and I had a meeting in New York. We worked out a plan whereby we agreed to spend three weeks in June making the rounds in New York, asking Steve's top business and personal contacts to donate towards the matching pool. By the end of June, we had commitments approaching $400,000, and with some mop-up work over the summer we surpassed our goal.

We decided to hold a small conference at the Rockefeller estate that summer, attended by Jim, Steve, many of the donors, and the three microfinance leaders from India that benefitted from our efforts, in order to celebrate our achievement and create a vision for what came next that would include the donors and volunteers who had been involved up to that point. This move helped create a sense of momentum, community, and inclusion, showing that we weren't going to rest on our laurels or make this a purely staff-driven process going forward. At one point during the daylong gathering, I felt a little stuck as to how to conclude a session. Steve brilliantly suggested that we let Jim have the final word. Jim relished the opportunity and spoke well, summing up what we had concluded up to that point in the day and in the overall campaign.

This gesture satisfied Jim's desire to be heard and to be seen as a wise leader and progressive philanthropist.

After that meeting, the three Indian organizations performed extremely well, reaching their goals six months early. This allowed us to crow about how well we'd used our donor money, gaining further credibility as a result. What came next was in some ways even more exciting. In 2001, in the midst of a recession, we worked with Jim and a young staff member named Sharmi Sobhan to arrange a follow-up campaign. We set a more modest goal of raising $250,000, met it, and gave the money to other Indian organizations who were able to use it as collateral to borrow ten times that amount—more than $2.5 million—for relending to poor women. This time we demonstrated not only impact but also leverage.

Jim Greenberg's creative efforts continued. He recruited Bob Eichfeld, the retiring head of Citibank in Saudi Arabia (and former CEO of Citibank India), to join our team and ultimately our board, which he would one day chair. We didn't realize what a powerful team we were creating when we asked Jim and Bob to work together. Collaboratively they came up with the idea of starting a socially motivated investment bank in partnership with the largest Indian private bank and the largest foreign bank working in the country. It took quite a few years to actually launch what became Grameen Capital India (GCI) in partnership with ICICI Bank and Citibank India, which together contributed more than half of the million dollars needed to get it going (with GF putting in a roughly equal amount).

Throughout the process of setting up GCI, Jim and Bob seamlessly copiloted the process with my colleague Julie Peachey and brought in money and volunteer talent from around the world. Our impact and influence in both India and the United States grew significantly as a result of their contributions of time and ideas. Over the years, GCI became both a market maker and market leader, leveraging its $1 million capital base into $160 million in new financing for microfinance institutions In India. It also spawned an impact investing fund, Grameen Impact Investment

India, that is doing great work to this day. In fact, as I was completing this book, the impact fund closed its second in a series of innovative bonds, raising $1.4 million in much-needed capital to support vocational training in India.

Our success under the leadership of Jim and Bob also enabled us to create a global loan guarantee facility that was probably the biggest single success of my eighteen years leading GF. Bob took the lead on that program, working in concert with other volunteers, the staff, our grassroots microfinance partners, and a group of families that pledged between $1 million and $10 million of their assets to our fund. In addition, Jim and Bob helped us leverage their knowledge of the Middle East and an introduction made by our second chairman, the Lebanese-American businessman Jim Sams, to launch a major program and later a joint venture with Mohammad Jameel, the head of one of the most progressive and influential Saudi business families—an initiative that positively impacted more than one million of the Arab world's poor women.

Thus, a single offer to volunteer—in this case, by Jim Greenberg—tied to a single generous donation set in motion a series of high-impact projects that not only put a dent in poverty and got GF known as innovators, but left dozens if not hundreds of people feeling as if they had contributed their ideas, talent, and time to make it all such a success—which led them to talk about it more and gain new recruits for GF. Jim added immeasurable value to our organization. His contributions are a powerful example of the good things that can happen when you don't just accept the help of volunteers but actually encourage them to use their leadership, creativity, and talents on behalf of your organization.

Bankers Without Borders

GF WAS FAR FROM PERFECT. We sometimes struggled to successfully leverage volunteer interest and talent. For every positive example like our engagement with Jim and Bob, there were several that turned out more ambiguously or awkwardly. Still, we had a quirky tendency to involve volunteers in ways most organizations our size would shudder at.

To rationalize our use of volunteer talent, in 2007 we hired an experienced executive named Sal Pappalardo as our chief operating officer. One of his mandates was to better organize our robust but rather ad hoc volunteer program under the banner of Bankers without Borders (BwB). Sal got a pilot grant from J.P. Morgan, and the results were so positive that the firm committed $3 million over three years to scale it up—a promise they laudably honored despite the global financial crisis that quickly followed their pledge of support. We used the J.P. Morgan grant to hire a brilliant woman named Shannon Maynard to run the program, beginning in January, 2009.

One of Shannon's first goals was to recruit 300 professionals into a reserve corps of volunteers. Information about these individuals would form the beginning of a proper volunteer database, including the skills each volunteer had, the languages they spoke, their contact information, and more. It required nearly thirty minutes for a volunteer to register; it was not meant to be super easy, something people could do on a whim. So we were pleasantly surprised when nearly 3,000 volunteers registered in the first twelve months, including many out-of-work Wall Street employees looking to gain a foothold somewhere.

In the years to come, BwB would deploy thousands of volunteers to hundreds of organizations, including GF, with greater than ninety percent satisfaction on the part of both the volunteers and the host organizations. By 2017, under the direction of Shannon's incredibly entrepreneurial Bangladeshi-American successor Sabrina Quaraishi, BwB had become a profitable social enterprise housed within GF, with some revenue coming from host organizations willing to pay a modest finder's fee for volunteers we found for them and more coming from corporate clients willing to hire us to create meaningful opportunities for contribution, professional development, and team-building for their high-potential young professionals. (Shannon Maynard now leads the Congressional Hunger Center, a small but mighty organization that she is taking in exciting new directions.)

The BwB story is one of the achievements of GF that I'm most proud of. We successfully turned a rather casual volunteering project into one of our signature programs. BwB is a fine example of GF's ability to improvise and innovate, which continues to this day under the leadership of Steve Hollingworth and Lauren Hendricks.

Other nonprofits should consider following our lead by developing their own disciplined, creative, and flexible ways to engage volunteers, thereby amplifying the human and financial resources available to advancing their missions. Integrating dozens or hundreds of opinionated, accomplished, and passionate people into an organization can sometimes be complicated and occasionally contentious. But it can also have a big impact, creating an army of evangelists who can speak about having generated meaningful change through their personal engagement with you.

Incubating Ventures, Then Letting Them Go

AN ONGOING STRUGGLE of most successful nonprofits is "growing to scale." Many organizations are excellent at innovation or at field-level service delivery to clients, but struggle when it comes to reaching large numbers and having a society-wide impact. The fundraising and management challenges are often daunting and frequently insurmountable.

One method that can work is spinning off an effective program or social enterprise so that it can become an independent entity with its own sources of funding. This approach avoids the problems that can arise when a highly effective team within a larger organization struggles to remain nimble and cohesive while having to conform to policies and a culture that may not be consistent with what the program needs or wants. The spinoff approach can also make it easier to attract talent: Many of the most able leaders want to be the CEO of something, rather than "merely" a program director. They value the autonomy, and in some cases the celebrity, of being in charge and reporting only to a board of directors.

Muhammad Yunus had this insight in the late 1990s. He began spinning off successful pilot programs that had been incubated within Grameen Bank's special projects unit. Thereafter, he seeded and nurtured a series of independent organizations that shared the Grameen name and included him as the board chair, but were otherwise on their own. Among other benefits, this limited the potential liability that Grameen Bank would have faced if it had kept those ventures under its own organizational umbrella. Grameen Foundation itself was an example of this—a free-standing effort to tap into the U.S. philanthropy and talent market to advance Yunus's ideals. Other examples of the scores of organizations Yunus launched were Grameen Shakti (Energy), Grameen Telecom, Grameen Fisheries Foundation, the Yunus Centre, and Yunus Social Business.

As GF neared the completion of its first decade of existence, we sensed an opportunity to follow the same path. We ended up spending much of our second decade setting up our strongest programs as independent organizations, or orchestrating their absorption by another organization that was better positioned to scale up the innovation. Here's a list of some of these successful spinoffs.

Mifos. Our technology team created innovative open-source code and tools to help microfinance organizations design their own loan-tracking software quickly and easily. Known as Mifos (short for "microfinance open source"), this project has thrived as its own entity under the leadership of Ed Cable, who emerged as the organization's improbable, fearless, and energetic social entrepreneur. Our former board chair Paul Maritz provided essential guidance and generous financial support both before and after it became an independent entity. As of late 2018, Mifos had touched the lives of more than ten million people through organizations using Mifos X (its latest version) and related software tools.

Taroworks. Another technology-oriented GF initiative, Taroworks was focused on developing and promoting an app that allowed field-based workers to use mobile phones to document and share their activities, results, and learnings. Taroworks reached profitability in 2017 and is now one of the leaders in its field, having been used by more than a hundred social enterprises in forty countries.

Growth Guarantees. Our innovative loan guarantee program leveraged more than $240 million of commercial capital to help scale microfinance institutions and fair trade cooperatives over a ten-year period. We wound it down in 2015, but not before training a handful of organizations, including Habitat for Humanity, in how to design similar programs of their own. Some of those efforts continue to this day.

Progress out of Poverty Index (PPI). Our efforts to design a globally applicable version of the Grameen Bank's "Ten Indicators of Poverty" to ensure cost-effective accountability for poverty reduction outcomes were a huge success. Under the leadership of Nigel Biggar and later Julie Peachey, and with strategic guidance by Peter Cowhey (today the chairman of GF), we popularized a ten-question survey based on national census data that would correlate to a respondent's poverty level and could be filled out in less than ten minutes. Mark Schreiner, a gifted economist with a practical orientation, was a key ally who developed the prototype and helped us spread it across the world. Later, we transferred GF's team, systems, donor relationships, and intellectual property related to the PPI to Innovations for Poverty Action (led by my occasional sparring partner Dean Karlan), where the international rollout has continued to go well. The tool has been rebranded as the Poverty Probability Index.

RUMA. This is an Indonesian social enterprise that GF incubated for two years while its dynamic founder, Aldi Haryopratomo, pursued a master's degree at Harvard. In return for our sweat equity and financial support, we received some shares in RUMA, which we were ultimately able to sell for more than $4 million while being assured that the organization's social impact focus would remain in place or be further strengthened.

Grameen Capital India (GCI). As I've explained, this public interest investment bank focused on financial innovation to benefit microfinance institutions and their poor female clients. After beginning operations in early 2008 under its dynamic leader Royston Braganza, GCI became an award-winning, trend-setting market maker and innovator, most recently launching an impact investing fund called Grameen Impact Investment India.

Grameen-Jameel Pan-Arab Microfinance. GF started this major program to support microfinance in the Arab world in 2001 using a grant of $2.4 million from Mohammad Jameel, the patriarch of one of the most respected business families in the Middle East. In 2005, it was spun off as a joint venture social business (as defined by Muhammad Yunus), supporting partners in reaching an additional one million female loan clients and undertaking a series of industry-building activities, such as translating essential manuals into Arabic for the first time.

PLAN Fund. This is a microcredit program started by Dallas City Homes, a low-income housing provider, with GF support in 1998. When the founders decided to shed the program, GF chose to absorb and run it for a time. Ultimately, we spun it off, and it was later absorbed into the Austin People's Fund, a respected Texas nonprofit focused on economic development in low-income neighborhoods around the state.

Perhaps in some small way the PLAN Fund helped sensitize people about the entrepreneurial talent and unmet demand for credit among low-income Americans, opening the door for the stunning success of Grameen America across the United States, first under the leadership of my Bangladeshi friend Shah Newaz, then, more recently, under that of Andrea Jung, the former CEO of Avon. Grameen America's experience lending more than $1 billion (in amounts averaging $2,000) during its first ten years with a default rate of less than 1 percent and a growing body of evidence of its positive impact on poverty is one of the great development success stories of our time.

Spinning off a successful program is rarely easy and sometimes quite controversial. One reason is that doing so may leave the organization in which the program was incubated in a weakened state due to the loss of the talent and prestige of the program. Another is that the separation makes it hard for the long-term impact of the incubating organization to be tracked, since the spunoff organization is usually under no obligation to provide detailed reports on its progress in the formats used by its original host institution.

Problems like these help to explain why the spinoff strategy is rarely practiced in the nonprofit world. In truth, most organizations try to ride their best performing, most celebrated, and most innovative programs for all they're worth, regardless of what's best for the initiatives and their societal impact. These flagship programs often effectively prop up other parts of the organization that are less successful or well-known—sometimes diminishing the societal impact of the best performing programs in the process.

Naturally, not every spinoff we tried at GF ended in success. The Grameen-Jameel joint venture ran out of steam and folded in 2015, though after a decade of achievement in advancing microfinance in the Arab world. Our Community Knowledge Worker program in Uganda and our Mobile Midwife initiative in Ghana would have naturally fit into government agencies in those two countries, and we worked hard to make that happen. But politics got in the way, and as a result both programs ran out of money and ceased operations.

Overall, however, our experience with giving successful programs the chance to have a life outside GF enabled us to have greater long-term impact and to attract, motivate, and retain the highest caliber of talent. And isn't that, ultimately, the name of the game?

A Partnership with Many Parents: The Microfinance CEO Working Group

AS OUR GROUP SETTLED AROUND A TABLE in a New York restaurant, the man sitting next to me ordered his usual drink—which in fact was decidedly unusual. "I'd like a vodka tonic," he told the waiter, then added, with a slight smile, "and I'd like five slices of lime with it."

This quirky request from Michael Schlein, CEO of Accion International, embodied one of my core beliefs, adapted from the leadership expert Dave Ellis, about how to lead a productive and contented life: Figure out what you want, take pride in it, and ask for it without apology. Indeed, I have come to appreciate many strengths and perspectives of peers like Michael and the organizations they lead over the years. In fact, despite the fact that Accion and GF have major philosophical differences, Michael and I have become good friends.

Accion International is widely seen as the more market-oriented rival to the network of Grameen organizations that I was long a part of. Accion's approach to microfinance and poverty alleviation is very different from Grameen's, and leaders of the two groups have sometimes been publicly and privately critical of one another. But Michael and I were able to slowly rise above that hostility, finding common ground on some issues and cordially agreeing to disagree on others.

This improbable détente was not simply based on our personal chemistry. Rather, it was the result of our choosing to unite against common enemies by joining a coalition formed in response to a challenge from an unlikely midwife: a blunt Pakistani-American with a high-pitched voice named Asad Mahmood.

Seven other microfinance network CEOs had joined me at that dinner in New York when Michael placed his unique drink order, along with Anne Hastings, the director of our tiny staff secretariat (and the former driving force behind Fonkoze, the Haitian organization I mentioned earlier). It was 2015. Over the preceding five years, I had become fond of each of these leaders, even though we did not always agree on substance or process. That night, we were having one of our traditional dinners prior to a quarterly all-day retreat. A few hours and many drinks later, I shared with the group the news that I was stepping down as CEO of GF, and I surprised myself by how emotional I became as I spoke.

To understand how and why I had become so attached to this group, you need to understand how it unexpectedly came into being. The origins of our coalition were threefold: a series of crises in late 2010 that threatened the reputation and operations of microfinance around the world; the retirement of a few leaders of global microfinance networks who tended to emphasize competition and zero-sum thinking rather than collaboration, and their replacement with more collegial successors; and Asad Mahmood's caustic and essential clarion call to us to put aside our narrow organizational agendas and think about what we could do more effectively together rather than separately.

An initial meeting was hosted by Asad in January, 2011, which I missed due to a scheduling conflict. I carefully studied the notes from that session and pondered whether and how to get involved. My mentors were all over the map about the value of working in coalitions. Several were skeptical; when they worked with others, they preferred loose associations that didn't constrain the options of individual members and didn't require much of a time commitment. Others saw more value in coalition building, especially when it yielded both tangible benefits (such as candid recommendations about hiring staff or joint efforts to achieve shared public policy goals) and intangible benefits (such as camaraderie and candid peer feedback on things like software packages and potential hires).

Still uncertain, I joined a follow-up conference call in February and supported the idea of an in-person retreat in March to see if we wanted to form a coalition of some kind. Since the retreat was held on a weekend when I had to be in Uganda, I called in to the meeting by speaker-phone for seven hours, racking up untold international roaming charges for GF.

Ultimately, I became one of the most active members of the Microfinance CEO Working Group (MCWG)—a name that I originally proposed as being intentionally and usefully ambiguous. (Today it is known as the Partnership for Responsible Financial Inclusion.)

One of my earliest proposals to the group was that we collectively write an open letter to the global microfinance industry. It took us months to agree on the wording, but it ended up being a powerful statement of our solidarity with each other and of our intentions for reforming and advancing our mission-driven industry. As time went on and we embarked on more initiatives together, I felt a growing sense of affinity for the group and its individual members, along with a feeling of agency that I often lacked in my own organization during my final years as CEO. The group thrived, largely because everyone contributed. Another essential element was having a tiny, talented, and hard-working secretariat housed at the Center for Financial Inclusion (a think tank based at Accion) to keep us on track. I was honored when, during a public presentation at the London Microfinance Club in 2013, the MCWG asked me to make the kick-off presentation on our behalf before a question-and-answer session with the audience. Soon thereafter, I was elected co-chair of the MCWG.

Our substantive accomplishments were significant. We publicly endorsed a campaign to promote consumer protection standards for microfinance clients, and engaged in friendly competition to see which of our organizations' networks had the most affiliates certified as meeting those standards. We quietly worked to have local officials of member organizations in several countries collaborate to defuse conflicts with government agencies that could have been debilitating or even fatal. We developed model legislation for regulating microfinance in partnership with the law firm DLA Piper. We actively supported an initiative to define sound practices for advancing the interests of poor clients of microfinance—one that had been catalogued in the Universal Standards for Social Performance Management but that we as leaders had previously done very little to contribute to or to advance.

Some unexpected collaborations took place involving the group members. In one memorable example, Michael Schlein invited me to address his senior leaders on a date that happened to coincide with my twentieth wedding anniversary. "There aren't many things that would take me out of town today," I said in my talk, "but this invitation is one of them." Michael returned the favor by agreeing to speak at the farewell gala GF organized for me a few years later—something he did very effectively and generously.

As our 2015 dinner broke up, each member came over, gave me a hug, and offered some words of encouragement and affirmation. I was the last one to leave. I spent half an hour sipping a glass of red wine and reflecting on the accomplishments of the group, what I had learned from it, and what its future held. I felt sadness, gratitude and uncertainty. A few minutes after eleven p.m., I left the empty room.

This unexpected partnership had turned into a surprising source of learning, growth, and satisfaction for me. If you have the opportunity to join, or to help launch, a nonprofit consortium that offers you support, empowerment, and personal growth, and that can help your organization fulfill its mission, take advantage of it.

PART THREE: CARING FOR YOURSELF

14

Life in Balance

Tips for maintaining your physical, mental, and spiritual well-being while leading a nonprofit organization

IF YOU HAVE BEEN DRAWN to working in the nonprofit arena, it means you are a person dedicated to causes bigger than yourself. You want a life devoted to helping others, whether that means providing poor people with the tools they need to escape poverty, supporting marginalized groups in their quest for equal rights, ensuring that future generations will have a safe and healthy environment to live in, or helping your fellow humans in any other way.

If you are one of the millions of people who fit this description—thank you! Our world is in desperate need of people with this kind of dedication to others.

But there's an inherent danger in pursuing a career based on selfless devotion to others—namely, the danger of failing to care for yourself sufficiently. Far too many people in the caring professions—not just nonprofit workers and managers but also doctors and nurses, social workers and psychologists, clergy and counselors—become so single-minded in their dedication to their chosen cause that they lose touch with their own needs. Little by little, they develop flawed assumptions, habits, mental frameworks, and ultimately lifestyles that take a physical, psychological, and spiritual toll. The results can include exhaustion, loneliness, depression, frustration, suppressed anger, anxiety, paranoia, and finally burnout.

Ironically, these selfless individuals end up harming themselves so badly that they ultimately become no use to anyone else—and least of all to themselves.

In this chapter, I'll describe some of the ways I gradually learned to take better care of myself while continuing to devote my career to serving the needs of the world.

The Productivity Paradox

ONE OF THE TRAPS nonprofit leaders fall into is to become so driven by the desire to produce good results for their organizations that they overwork themselves. They spend crazy hours in the office, give up evenings and weekends for work, make themselves available 24/7, skip activities with family and friends, and fail to take time off for holidays and vacations. They believe that, in this way, they can make themselves and their organizations as productive as possible.

In reality, the odds are great that leaders who behave this way are actually *reducing* their productivity. Working too long and too hard gradually saps your creativity, openness, clarity, and empathy. Perhaps without realizing it, you become a little like a hamster spinning the wheel in his cage, expending energy without producing much in the way of meaningful results. The same phenomenon can happen to hard-driven people in any field—which is why wise leaders in for-profit as well as nonprofit organizations often *insist* that their team makers take time off to recharge and refresh themselves and engage in other forms of self-care. They've seen how productivity drops when people refuse to do so.

As the saying goes, "It's possible to do a good year's work in eleven months—but not in twelve."

I think of this as *the productivity paradox*—and I can vouch for its reality based on my own experience.

Three of the most productive and satisfying periods in my career were preceded by taking a long break from work. In one case, during the summer of 2004, I took a three-month sabbatical from Grameen Foundation after seven often grueling startup years. For the first and only time during my eighteen years at GF, I almost completely unplugged from my work. When I came back after Labor Day, I felt so energized and refreshed that I was able to help lead the organization on its next steps to becoming an international humanitarian powerhouse whose board, middle management, and finances were much stronger by year end than they had ever been. (Much of this was due to how colleagues like Barb Weber, Craig Sarsony, Peter Bladin, and John Anderson stepped up during my absence—another reminder of the power of effective delegation.)

In another case, I spent almost an entire month travelling in Russia, a place where I had no programs to monitor; it was a prospecting tour that yielded no partnerships or projects for us. After returning from that stimulating trip, I worked intensively with Steve Rockefeller to raise the bulk of the $1 million needed to make our first loans to Indian microfinance institutions (as described earlier in this book), establishing our credibility in the country with the world's largest number of poor people and laying the foundation for several other successful fundraising efforts.

In the third case, after announcing my intention to step down as CEO of GF and activating my succession plan in May, 2015, and after spending a month putting it into place, I took July and August off and disconnected from the organization. After my return, the final months of 2015 were some of my most productive ever. For the first time in almost twenty years, I was free from the burden of making the hardest decisions and worrying about the safety and support of 200 employees and 20,000 volunteers as only a CEO can. I was able to do the things I liked the best, and avoid those that I had tired of or had never liked in the first place.

How can I explain these periods of productivity after stepping away from my core responsibilities for an extended period? I think there are several contributing factors.

First, in each case, the people I reported to gave me their blessing to take the time off, which was a vote of confidence in me and in the team I had assembled. Everyone responded to these affirmations positively.

Second, I chose the right people to assume my responsibilities during my absence. In some cases, their loyalty to me and their desire to show that the trust had been well placed motivated them to be ultra-productive.

Third, during each of these absences, I did not try to manage things by remote control, even in those cases where I stayed in touch a bit. I understood and abided by the unwritten rule of delegation: If I was going to give others the burdens that I normally carried, they needed the ability to make decisions and do things their way.

Most important, taking the time to rest, play house husband, reconnect with friends, and temporarily arrest the growth of my pile of unread books gave me an opportunity to reflect on my inner life and my journey in ways that led to greater self-awareness and creativity.

You may or may not get the chance to take an extended break from your work. If you do, take advantage of it. If you don't, force yourself to take off the time that your organization makes available. A week or two away from the daily grind is essential to your mental and physical health, and to maintaining your creativity and productivity for the long run. And even something as simple as taking a meditative walk each day during your lunch break can make a big difference.

The Nourishing Magic of Music

AT SOME POINT IN THE EARLY 2000S, I found myself in a bit of a professional funk—one of those times when the many little problems that constantly crop up for a nonprofit leader seemed to add up to an overwhelming burden. Even things I would normally enjoy greatly did little to improve my mood.

During this period, I went on a business trip to New York. My wife Emily joined me, something she rarely did, and we stayed for the weekend. We attended a lively Sunday brunch with a group of some local nonprofit colleagues and associates, including David Bornstein, the prolific social entrepreneurship author and future founder of the Solutions Journalism Network. The conversation was fun and positive. But my funk barely lifted.

Our next stop would be a play on Broadway that Emily had selected. I wasn't excited. It felt like just another thing to do before the overwhelming challenges of leading GF would be front and center again Monday morning. I recall wondering whether I would toss and turn all night after we returned home, as I tended to do on Sundays when the new work week beckoned.

The play Emily had chosen was *Mamma Mia!* Never having heard of it, I figured it was a drama about Italians in New York.

In reality, of course, *Mamma Mia!* is a jukebox musical built around the songs of the seventies Swedish rock group ABBA. And that afternoon in the theatre—much to my surprise—turned into one of the most unique and memorable experiences of my life. It wasn't just that the show had great comedy, acting, and singing, nor was it the fact that I, like everyone who came of age in the seventies, knew most of the songs. It was something ineffable and yet unmistakable about the performance. The experience felt like a wave of lightness and celebration washing over me, relieving me of my worries and making me smile and feel glad to be alive. Even more strangely, the feeling of silly joyfulness persisted long past the curtain call when the performers took their bows. It lasted for weeks, even months. In some sense, it lives on in me to this day. Never before had I experienced a performance like it.

Several years later, I had a second experience that recalled my *Mamma Mia!* moment.

Emily and I were concluding a nice vacation on the West Coast by walking around San Francisco on an overcast afternoon. It was one of those days when we try to talk and act as if we are having a good time when, in truth, neither one of us can wait for the day to end. There was nothing really wrong with our day, but there wasn't anything right about it, either.

Then, everything changed. It happened in the city's famous waterfront district, when we chanced upon a group of musicians playing at the intersection of the Embarcadero and one of the piers lined with stores catering to tourists. There were nine of them, playing Motown songs with just enough talent so as not to detract from the joy they so clearly took in performing them. We joined the hundred or so people in front of their makeshift stage, and within a few moments we found ourselves starting to enjoy our day for the first time. When the band took a break, we decided to get a cup of tea and wait until they played another set. It was hard to stop smiling while they performed, and those same smiles break out uncontrollably whenever we recall this experience.

My afternoon at *Mamma Mia!* and the street music of San Francisco were both examples of the infectious power of music. But for some reason, it wasn't until 2007 that I drew the obvious conclusion: Live music, especially in intimate venues, has an incredible ability to both calm and invigorate me. Realizing this gave me a tool I could use to dramatically improve my life. Tapping into the power of live music makes stress disappear for a time, and makes my mood measurably better for hours, even days.

Since then, I've gone out of my way to build experiences of live music deeply into my life.

In January, 2007, I travelled to Key West, Florida, with a few dozen family and friends to celebrate my fortieth birthday. Being with so many people who were important to me in a tropical locale far from the winter cold was enjoyable enough. Then, during the week, we spent several nights listening to a group called the Carter Brothers Band play a delightful fusion of bluegrass, blues, folk, and rock that transfixed me—which was especially surprising since bluegrass, in particular, was a genre I knew little about, except that (in my mind) it was like country music, but worse.

Over the next few years, we became friends with all four members of the band, including Danny and Tim Carter, and then with dozens of their friends, fans, and fellow musicians in Key West, Tennessee, North Carolina, and beyond. I became the volunteer president of their fan club, setting up a website and hawking merchandise whenever they played.

Those moments listening to the Carter Brothers' music—and especially dancing to it, once I got over my fear of looking foolish—gave me a glimpse of another reality that made every other reality feel different. It wiped away the Alex who was prone to take himself too seriously and to demand nothing less than perfection from himself—and thereby helped to sustain me through some of the most taxing and difficult years of my career.

I'm so grateful that I had the opportunity to discover the healing and revitalizing power of music, and that I have had the resources and made the time to incorporate music so deeply into my life.

Perhaps music can do something similar for you—although, in your case, it might not be funky bluegrass music like that of the Carter Brothers Band, but rather punk rock, hip hop, Broadway show tunes, the organ music of Bach, or the operas of Verdi. If music doesn't have your healing magic, maybe you'll find it in painting or sculpture, poetry or science fiction, knitting or quilt making, or any other art form that can take you to a different place, spiritually if not physically.

Whatever kind of creative expression moves you most, embrace it and make time to experience it as often as possible. Enriching your life through creating or appreciating art is a great way to restore the balance you need to go on serving others through the daily work you do.

Just Move! The Importance of Exercise

EVER SINCE I WAS A KID, sports have been important to me. I was a decent baseball, tennis, ping pong, and squash player; I liked basketball a lot more than it liked me. During the three years when my family lived in Brigantine, New Jersey, I took to gathering the neighborhood kids together to play baseball, soccer, and street hockey on a regular basis. It was perhaps my first experience of leadership. I was the best athlete among those roughly my age, though not by much.

However, when it came to playing in school or in the organized leagues for youth that are so important in small towns like Brigantine, I often felt out of my depth and froze up. That was my first experience of realizing that in my little neighborhood, I had been a big fish in a small pond.

It was also in Brigantine that I began following professional sports. I recall lying in bed with my mother, watching the Philadelphia Flyers on a tiny television as they won their second consecutive championship in 1975. The next day, classes were interrupted so the students could watch the victory parade on TV. The names Bernie Parent, Bobby Clark, and Rick MacLeish were on everyone's tongues. When a goalie stopped a shot in street hockey, everyone yelled, "Parent save!" I was hooked on the Flyers from that point on. Sadly, they have yet to win another championship.

Likewise, I began following the Philadelphia 76ers in basketball and the Phillies in baseball—the latter my greatest love. I noticed how team sports at every level have a way of pulling communities and people together, across lines of age, gender, ethnicity, and wealth. I also saw how my most important sports moments stick in my mind forever. There was the time my friend Scott Hickey and I led an improbable baseball comeback from a 9-0 deficit against a team representing another sixth-grade class on a gorgeous spring day in Central Park—and the time in my early thirties when I was overmatched in a singles tennis match against my friend Jeff O'Malley and somehow won (though helped, I must admit, by a disputed line call).

I played in a squash league in Dhaka, Bangladesh, with others from the American Club. My most exciting match was the time when I lost the first game badly, rallied to win the next two, and after tiring and losing the fourth, somehow pulled myself together to win the fifth, deciding game.

After I returned home to the U.S. and started GF, I went to a gym on occasion despite the cost and the distance from my apartment (at the time, Emily and I did not have a car). Being active became important to me for both physical and mental reasons. The pressure of running an underfinanced nonprofit at the request of a future Nobel laureate made me unbearably tense at times, and physical exercise helped to relieve that stress and relax me.

At one point, after losing a lot of weight through a process described earlier in this book, I began running outdoors for the first time in years. I discovered that I actually enjoyed that form of exercise, and I noticed how much easier it is to run when you aren't carrying around an extra twenty-five pounds.

During the second half of my thirties, I made a habit of exercising for forty-five to sixty minutes six times per week, regardless of whether I was busy or not, travelling or not, or any other consideration. I have continued that to this day. I occasionally joke that, even if my doctor told me that aerobic exercise was physically *unhealthy*, I would still do it for its stress-reduction value. On the rare occasions when I miss two straight days of exercise, I become borderline obsessed with how to work at least an hour of exercise into the third day.

As you can see, sports and exercise have been important to me for a variety of reasons. But there have been a few times when I experienced something extra special during sports or exercise—what some athletes and musicians call flow. This is a moment when your performance and your trust in your mind and body rise to such a high level that you feel like a different person. Such moments are really unforgettable. I can still vividly recall, for example, the intense joy I experienced when playing pickup basketball during my senior year of high school with reckless abandon, my usual tentativeness completely forgotten.

Or the time when I somehow managed, through sheer instinct, to sprint to the perfect location to catch a fly ball hit to deep left center field, my arm and body fully extended and racing at my top speed. Or the time I ran a marathon at age fifty-one, a transcendent 26.2 mile journey in which I never experienced a moment of cramping and cut more than thirty-one minutes off my personal record time.

Those rare, brief glimpses reminded me that, like all human beings, I have the potential for joy, self-trust, and excellence far beyond what I normally experience. They convinced me that, with effort and discipline, I could tap into those higher powers a little bit more every day.

"LIFE IN BALANCE" may sound like a lofty goal. It's certainly not an easy one to attain—especially for those us with highly demanding lives, like most leaders in the nonprofit arena, or, say, single parents living on modest incomes in crummy neighborhoods. We're all sure to spend days, weeks, even months "out of balance" when short-term crises demand our fullest attention and energies.

But life gifts like music, the arts, sports, and physical activity—and even just time spent away from work, being with friends and family or doing nothing at all—can have amazing restorative powers. They help us remember that problems, worries, and self-imposed limitations are rarely as serious or inescapable as they initially appear. They send me to what Emily calls "my happy place," and when I return, the world often looks very different—more inviting and less formidable.

Eight Favorite Tips to Help You in Your Quest for a Life in Balance

1

Don't let anyone else dictate what work/life balance means for you. Discern how you want to calibrate your engagement in all the things that compete for your time, your energy, and your soul, and reassess those priorities periodically as your life evolves. The right path to work/life balance is for you and you alone to determine.

2

Commit to de-cluttering your life on a regular basis. Clear away letters, papers, articles, books, and other objects that are distracting you. As an alternative, if possible, identify someone who can do it for you or help you do it—for example, an office assistant or a life partner.

3

Become mindful regarding your tendency to perfectionism. There are times it's unnecessary—when *good* is really *good enough*. Other times, details are crucial—meaning good is *not* good enough. Make an effort to distinguish the two situations accurately and to handle them appropriately.

4

SCHEDULE ACTIVITIES in a way that's conducive to a more balanced life. For example, meetings lasting fifteen, forty-five, or seventy-five minutes naturally leave time for a fifteen-minute break to write up notes, think about next steps, go for a short walk, or simply to daydream.

5

WHEN CONFRONTED WITH A MASSIVE TASK, remember the saying, "How do you eat an elephant? One bite at a time." Choose one small part of the project—preferably one you can easily imagine tackling—and just start working on it. You may find that the job is easier than you imagine, and even limited progress may give you a sense of momentum and possibility.

6

WHEN TRAVELLING ALONE ON BUSINESS, don't feel obligated to visit tourist sights or to buy gifts for your life partner unless you or they truly desire it. Get home faster, rest more, and save your money instead.

7

WHEN YOU ARE WORKING on managing your weight or improving your eating habits, don't be too harsh with yourself if you break your own rules occasionally. Shame and anger can lead to a more serious case of backsliding. Rather than chastise yourself, just resume your regimen the next day without any self-reproach.

8

FIGURE OUT WAYS to fit daily physical exercise into your schedule while travelling. If necessary, sacrifice a bit of work time spent in meetings or managing projects in favor of letting your body release its stresses through activity. Simply walking up a flight of stairs rather than taking an elevator makes a difference if you do it frequently enough.

15

Beginner's Mind

Practical advice for remaining a lifelong learner, so that your leadership skills are continually evolving and improving

SOMETIMES IT TAKES a friend or colleague to articulate some insight that I am having difficulty getting a firm handle on. A few years back, I was having lunch with Steve Graubart, a consultant who did a lot to help me close the $10.6 million transaction in support of Yunus's telecom project in Bangladesh described in chapter seven. That assignment and how Steve often had to prop me up along the way sometimes felt like an "Instant MBA" gained through experience and effort rather than study. In that education, Steve was as much my professor as an advisor.

Steve was also good about keeping up with business contacts, including me. We would have lunch every few years, and occasionally play tennis or go to a hockey game together. Twice I tried to recruit him to be Grameen Foundation's chief financial officer, though I never succeeded (probably in part because we didn't pay enough).

One day, over a lunch of mediocre Thai food, Steve and I shared some stories about our current professional challenges and achievements. But then I veered into a different subject, one that I was excited to discuss—namely, my relatively new avocation as the volunteer fan club president for the Carter Brothers Band. After describing the group and its music, I tried to explain why I found this hobby so enjoyable—and so personally valuable.

"One thing this fan club effort has taught me, or reminded me, is how important it is for me to always be doing at least one thing that I'm a beginner at," I said. I wasn't quite sure why this was the case, but before I could struggle to try to explain, Steve's face lit up.

"Yes, that makes so much sense!" Steve exclaimed with a big smile. "I think they say in Buddhism that a beginner's mind is a learner's mind. So I totally get what you're saying. You like being a beginner, because that makes you a learner."

Catalyst of Curiosity and Wonder

OVER THE YEARS since our lunch, I have reflected quite a bit on Steve's pearl of wisdom. Being a beginner at something you care about usually brings with it a particular array of experiences. It involves observing and talking to people with more mastery than you have; getting relatively comfortable with looking uninformed and even foolish; struggling to break down complex subjects into digestible component parts; drawing encouragement from incremental progress; and generally being a sponge focused on absorbing and using as much new information as possible. The underlying attitude that links all these behaviors is *humility*—which I've found is an enormously valuable mindset to practice. Humility is essential if you want to develop the learner's mind that Steve referred to.

Once the learner's mind is activated in one domain of your life, it tends to spill over into others in healthy ways. It encourages you to push back against complacency in areas where you have some mastery but could benefit from more. It catalyzes curiosity and wonder, two qualities that tend to get snuffed out and replaced with know-it-all arrogance when people spend most of their time engaging in activities that they believe they are good at, especially if they don't spend much time around people with more mastery than they have.

Being committed to learning, growth, and continuous personal development is especially important for a leader. Running an organization can be taxing, making you feel as if you have little time to further develop your skills. Training and managing staff members with less experience and knowledge than you may create the misleading impression that you know everything there is to know. And if the people around you are prone to flattery, the natural human tendency to complacency gets exacerbated further.

Fortunately for me, I've been able to find ample opportunities to thrust myself into positions where I have new things to learn.

I recently took on the challenge of teaching undergraduates at the University of Maryland. Being a professor is something that I always felt I would love to do, but when I began teaching in 2016, I struggled to do it consistently well. In fact, sometimes I stunk at it. I quickly realized that giving a guest lecture in someone else's class was far different from—and much easier than—designing a syllabus and leading a classroom of today's teenagers through it over the course of four to five months.

My students and the challenges they bring me keep me on my toes and continually searching for useful techniques, theories, and insights related to education. With the help of terrific graduate teaching assistants such as Kate Raulin and Julia Clark, I've tested new ideas in the classroom and studied how they worked out. I've devoured books, talked to people about teaching (especially some of the other terrific faculty at the Do Good Institute), and sat in on classes taught by others, all in an effort to improve my own classroom performance. And the same hunger for knowledge and insight has trickled into other areas of my life, feeding my hunger to be a better professional, writer, husband, friend, marathon runner, music lover, and sports fan (among other things).

As I was completing the first draft of this manuscript, I became fascinated by an activity I had never done much or done well: cooking. I discovered that I loved trying new recipes, learning my way around the grocery store, figuring out how to use kitchen gadgets, and making (and learning from) silly rookie mistakes. I am sure that the learning mentality that I applied in the kitchen each evening influenced my writing, teaching, consulting, and other activities.

I also recently became certified as a Court-Appointed Special Advocate (CASA) for children in the foster care system in Prince George's County, Maryland. This is a special type of volunteer post that allows an individual with appropriate training to work on behalf of abused or neglected kids, helping them find safe, healthy homes in which they can grow and thrive. Being an eager rookie in this new domain has been an eye-opening experience. I met and learned from those in my training cohort, most of them purposeful and pragmatic African-American women in their fifties and sixties, as well as our trainers, who were deeply versed in the intricacies of the legal system and how it needs to be navigated to improve the chances a foster child gets a decent shot at a normal adult life. It was exciting to learn how the training put me in a position to use some of my strongest qualities—being consistent, organized, and dependable—to benefit a child in need of social support. I spend a lot of time these days encouraging my friends around the country to get this training from their local chapter of the National CASA Association.

Some people find being a beginner frustrating rather than invigorating. Trying to learn something new without a good mentor, teacher, or online resource can be overwhelming. But, for me, the habit of always being invested in some new activity or discipline has helped feed my hunger to learn and grow. It's also a trait I admire when I see it in others. I was struck, for example, when I visited a team of professionals at the Bill and Melinda Gates Foundation led by a talented man named Rodger Voorhies to tell them something about our work at GF. They listened intently, took copious notes, and asked a slew of questions about our presentation, as if they were sure we had new information that could help them do their jobs better. The fact that this hunger for learning was exhibited by such experienced and accomplished professionals from one of the world's biggest and most influential foundations was particularly impressive to me.

Experiencing Diversity

ANOTHER WAY TO NURTURE your own readiness to learn, grow, and develop is to make a deliberate effort to expose yourself to new places, new experiences, and new people. In particular, seek out connections with others who have significantly different backgrounds, values, and beliefs than you. You're sure to learn things that will broaden your mind and deepen your understanding of the world—and of yourself.

Experiencing this kind of human diversity isn't something that will happen automatically. If you're like most people, you're prone to make decisions that put you around others who think like you, vote like you, talk like you, and act like you. This is natural and often unconscious, but it has a big impact on our knowledge and our worldviews. It is also a barrier to personal and professional growth and fulfillment.

When my family moved from a small town in South Jersey to New York City after I completed fourth grade, my parents decided it was no longer possible for them to just let me and my brother roam around town after school and during the summer. An after-school program and summer day camp beckoned. My stepmother suggested an unusual choice for someone of upper-middle-class background: a camp run by the Lenox Hill Neighborhood Association. It was a place mostly frequented by working-class kids from a wide variety of ethnic groups. Virtually all of them, except for my brother and me, received some kind of subsidy from the city government to go there.

Sending us to the Lenox Hill camp was my parents' way of ensuring that, in a metropolis stratified by race and class, we were exposed to people from diverse backgrounds from an early age. The experience helped us to transcend these barriers more easily than most of our peers. It's important to note that my parents didn't tell us the reason they chose Lenox Hill until years later. To us, it was just a place to go and play with kids our ages as we waited for our parents to come home from work during the school year, and to spend our summer days when school was out.

While I focused on sports and my brother on building things in woodshop, we both made friends with some real characters. One was the pudgy, affable son of a newspaper stand owner whom everyone called Charlie Tuna. He loved to play punchball (a variation of baseball for kids who couldn't afford bats or gloves), and we would occasionally pay a visit to his father's stand to buy a pack of gum or candy. Our other buddies included a nimble and skinny Puerto Rican kid named Joaquin and a tall, lanky black boy named David whose athletic prowess, honesty, and understated dignity won our respect. Whenever there as a dispute on the playing field, all of us turned to David to render the final verdict, regardless of which team he was on.

I learned some street smarts at Lenox Hill: how to talk your way out of a fight you would likely lose; what it took to earn people's respect in a cross-cultural environment; how sports can be a great equalizer; and, most of all, how fascinating it is to have friends who experience the world differently than you.

As I went through life, it became natural for me to rub shoulders with people much older, younger, poorer, or richer than I was, as well as people of different faiths, ethnicities, and political persuasions. I wasn't intimidated by the idea of going to Bangladesh right after college, despite the need to master a foreign language and the religious and ethnic differences I knew I'd encounter. Likewise, becoming close friends with a bunch of bluegrass musicians and fans from the South, despite my northern upbringing (and lack of musical talent) was easy and fun for me. I've made a career and a happy, interesting life out of being around some of the world's poorest people as well as more than my share of billionaires.

One of the secrets of being an effective and fulfilled nonprofit leader is to keep learning, developing, and growing. Finding ways to maintain your beginner's mind is one of the best antidotes to becoming complacent, bored, or arrogant—and a great path to continually rediscovering the fun and excitement in your life and your work.

Seven Favorite Tips to Help You Retain Your Beginner's Mind

1

AS A GENERAL RULE, most people are too cautious. Push yourself to take calculated risks in how you act, speak, and relate to others. At the same time, work throughout your life to improve your ability to discern how and when you need to be risk-averse.

2

TO OPEN UP YOUR MIND AND SPIRIT, find a place that allows you to temporarily slip into a different persona and way of living. For me, such a place is Key West, Florida; for my wife, Emily, it is skiing, virtually anywhere. For others, it may be a particular stretch of beach or a neighborhood with a unique vibe. Find your place and visit it as regularly as you can.

3

TRY TO LEARN A NEW LANGUAGE every ten to fifteen years, and find opportunities to practice languages you've already learned so your fluency can stay reasonably fresh. This will require you to overcome your fear of looking foolish—which is a liberating activity in itself.

4

EXPOSE YOUR MIND to books, articles, films, and presentations that challenge your political ideology, your religious faith (or lack thereof), and your social values. Listen with an open mind rather than devoting your energy to looking for ways to refute what you are hearing.

5

SEIZE EVERY OPPORTUNITY to visit or work in a different country or culture, especially early in your career. Avoid making quick judgments about the customs you encounter. Instead, remain open and curious, trying to expand your conceptions of what is possible and beautiful, right and wrong, effective and offensive.

6

WHENEVER YOU HAVE THE CHANCE to spend significant time at the grassroots level where the social issue or problem you are trying to address professionally is most robustly manifested, seize the opportunity and extract as much isight and understanding from it as possible. Don't rush through it despite all the other demands you have on your time; instead, linger for as long as you can.

7

AFTER ANY MAJOR PROJECT IS COMPLETE, schedule a post-mortem. Invite all participants to discuss what went well, what didn't, and the lessons for the future. Welcome divergent and unpopular views rather than driving them underground. This practice helps promote a learning culture focused on continuous improvement throughout your organization.

16

Learning Acceptance

Separating what you can control from what
you cannot—and managing effectively and wisely,
whether you're in control or not

WITH ALL THE DASHING around the office, the country, and the globe that I did during the middle 2000s, there was not a lot of time for self-examination. But insights into the life I was leading would come to me nonetheless, often at odd moments. In two cases, they involved the realization that certain semiconscious goals of mine were unrealistic, undesirable, and even silly, given the line of work I had chosen.

One of these goals was the dream of having a less pressured, more peaceful life—a life that provided me with many more opportunities to think, study, learn, and reflect.

Sometime in 2005, I was in the midst of one of the frenetic periods typical of my work at Grameen Foundation. I was preparing to meet one of the top venture capitalists of Silicon Valley. "Tim" was a strong ally, but his relationship with GF was complex and tricky to manage; the purpose of the meeting was for me to persuade him to support a new program we were hoping to launch, one that was quite different from the ones he'd backed in the past. My schedule called for me to travel cross-country to San Francisco, complete my last-minute preparations for the pitch I'd be making, hold the meeting, and then somehow find time for follow-up actions while being simultaneously plunged into preparations for my next meeting, just hours away.

This was my life as head of GF, and while it was rewarding and meaningful, I also found it rather stressful and sometimes unpleasant. Deep inside, I hoped it was a temporary condition. Without having a conscious plan to bring about change, I had a feeling that, if I did this work well enough for a few more years, I would get to the other side—a place of success where my days would be filled up with very different activities. I would be able to spend my days sitting in my office, doing things like thinking, reading, and writing. I would also meet with my staff members to mentor and advise them—because they would be the ones flying around the country, wrangling donors and doing all the other high-pressure things that I used to do.

The night before my meeting with Tim, I was sitting in front of my computer in a nondescript Days Inn a few miles from his office, working on my notes for the meeting, my stomach churning. As I worked, a part of my mind was dreaming about the idyllic future I imagined: *One of these days, I'm going to put all this craziness behind me.*

But somehow, this particular night, my brain was ready for a reality check. I looked up from my computer and suddenly experienced a moment of clarity: *Actually, that life of quiet reflection in my office is* not *going to happen! This is my life.*

As soon as that realization hit me, the obvious logic behind it fell into place.

As long as I was CEO of GF—or filling a similar leadership role in another organization—I would always be required to spend my time traveling, meeting with supporters, winning their confidence, developing strategic plans, performing feats of persuasion, and dealing with complications in our relationships. That's what it means to be a CEO! And somewhere deep inside me, I *knew* that was the case—after all, I'd seen a number of my peers in action as they managed their nonprofits effectively, and the lives they lived were basically the same as mine.

Of course, that didn't mean that the details of my work would never vary. If I continued to succeed at growing GF's reputation, resources, and capacity, the quality and capability of the average person I would meet with would continue to grow as well. But that wouldn't reduce the pressure on me. Just the contrary—it would make the meetings I participated in even more difficult to pull off well, and the stakes for our organization even higher.

At the same time, I would be able to attract more and better people to work with me. They would take on meetings that were important, but not important enough to merit my attention, and they would help me prepare for the high-level meetings that I would be focused on. That support would relieve some of the pressure on my schedule and enhance my ability to improvise and perform well. Add it all up, and it was a wash. My future as CEO of GF would not be a hellscape of ever-increasing stress . . . but neither would it be a nirvana of peaceful contemplation. I thought again, *This is my life!*

In this moment of insight, I received a customized version of the age-old insight bordering on cliché: *It's not the destination, but the journey*. Rather than believing that I would start enjoying life at some unspecified date in the future, I'd better start figuring out how to enjoy it here and now.

As a secondary benefit, I also received a helpful emotional adjustment. Rather than wallowing in my desire for a quiet, reflective future—and a growing sense of bitterness over my stressful present—I began to see the humor in my situation. The image of myself as a wise, elder statesman poring over leather-bound volumes in a wood-paneled office and occasionally offering pearls of insight to grateful young staff members began to appear like the silly daydream it was.

From that day forward, whenever I caught myself longing for that fantasy future, I would pause to picture it—and generally burst out laughing. Then I would put my head down and get back to work.

Accepting my life for what it was represented a big step on the way to wisdom and happiness for me.

People Are Who They Are

THE OTHER INSIGHT I GAINED at this time involved people and how I related to them. I realized that, on some level, I had been assuming that my job as CEO was to get everyone in my organization, as well as our outside supporters and partners, to behave basically the same way—essentially, the way I did on my best days. I expected everyone to be motivated, demotivated, amused, saddened, inspired, and troubled by roughly similar things as I was.

Looking back, I can understand why I made this assumption. After all, I knew myself much better than I knew anyone else—so when it came to interpreting the words and behaviors of the people around me, it was natural for me to fall back on my own psychology as a source of insight. Furthermore, assuming that everyone is fundamentally the same is very tempting for a leader. If it were true, the challenges of leadership would be so much easier than they really are!

It sounds laughable now, but this was the essence of my original approach to managing and interacting with people in the workplace. Of course, it didn't work. Instead, it led me to try to manipulate, cajole, or even lightly bully the people around me into acting the way I expected them to and wanted them to. And when they didn't, I got annoyed and angry at what I considered to be their inexplicable and unreasonable behavior.

I came to realize how silly my assumptions about human behavior were, and to gradually adopt a more realistic point of view, by observing the leadership style of John Anderson, the chief operating officer of GF in the mid-2000s, whom I briefly introduced to you earlier.

John was winding down a successful career as a management consultant, and he took on our COO role as a kind of public service capstone to his career. John enjoyed the opportunity to be around young people during the final years of his working life. He also liked having something at stake bigger than his golf score or getting a cheap dinner on the early bird special.

As I observed John building rapport with staff, their families, and many others whose lives he touched—for example, the people who worked in our building as security guards and janitors—I noticed that he approached his professional relationships much differently than I did. He didn't assume that all people are (or should be) fundamentally the same. To him, every person was a riddle to be solved, joyfully. He worked to deeply understand the motivations, values, and biases of each person he encountered. This enabled him to tailor his approach to working with each one as a way to build rapport with them. Most important, perhaps, John seemed to enjoy the process of getting to know people and their quirks as much as the leadership benefits he derived from it.

Over time, John began advising me based on his insights into human nature. For example, when I was planning the delivery of an important message, a piece of feedback, or a decision to a particular person, he would call upon his knowledge of the unique characteristics of the individual (as well as his understanding of me) to help fine-tune my plans. Should I conduct the conversation in person, over the phone, or over a drink? Should it take place in a group or in a private setting? In my office, in theirs, or in a neutral location? Should I deliver the message early or late in the conversation? Or would a written note work better?

For a while, I responded to John's advice on matters like this with impatience. It took time and energy to understand the riddle that each person represented, and then a lot of mental power to figure out how to use those insights to work most effectively with them. I felt this was a distraction from my "real work."

Gradually, I came to think about all this very differently, and my own behavior slowly changed as a result. I began to appreciate the fact that getting to know people deeply, including their strange and unexplainable qualities that differed from my own, was actually an important part of my real work. Over time, it became less of a chore, less of a means to an end, and more of an end in itself. I began to take joy in unraveling people's unusual qualities, and then adapting my management and communication style to them. A new colleague meant another new mystery to dive into, rather than being someone to cajole into being exactly as I would like them to be.

John Anderson was one of the wise men of GF—someone who powerfully shaped the organization, and shaped me as well.

I will never be as good at solving the riddle that each person represents as John is, or as good as some of my other mentors and colleagues, like Bob Eichfeld, Norm Tonina, and Jennifer Meehan. But at least I now understand and accept the reality that people are who they are—and that this is not a problem to be fixed or an annoyance to be tolerated, but one of the joys and delights of a life well lived.

Shake Off the Sense of Entitlement

SOMETIME AROUND 1999, my colleague Nigel Biggar asked if he could come into my office. In one sense, this was just a formality, since I had an open door policy. But I wasn't always friendly to everyone who ventured in. In fact, I could often be short with people, especially anyone who wasn't a GF donor (and occasionally, I regret to say, even with those who were).

But Nigel, who ran our Latin American programs at the time and later would manage our work on tracking social impact, never seemed to take offense at my mini-tirades; in fact, I think they rather amused him. Although he was serious about his work, he was also deeply curious about many things in life, and had a personal style that was happy-go-lucky and slightly bohemian. Satisfying his curiosities seemed more important to him than fretting over his boss's occasional ill temper—which made him easy and pleasant for me to deal with. Of course, I invited him in. He shut the door behind him, signaling that this needed to be a private conversation.

"Alex, I got my letter that informed me of my raise," Nigel said.

For an instant, my heart sank. We were starting to grow as an organization, and demands for increased pay were becoming more common. I had just decided on staff raises after a formal performance review process, and I feared the increases I'd approved would strike my hard-working staff as too little, too late. If even mild-mannered Nigel was going to complain—if Nigel was in fact going to be *the very first person* to complain—I was in for a tough couple of weeks. I braced myself for Nigel's next sentence.

"I just wanted to thank you for the raise," he said. And then he smiled, shook my hand, and walked out of my office. I was dumbfounded and grateful.

For many years thereafter, Nigel would repeat the same gesture after annual raises came out. What his behavior said to me was that Nigel didn't feel he was entitled to a raise—so when he got one, he wanted to express appreciation.

I think Nigel was on to something.

One of the secrets of a contented, fulfilling existence is to eschew feelings of entitlement. Don't participate in conversations where you or others engage in self-pity. When you find yourself in such a discussion, listen if you must, but resist the temptation to engage or agree. Instead, try to change the subject as soon as possible. Focusing on the things you think you *ought to* have—and bemoaning the gap between that and the things you *actually* have—is a recipe for unhappiness.

I can testify to this from personal experience.

When I lived in South Asia during my twenties, I developed a few personality quirks and views about being a professional that did not serve me well. Some dealt with feelings of entitlement. I felt that people and organizations owed me certain things. Thus, when I didn't get them, I thought it was a good idea to be indignant, and that when I did get them, it was unnecessary to be thankful. This attitude applied especially to subordinates, contractors, consultants, and vendors. When a subordinate performed well, I figured that was what they owed to the organization and to me as their manager. I feared that thanking them might cause them to relax, let up, and drift into complacency. So I was very stingy about expressing gratitude or praise.

Many things shaped my warped thinking about this topic. I saw how hard people worked in Bangladesh while receiving little money and affirmation in return. By comparison, I felt that everyone in the United States seemed to be overly compensated and, on top of that, expected praise and raises as a matter of course. I felt it was my right—maybe even my duty—to push back against this trait of American society. The same attitude was also modeled by some of my early mentors. This was not one of their better tendencies, but I initially adopted it as my own anyway.

It took me some years to unlearn this perspective. Over time, I taught myself to not expect raises or praise for myself, to express appreciation for things that others might feel they were entitled to, and to enjoy it when people like Nigel thanked me for whatever I gave them. I discovered how much happier I was when I channeled my inner Nigel, learning to be delighted when I received something and unaffected when I did not.

I have found myself able to take pleasure in things that I would once have felt entitled to. I have also learned the wisdom of giving praise to people even for meeting modest expectations, because doing so is more likely to motivate them to try even harder next time, rather than causing them to become complacent (as I'd once feared).

I still have a few latent feelings of entitlement that do not serve me well. But with every passing year, I find it a little easier to shake them off.

Learn to Be Grateful—Even When You Get What You Want

I'VE ALWAYS LOVED NEW YORK, and I've grown to like the Washington, D.C., area, which I've called home for all but six years of my adult life. I've also had many good experiences in Silicon Valley and southern California. Each of these regions has cultural aspects that impress me and others that annoy me. In New York, getting rich, especially through real estate or finance, is overvalued by too many people and ends up frequently being the subject of conversations. In Washington, political power is an obsession that enjoys the same inflated status as wealth in New York. In Silicon Valley, the universal currency is being tech-savvy and entrepreneurial. In Los Angeles, it's being famous or close to those who are.

Another culture I've come to know well is that of the global humanitarian community. This is a culture that spans local and even national boundaries. It has its own charming elements, including a certain quasi-jaded idealism and a sense of subdued moral outrage, as well as some absurdities that are rarely remarked upon.

Like many people these days, international development professionals are, or at least claim to be, perpetually busy and overcommitted. I take these complaints with a grain of salt. But I find one strain of self-pity that's characteristic of nonprofit leaders to be particularly off-putting. Early in their careers, they often complain that they are not given enough opportunities to provide leadership, to test their own ideas, or to travel to far-flung locales to meet with their peers, partners, government officials, and the intended beneficiaries of their work. I certainly uttered my share of those complaints early in my career. But those who later get the chance to do those types of things often start complaining about them—all with no sense of irony.

The result is an endless stream of dull conversations in which senior nonprofit leaders bemoan the burdens of attending conferences, spending time with colleagues, grassroots leaders, and government officials, making decisions that have the potential to do good, and traveling the globe. It's rare to hear them express gratitude for the opportunities these represent—to work with extraordinarily gifted and able people, to learn continually, and to see the world, all without spending a dime of their own money. When I find myself in conversations like these, I tend to withdraw or try to change the subject. If I know the people I am talking to well enough, I might try to find a nonjudgmental way to point out the absurdity of complaining about things that most of us craved earlier in our careers.

I don't mean to be overly harsh about self-pity. It sometimes has its place when we need to vent or to process an emotionally difficult situation. However, it is best done privately with a loved one or a therapist. You might even want to set up the conversation by saying something like, "I am going to engage in a little venting and self-pity over the next few minutes as a way to get myself back on track, and I would appreciate your being empathetic."

The sense of entitlement, too, has its place. There are certain things that people *should* feel entitled to, such as having their opinions taken seriously in the context of a business or community meeting that they have been invited to. When you're deprived of something you have a right to expect, the issue is not so much that you express feelings of entitlement, but rather *how* you do it.

In truth, when you find yourself repeatedly complaining about something that you voluntarily engage in—such as your job—you should probably ask yourself a few questions: Are there people who envy the things I'm complaining about? What am I gaining by engaging in self-pity, and what am I losing? Is there something I should be doing to improve my situation—and if so, why aren't I doing it instead of merely complaining?

In my experience, most people who take the time to answer such questions honestly soon come to realize the futility and self-destructiveness of self-pity and entitlement—and to appreciate the wisdom of learning to accept and be grateful for the realities of their lives.

Four Favorite Tips to Help You Practice Learning Acceptance

1

MAKE TIME EACH WEEK to write down a list of at least ten things you are grateful for at that moment.

2

IF YOU TAKE RISKS in your personal and professional relationships with others—as you should—make peace with the fact that some of those relationships will suffer. Your highest priority should not be to avoid upsetting or offending others. If it is, you are likely to become too cautious in your dealings with other people, sacrificing your spontaneity and freedom in the process.

3

WHEN PREPARING FOR A TRIP OR A HOLIDAY, don't stress yourself out by needing to get everything done perfectly before you leave. Misplaced perfectionism drives you and your colleagues crazy, undermines your sense of enjoyment, and robs your colleagues of the opportunity to handle problems in their own way.

4

UNLESS YOU ARE EXPERIENCING profound poverty or other types of vulnerability, it's likely that your life is significantly better than that lived by the majority of human beings throughout history, as well as most living today—even if only because you have reliable access to food and shelter. Strive never to take such advantages for granted.

17

Living Generously

You were drawn to nonprofit leadership because of a desire to help and serve others. Here are tips on how to live and work every day in that spirit

RETURNING TO WASHINGTON in the fall of 1989 was quite a change after living in Bangladesh as a Fulbright scholar. I was earning a monthly after tax paycheck of around $1,600, which seemed like an incredible sum after my time in Bangladesh. My part of the monthly rent for the apartment I was sharing with my then-girlfriend Jennifer amounted to $350. I remember wondering what on earth I could possibly spend the remaining $1,250 on—not just this month, but *every* month!

My job also called for some big adjustments. I felt woefully underprepared for my new role as legislative director for RESULTS. To deal with this, I learned to fake a sense of confidence, all the while worrying that my new environment would expose my underlying mediocrity.

With the benefit of hindsight, having to feign a sense of confidence took its toll on me, as I imagine it does on many young professionals given outsized responsibilities. As a twenty-two-year-old with limited life and professional experience, I was quite rough around the edges. What's more, everyone involved felt that the stakes were huge. That's a tribute to the environment that Sam Daley-Harris created, which fostered a sense of agency and urgency among those he touched and inspired.

Confessions of a Former Brat

I RESPONDED TO THIS SITUATION by working very hard, reading everything, adopting mentors, and finding temporary escape with a parade of eclectic girlfriends (ending, happily, with Emily, the love of my life). It all worked fairly well. But the challenges I faced also brought out some of my darker qualities, which were more pronounced in my younger days.

The truth is that I frequently played the role of an arrogant brat. It was bad enough that I picked fights in my dealings with colleagues, volunteers, and those we were seeking to influence—on one notable occasion, with virtually the entire staff of Senator Mitch McConnell. But my worst behavior, I am sad to say, was directed towards RESULTS founder Sam Daley-Harris himself.

As I observed Sam managing the staff and leading RESULTS, which by the early 1990s included national organizations in six other countries, I focused more on his flaws and mistakes than on his achievements and the guts, smarts, and diligence they reflected. Sometimes I was actively supportive of him, dutifully trying to build on his accomplishments, manage his miscues, express empathy, and extend friendship. But just as often, I was harshly judgmental in an immature, know-it-all way. Behind Sam's back, I undermined his leadership. On a couple of occasions, I seriously contemplated how to assemble a coalition of disaffected staff and board members to affect a coup-d'état that would bring in a new leader—possibly me.

Looking back, what horrifies me so much about my behavior at that time is that I *thought* I understood what it meant to be a leader. In reality, I had no idea.

Years later, I would find myself in a situation like Sam's—the founder of a startup lacking much of the necessary training, pedigree, financing, and expertise but determined to make it work anyway. That experience would teach me just how tough the challenges Sam had faced really were. But as a young staffer, I vastly oversimplified the demands of leadership and found Sam sadly lacking in many ways. It was unfair and it was not right. And worst of all, I was absolutely sure my assessment was correct.

This story has a happy ending. As I learned through direct experience what leadership was really like, I gradually became one of Sam's staunchest supporters and allies. When he came under attack for the strong stands he took, I publicly defended him. When he didn't get enough credit for his role in putting microfinance on the world map, especially through his leadership of the Microcredit Summit Campaign, I made sure more people knew about his contributions. When RESULTS staff and volunteers came to me to complain about him, as they occasionally did, I listened but tried to help them see him from a more generous and realistic perspective. And though Sam and I did not always agree on strategy or tactics (and still don't, even today), we ultimately became good friends.

In time, I got a dose of my own medicine. During my years with Grameen Foundation, I had to endure my fair share of young, mostly male, staff who were whip-smart and committed, but also arrogant and judgmental, and who at times used their influence to undermine me as the leader of the organization. Like most nonprofit executives, I had my own "Alexes," and I suppose I deserved them.

A few years back, a friend who admired what I had accomplished in my career confided in me her worries about her highly intelligent son. She was concerned because he demonstrated, on occasion, some qualities that were all too familiar to me. I knew exactly how to reassure her. "Well," I said, "when I was in my twenties, I was a lot like your son—only worse!"

She smiled and exhaled.

Many of us start our lives and careers with a little bit of the brat inside us—sometimes with a lot. In many cases, it's a temporary affliction. The cure lies in being sensitive, honest, and open to learning from our mistakes.

It also requires developing a greater degree of generosity—towards the people around us—with their flaws, foibles, and wonderful qualities—and even towards ourselves.

To leaders who must deal with talented but challenging junior staff, I recommend not confronting them unless it is essential. Instead, have confidence that they will find their way, while at the same time trying to surround them with people who make them uncomfortable when they indulge in their most immature and unprofessional behavior.

As for the Young Turks themselves, I urge them to be less judgmental and more curious when it comes to assessing leadership.

The Secret Discipline of Generosity

ONE OF THE MOST POPULAR and influential career guides of recent decades is Adam Grant's *Give and Take: Why Helping Others Drives Our Success* (Viking, 2013). Grant's overarching message is that people who are generous tend to be happier and also—perhaps surprisingly—more successful as measured by traditional indicators such as wealth and job title.

By the time I read Grant's book, most of his message had become part of my personal DNA. But I certainly didn't start out that way.

In my youth and through early adulthood, I was often stingy in praising others. I was also rather tightfisted when it came to money. I skimped on donations to nonprofit organizations, figuring that my volunteerism was enough. I gave meagre tips to people who served me at restaurants, since I could always find some flaw in how they performed. And I sometimes contributed less than my share to paying the bill when out with friends, especially if I figured others in the group earned more than me. I believed that giving too much away too soon was a sign of weakness, low standards, or wastefulness. Like many people, I often operated from an underlying assumption of scarcity.

During my thirties and forties, I came to see giving to others not as a sign of weakness or low standards, but as another expression of my desire to contribute. I started looking more thoughtfully at my life and realized that, while I was not rich, I had enough of everything I needed. What's more, when I reflected on my past experiences, I found I had no regrets about times when I'd chosen to be "too generous," but many regrets about not being generous enough. So I gradually shifted my habits, posture, and worldview.

Now my advice to anyone getting started in life and work, is simple: Err on the side of generosity with your money, your time, and your treatment of other people. The universe will pay you back manyfold. Here are some examples of how I try to practice the discipline of generosity.

For the last fifteen years, I have always sought to offer written or verbal praise when it was deserved—or even when it was *almost* deserved. I typically tip more, give more, and pick up more of the tab than my first instinct tells me is appropriate. I truly have no regrets from any of the dinner bills I have picked up, the compliments I have given, and the times I've put twenty dollars in a musician's tip jar when five bucks would have sufficed.

I've also noticed that some of the most contented people I know are those who try the hardest to make other people's days joyful and fun. Two of the most prolific are the late Emalyn Mercer and Joan Robbins, women I met through my musician friends, Danny and Tim Carter.

Their actions often take the form of thoughtful gifts—a touching letter or email out of nowhere, or an act so considerate that one would normally expect it only from a spouse, parent, or close sibling. For example, I have observed Emalyn and Joan fly around the world to surprise a friend who was performing music, or to support a charitable cause that a friend is passionate about. These are women who would share the last few dollars in their purses if you needed it, and do it with joy.

Like any other life strategy, the discipline of generosity can be overdone or misplaced. On occasion, being overly generous with money can be culturally inappropriate or signal that a relationship is more transactional than the other person thinks. For example, I once became friends with two Swedish tennis instructors. At the end of one visit to the place where they taught, I debated whether to tip them, then decided I should err on the side of generosity. Unfortunately, my well-intentioned gesture mildly offended them, sending a false impression about our friendship. So be sensitive about your giving—but don't let that discourage you from being as generous as you can be.

Sometimes, being generous can involve acts that few would think of in those terms. Here's an example I learned from Susan Davis.

When you are in the audience for a speech or presentation, and you notice that the speaker seems a bit uneasy or nervous, start clapping when they say something that touches you. Most likely, others will follow suit. The resulting round of applause will probably relax the speaker and help ensure they do their best from then on. I am especially focused on playing this influential role when the speaker is someone I know and like and want to succeed. This can also work when you start a round of applause for musicians in small venues after they finish playing a song—try it sometime!

I recall once when a woman named Laura Foose, the head of an influential microfinance industry body called the Social Performance Task Force, took the podium to speak at the opening session of a conference that she had helped organize. The preceding keynote speaker had been a little boring, and the gathering was still in that awkward phase before it hits its stride.

I thought the world of Laura and figured she would be a little nervous, as I would be with the ice not really broken yet. So when she said, "Good morning, everyone, my name is Laura Foose," I started clapping, as if to say, "You are a great leader in our field, and we all admire you!" Like a charm, virtually everyone else—about 200 people in all—joined me in the ovation. Even though I was sitting in the back of the ballroom, Laura noticed that I had gotten it going, which she acknowledged by catching my eye and smiling. As expected, everyone in the room, including Laura, seemed to relax. I took satisfaction in having helped speed that process along.

The Flip Side of Generosity—Frugality

I HAVE EXTENDED my generosity discipline to the way I negotiate my compensation with nonprofit organizations I work for. I don't claim to be in a league with people like Muhammad Yunus, who take salaries that are a tiny fraction of their so-called market value. Yunus also takes a pass, as a matter of principle, on receiving ownership shares in the for-profit social ventures he starts. If he had behaved in a way most people would consider rational, those shares would have probably made him a billionaire by now.

Yunus's generosity in these matters is extraordinary and exemplary. And while I wouldn't compare myself to him, in most cases I have chosen not to push for the highest salary I could from my employers. This was possible, in part, because Emily and I have opted for a relatively simple lifestyle. (I sometimes joke that I decided to limit myself to one house, one car, one wife, and one cat.) Not having children preparing for college, as many friends my age do, has helped to make me a bargain for most of my employers and, more recently, my consulting clients. I have no regrets, only gratitude that I have been able to do work that was meaningful for me and get paid more than I ever thought I would for such work.

In the process, I have come to believe that compensation for senior executives in nonprofits should not be set solely based on the market (i.e., what other organizations of similar size pay for comparable roles). Rather, it should be *negotiated* based on a variety of factors, including the life needs that a potential employee has at the time. What they actually need is itself influenced by many factors, including, for example, the number of school- and college-aged children they have and the amount of wealth they've inherited or previously earned. Using that logic, there might be times when the CEO is not the highest paid person in the organization, which was occasionally the case when I was leading Grameen Foundation.

For years, the so-called market rate for a CEO in an organization the size of GF was at least $50,000 to $75,000 more than I earned. I never asked the board to close the gap. Similarly, after leaving GF, when I became CEO at the American India Foundation (AIF), I shocked the board by not asking for a raise after my first year, since it would not be until the second year that revenue went up (by twenty percent, as it turned out). This left more in the raise pool for some of my colleagues who had greater family needs and were being paid much less than I was. Later, when I asked the board of AIF for permission to teach a class at the University of Maryland and become an affiliated faculty of its impressive Do Good Institute, which would take up a bit of my time during working hours, I told them I would donate my entire $5,000 stipend to AIF. This also surprised them, but I never considered any other option.

A corollary to being moderate in your salary demands is to be frugal when spending money on behalf of the nonprofit organization that employs you. This is a form of generosity in that it leaves more resources to go directly to the cause you are dedicated to serving.

Frugality of this kind requires, of course, that you never claim benefits or expenses beyond those allowed by your organization's policies (which themselves should be reasonably strict). But go one step further. If you want to be a leader who embraces the values of modesty and mission-orientation, be *more* frugal than policy requires. For example, when you're on a business trip, occasionally stay with friends instead of in a hotel, or use frequent flyer miles in lieu of a paid airline ticket. People will notice that, and some will imitate your actions, which will help make your donated dollars go further.

Sometimes it can be tricky to calibrate the organization's culture so that it accurately reflects both the financial realities you face and the desire for generosity and mission-centeredness. During GF's early years, we engaged in what some would call extreme frugality. If someone was departing on a plane early in the morning or arriving late at night, the one employee who owned a car—at the time it was Jacki Lippman—would be expected to perform pick-up or drop-off duty, all without getting reimbursed for mileage or gas. (As Jacki was not a morning person, she sometimes let other staff use her car to perform this duty if it involved an early drop off or pick up.) Most people embraced the sense of adventure these casual practices created.

In 2004, when our fundraising picked up and we began hiring people from corporate America, there was pressure to loosen up. Not doing so would have projected an aura of amateurism and emphasize self-sacrifice far beyond what any of our competitors required of their employees. It felt as though attracting the best talent demanded that we grow up. And gradually we did.

Looking back, I wished that we'd retained a little more of our hyper-frugal culture (though we never got extravagant by any means). When grant dollars got tight in my final years as CEO, we needed to rein in some of the spending habits we'd acquired, which is painful to do and usually deflating to morale.

I made an effort to encourage frugality at GF during mainly through peer pressure rather than policy requirements. For example, I decided to create a fictitious persona, Mr. Kripon, to highlight ways of saving money for my colleagues. (In the Bengali language, *kripon* roughly translates as "miser.") Over the years, I posted stories about Mr. Kripon's cash-conscious behaviors on the office bulletin board. For instance, I often took the bus back home from the Baltimore airport, even though catching a cab was allowed. On business trips, I sometimes bought a sandwich at a grocery store for dinner rather than going to a restaurant. A few of my colleagues told me that they had been unaware of some of the ways one can travel cheaply until I brought them to their attention through my Mr. Kripon posts, and that they'd started using those techniques both professionally and personally while coming up with their own creative ideas to save the organization money.

Be Generous with Yourself, Too

LEARNING TO LIVE GENEROUSLY is an essential skill for anyone who wants to be truly satisfied and fulfilled. But sometimes, life simply demands that you devote full attention to self-care. When that happens, heed the message that your body, mind, and spirit is sending, and figure out what you need to do to be generous to yourself.

Midway through 1991, my world began to crumble, piece by piece. I went into the only prolonged period of sadness I have ever known.

I am normally an optimistic, upbeat, high-energy person. My typical week is six days that are generally pleasant and satisfying, though often hectic. If one day per week is a downer, it's nothing that a good night's sleep can't fix. But for six months in 1991, this pattern was reversed. Six days per week were now filled with feelings of melancholy. Even the occasional day which was enjoyable had a dark cloud hanging over it—the foreboding sense that my life would soon return to the new normal of sadness.

I don't really know what the most important precipitating factors were. My mentor, Muhammad Yunus, was dealing with two major crises that potentially imperiled Grameen Bank. One was a major cyclone that had devastated Bangladesh in late April. The other was an effort by disgruntled employees to form a labor union that would have infused politics into the bank for the first time. The prospect of seeing the foundations of the flagship anti-poverty institution I had aligned myself with crumbling was deeply unsettling to me.

Around the same time, I dislocated my shoulder while bodysurfing, and a doctor told me might become a chronic issue requiring surgery at some point. I had begun dating Emily, but our relationship was not yet serious, and I was still smarting from two painful breakups the year before. A friend and mentor was struggling with mental health issues and had attempted suicide. And on the national stage, the Republicans had been in power for eleven years, with no end in sight, which laid a heavy damper on my liberal Democratic spirits.

Whatever the exact cause, I found myself, for the first time, laboring under a lasting sense of gloom.

I tried to be a good professional and leader despite the haze of melancholy that surrounded me, but it took a lot of energy to perform even reasonably well under the circumstances. I felt as if I was trapped in quicksand. While I took satisfaction in holding up most of my professional responsibilities fairly well, it was a joyless sense of achievement. I sought help from counseling with a social worker covered under my employer's health plan, but that fell far short of what I needed.

The low point came in the early fall. After making a commitment to date Emily exclusively, I sabotaged the relationship by impulsively sleeping with a young woman I'd met at a friend's wedding. Only by following my father's advice to the letter was I able to resurrect my relationship with Emily. (I sent her a dozen red roses the first day of the week, a dozen pink roses the second day, and a box of chocolates the third day. Then I offered to take the next flight to Reno to apologize to her in person.) My failure to live up to my own standards of honesty and fidelity deepened my sense of sadness, adding to it a powerful dose of shame and guilt.

My father had some other help to offer me. When I told him about my persistent sense of gloom, he used his professional network to find me an excellent psychiatrist in Washington. However,

I wasn't able to get my first appointment until February, 1992. I decided I would simply have to muddle through for the next few months, and I hoped the psychiatrist would be able to help me then.

Somehow, my fever broke in January. It was not a gradual return to normalcy, as one might expect. One day, while I was visiting Seattle to participate in a conference, I simply felt normal again. I had several pleasant and enjoyable days in a row, and somewhere inside myself I realized that these were not exceptional days but rather, the new (old) normal. Deeply relieved, I found myself looking forward to life with my characteristic energy and optimism once more.

The next month, my date to meet with the psychiatrist arrived. I felt a bit guilty explaining to him that the condition that had prompted me to seek his care had seemingly resolved itself. But he and I agreed that trying to get to the bottom of what put me in such a funk was worthwhile. So I saw him for about six months, and while I gained a number of insights from our meetings, only one specific conversation with him remains vivid twenty-five years later.

I described some of the events that had destabilized me during the spring of 1991, especially the troubling developments in Bangladesh, my friend's suicide attempt, and my shoulder injury. I tentatively asked my doctor, "Is it *normal* to be deeply troubled by things like this?"

I half expected him to turn the question back on me, as I thought his training might have led him to do. Instead, he simply said, in a way that was more human than clinical, "It was completely understandable."

That response affected me more deeply than I would have expected. I stopped feeling guilty about my weakness. Instead, I felt liberated by the knowledge that I'd simply responded in a normal way to some of the painful vicissitudes of life. I stopped being so hard on myself, and the last remnants of my melancholy melted away.

In the years to come, I returned repeatedly to that moment. I came to realize that sometimes I just need to hear a message of understanding, affirmation, and acceptance in order to regain my balance. I've gotten better at recognizing when those moments occur, and become braver about seeking out the help I need. I've been able to assemble a network of supporters—family, colleagues, mentors, friends—that I know I can turn to in times of trouble. They include not only my wife and parents, but also people like Susan Davis, Bob Eichfeld, Nick Arena, Donna Nelson, Julia Soyars, and Karen O'Malley.

Perhaps most important, I've also learned to offer some of the same kind of help to other people when I sense they're going through the kind of darkness I experienced back in 1991. Powered by the gratitude I feel for the many blessings I enjoy, I try to respond to their needs with empathy, understanding, and compassion, and with the honest recognition that times of sadness and even despair are not signs of weakness but simply a natural part of the human condition.

Being generous with others and being generous with yourself, I now realize, are two sides of the same coin.

Nine Favorite Tips to Help You Practice Living Generously

1

WHEN SOMEONE TELLS YOU about a painful or traumatic situation they are going through, resist the temptation to tell a similar story from your own life. Instead, listen attentively and show that you are comfortable with them emoting if they want to. At some point, simply ask, "Is there anything I can do to help you now?"

2

AN APOLOGY THAT INCLUDES the words "if" or "but" is actually *not* an apology, and sometimes it is worse than saying nothing at all. Avoid cluttering and diluting your apologies. On the other hand, when *receiving* an apology, accept even an imperfect effort graciously, as it may be the best a person can do.

3

WHEN SOMEONE HAS LET YOU DOWN, avoid reminding them of their transgression, especially if they have made amends. This includes making jokes about what happened. Otherwise, you may be contributing to the negative pattern repeating itself.

4

WHEN YOU LEARN something interesting or valuable from your interactions with someone—even something small—let them know. Don't assume that hearing such feedback won't matter to them. It probably will.

5

IF YOU ARE A LEADER AT WORK, be willing to roll up your sleeves on occasion and happily do "grunt work" that some people would consider "below your pay grade." Rather than diminishing you in the eyes of others, your humility and lack of pretense will likely impress them.

6

WHEN YOU TRAVEL, do what you can to treat yourself well. Figure out what you want from airlines, trains, cabs, and hotels, and, without a spirit of entitlement, ask for those things. You will be surprised how often you will get what you ask for.

7

WHENEVER YOU VISIT SOMEONE'S HOUSE for at least one meal, and certainly if you stay overnight, bring a house-warming gift of some kind. If you forget, send a gift with a handwritten thank-you note within a week of leaving.

8

IF YOU OBSERVE SOMEONE being bullied while traveling, stick up for them if you can do so reasonably safely. If you help to improve the situation, you'll feel good about it for a long time. If you fail to act, it may haunt you.

9

SPEND MONEY LIBERALLY and without guilt on a few things that bring you joy, and be frugal in all other areas. Periodically reevaluate whether the things you have been splurging on still bring you joy. If they don't, scale back or discontinue spending on those things, and channel your spending toward other things that bring you more satisfaction.

18

Letting Go

One of the hardest challenges for any leader is handing the reins over to others. Here is advice on how to do it

AT CERTAIN TIMES IN MY LIFE, my beliefs about God and the supernatural have been tested. My father's death provoked some of those moments.

He died on November 3, 2004, and we had a memorial service later that month, at which I presided and gave the final eulogy. A few weeks later, when I was in Northern California with Emily's family, I asked my in-laws, Duane and Mary Wainright, to arrange a meeting with their retired family priest, Charlie Poole. I had something I needed to discuss with him.

My father had not believed in God; he was an agnostic, or perhaps an atheist. The topic never really came up between us, though he had no problem with my evolving Christian faith. Now I was troubled. I needed to make sense of passages in the Bible that seemed to suggest that, unless a person accepted God, they were condemned to Hell after they died. Did this apply even to an ethical humanist like my father, who'd helped people his entire life?

Father Poole and I sat down one afternoon in late December at a coffee joint near the thrift store where Duane and Mary volunteered, which was affiliated with their church. I explained my dilemma, which I am sure Father Poole had heard before in many forms over the years as a practicing Episcopal priest. In response, he handed me a sheet of paper with more than fifty Bible verses, all with a common message—that God forsakes no one. He loves and embraces us all. We didn't discuss or debate any of the Bible verses that seem to contradict those.

Towards the end of our discussion, Father Poole made a prediction: "Your father is okay, Alex. And sometime soon, he will signal that to you."

About six months later, I was walking from Union Station in Washington to meet Emily at La Loma, our favorite Mexican restaurant. While I was crossing in front of a federal judiciary building, for some reason I recalled Father Poole's prediction that I was going to get a signal from Dad. I met Emily at the restaurant, and we took a seat outside, as it was a warm summer day. At some point, one of the owners, a bald man with a wide smile, came up behind me and gave my shoulder a big squeeze. This embrace was completely out of character for our friendly but polite relationship.

I immediately realized what had happened. This embrace was a message from Dad. He was telling me that God had not forsaken him, but rather had welcomed him into His kingdom. (A God who would do that has become easy for me to worship, despite my agnostic upbringing.)

I've told and retold this story to family and friends. Some have been incredulous, but others have described similar experiences of being touched by loved ones who had passed.

About fifteen months later, I was sitting in that same restaurant, waiting for Emily to arrive for dinner, when a question popped into my head: Was our extended family's new tradition of having me sit at the head of the table during the holidays okay, or was it presumptuous—since that had formerly been my father's seat? It was a question I'd been wondering about, on and off, for the last few months, ever since my stepmother had spontaneously invited me to take that chair at one of our family gatherings.

Just as I was turning this question over in my mind, that same bald restaurateur, standing thirty feet away, caught my eye and waved at me with a big smile on his face.

My father was using his channel on Earth to tell me he was pleased to see me sitting in his chair. I never worried about it, or about my father, again.

Leaving Behind a Big Chunk of My Life

LETTING GO OF SOMEONE as important and influential in life as my father was not easy for me. I'm glad that Dad took advantage of his supernatural connections to send me messages of reassurance from beyond.

But letting go of things that are precious to us is never easy, even when it involves an organization rather than a person of flesh and blood.

For the first fifteen years I ran Grameen Foundation, the thought of working anywhere else was the furthest thing from my mind. I studied other nonprofits and their leaders to pick up useful ideas, and occasionally envied one of my peers or was thankful I was not in the shoes of another. But unlike most of my counterparts from the private sector, I focused less on how we matched up with our competition and more on whether we were meeting our own goals for excellence and impact. I wanted to be great by my own definition rather than the best in comparison to others (though of course I wanted to measure up to Muhammad Yunus's expectations for me, and still do today).

Still, the spirit of competition can be a powerful motivating force, even in the nonprofit world. I chuckled when Premal Shah, the charismatic and brilliant cofounder of the innovative nonprofit Kiva, recently introduced me before giving a talk to his staff by saying, "I've sometimes asked my team members, 'Why can't we be as innovative as Grameen Foundation?'" I laughed because, at the same time as he had been haranguing his colleagues with statements like these, the GF board of directors was scolding us for falling behind Kiva when it came to innovation!

In fact, I never even remotely entertained the thought of leaving GF to join a different organization until after 2012.

A growing number of signals pointed in the direction of my stepping aside. I observed peers hanging on to their roles so long that the organizations they led were indistinguishable from them as leaders. Some seemed to remain as CEOs in part because they had no idea what else they could do. I wondered whether that applied to me. Our chairman Paul Maritz once said during my performance review that he had been tempted to write the following in my formal evaluation, "What is Alex going to do when he grows up?" I took it as a compliment—but also as a challenge to begin thinking about the next stage in my life.

There were other, more painful circumstances that encouraged me to think about leaving. In the years following the 2009 financial crisis, I had to deal with several rounds of layoffs among our U.S. staff, exacerbated by our commitment to basing more of our team in the field while also dealing with the fallout from the global financial crisis as well the completion of several large projects funded by the Bill and Melinda Gates Foundation. Few things weaken a leader's resolve or his or her standing in their organization as much as reductions in force do.

In February, 2015, I attended a meeting in Seattle with leaders from our staff and board, along with some expert advisors. At one point, I presented a two-page written summary of what I thought our strategy should be going forward, and how we should talk about it. I asked everyone to read it. Then we went around the table, and everyone offered comments. With a few exceptions, the members of the group dismissed or discounted most of my ideas. This episode helped me realize that I was increasingly out of step with many of the great people I had attracted to GF. Around the same time, we completed the arduous and stressful work to finalize a one-year budget and a three-year operating plan. I woke up one morning in March and told Emily that I was crystal clear about one thing: that I would never lead GF through another strategy or budgeting process as its CEO.

On April 1, I told my senior staff that I would be stepping down later that year. It happened to be the eighteenth anniversary of the founding of GF.

Organizational transitions are never easy, and transitions that involve the departure of the founder can be especially hard. I'd witnessed this process go so badly in another organization that the chair, who had previously served on the GF board, resolved never to be involved in a nonprofit again for the rest of her life.

I had a visceral sense of why founders often botch their departures. In his first year as our board chairman, Bob Eichfeld had asked me to write an emergency succession plan—a memo outlining what the organization's remaining leaders should do if I suddenly died or was incapacitated. (All nonprofits should have one of these in place, but few do.) I put off this exercise for months, as I found it hard to spend much time contemplating the prospect of having GF operating without me. Leaving GF voluntarily wasn't as traumatic as sudden death, but it was certainly an intensely emotional experience. I resolved to try to be the exception to the rule of messy founder transitions when my turn finally came in 2015.

My main tactic was unilateral disarmament. I took off the table the idea of serving on the board after I'd left the CEO role. I had come to believe that appointing a retiring founder to an organization's governing body was a lazy and potentially harmful way to keep a founder involved and supportive, because it almost inevitably undermined his or her successor. In addition, I said I would not serve on the search committee for my replacement, though I would advise it informally if asked. I also told the board leadership that I would be willing to leave the organization quickly or after a long transitional period, depending on their preference. The only thing I requested was some input regarding the timing and manner of the public announcement of my decision to step down as CEO—to which the board graciously agreed.

Once my successor, Steve Hollingworth, was identified, I praised him in a public post on our blog and wrote him a confidential, forty-page transition memo. I also contributed to the blog of InterAction, the respected network of international nonprofits, an article about how our transition was a model that others could follow. When I sensed a potential gap in terms of sending handwritten notes to top donors who made contributions at year end, I volunteered to come back on the first working day of 2016 and write dozens of customized thank-you letters before quietly slipping out the door at the end of the workday.

Were there a few awkward or tense moments during the nine-month transition process? Of course. I was struck by how some people in the organization that had always listened to my views stopped doing so once I was a lame duck. It got worse when my title changed from CEO to senior advisor, but this was the right decision, since it made way for my deputy, David Edelstein, to serve as interim CEO for the second half of the year—a role for which I gave him a grade of A+.

My thoughts soon moved to how we could make the transition fun and soulful for me and those who cared about GF. The default plan for honoring my service would have been to hold the welcome dinner the night before our fall board meeting and focus on people expressing appreciation for what I had done. As had been done with other retiring leaders, I would be allowed to invite a handful of friends and family to the occasion, at no cost to them or me. But given my desire to leave GF in the strongest possible financial position I could, spending more than usual on the pre-meeting dinner seemed somehow inappropriate.

Then I had an idea: Why not turn the farewell dinner into a big fundraising gala? We could have live music and lots of dancing after the requisite tribute speeches and roasts. I would pay for the musicians—my friend Stacy Brooks, a terrific blues singer, and her band, backed up by Danny and Tim Carter—and GF would come out several hundred thousand dollars ahead. Our board chairman

Bob Eichfeld immediately embraced the idea. In the end, 350 people turned out, nearly $450,000 was raised, and people loved the speeches, the music, and the dancing. The gala attracted a greater number of staff and board alumni than any other event in GF's history.

I savored that evening like few others in my life. Many people expressed their appreciation for my service in touching ways. For example, Wayne Silby, the father of the social investing movement in the United States, flew back from China to attend. People who had been disconnected from the organization for years showed up or sent a donation. Friends of limited means who led busy lives figured out how to get there.

I had long appreciated the importance of sending people off when they leave an organization with the class and effort that their contributions deserved—and in my own case, I had set in motion a process for GF to succeed.

However, in one small but important respect, I failed to take in the love and enjoy the moment, which turned into yet another lesson learned. The evening included remarks from about ten people who wanted to talk about what I had meant to the organization and to them. Then I gave my farewell speech. When finished speaking, I hurried off the stage while the crowd was giving me a standing ovation—both for my well-received and reasonably short remarks, and for my years of service.

I realized later that my hasty departure was a mistake. I should have just stood there for a minute or so, taking it all in, perhaps waving to the crowd and showing the emotions I was experiencing. But having never been on stage for a moment like that, I didn't linger. Instead, once back among the audience, I hugged a friend who was near the stairs down from the stage, turned and waved to everyone for a very brief moment, and returned to my seat.

Lesson learned: If I ever encounter a moment like that again, I'll try to anticipate what's coming and make sure to savor the ovation, which is its own form of thanking the people giving it.

Overall, I'm proud of the way we handled my leave-taking from GF. Later, when I left the American India Foundation after a much shorter tenure as its CEO, I went back to the GF playbook to ensure a smooth process—although leaving an organization as CEO after a nineteen-month tenure is much different than after an eighteen-year stint when you are also the founder. However, I did follow some of the same steps. I wrote a long transition memo, published a blog post praising my successor, Nishant Pandey, and worked hard every day I was on the payroll, even when I was a lame duck. Indeed, I closed one of the largest grants in the organization's history in my final days working for AIF.

I remain highly supportive of GF to this day. I have no title except founder, since president emeritus (which I was also offered) seemed superfluous. I have advised my successor whenever he has reached out for help. I have been especially impressed by the talent he has attracted, particularly when he brought on Lauren Hendricks as his deputy. The absorption of Freedom from Hunger that he orchestrated has made the organization stronger; it has been especially gratifying to see it now being a significant player in some of the poverty-stricken countries of Francophone Africa. Completing the sale of GF's stake in the Indonesian social enterprise RUMA, the foundation for which had been laid by my colleague Sean DeWitt and others a decade earlier, brought in a welcome infusion of growth capital and also served to replenish the reserves that had shrunk the aftermath of the global financial crisis and the conclusion of several large grants in the mid-2010s. Many of the programs and affiliated companies started during the last five years of my tenure as CEO have evolved nicely, especially the work on subsistence agriculture, Grameen Capital India, and the social enterprise Taroworks.

As a show of my solidarity with Steve and his team, I ran the Richmond marathon in 2018 as a fundraiser for GF after having promised myself ten years earlier to never run 26.2 miles at a stretch again. In response, many former staff and board members who had drifted away from the organization renewed their financial support.

HERE WE ARE, at the end of this journey. I hope you have enjoyed it as much as I have. Let me close with a final thought or two.

My doctor once summed up the causes of my good health as a combination of good genes, good habits, and good luck. I think he got it right. If you adapt his analysis to the secrets to living a productive and contented life, either as a nonprofit leader or in any other field, you could say that it is the result of unearned privilege, useful habits, and good fortune—also known as dumb luck. While I am far from the most accomplished person in my field, the degree to which I have experienced success has certainly been shaped by all three of those factors. This book has been about the one of those three that each person has control of: adopting and adapting habits—that is practices, mindsets, and techniques that you use repeatedly—that will serve you well.

While I think that many of the habits and ideas that I describe in this book could benefit you, I believe even more strongly that periodically taking time to seriously inventory, reflect on, and get objective outside feedback about your current habits, principles, and philosophy about life can change your circumstances dramatically for the better. It takes time and can be uncomfortable, but it is well worth it.

For those of you who have chosen a life of service or devote time to actively volunteering with one or more nonprofits, I believe this to be especially important—for you and for the many other people who benefit from your efforts.

Good luck, and let me know how it goes. I'd be delighted to hear from you about your own experiences in the world of mission-driven leadership. Please visit my website at https://www.alexcounts.com, where I will be posting additional lessons to supplement those in this book. And feel free to contact me at alexcounts09@gmail.com.

Epilogue: Leading in a Time of Crisis

THAT SETTLED IT. The meeting would definitely *not* go forward.

One fall morning in 2001, I was chairing a meeting of the executive committee of a microcredit program operating in the iconic New York City neighborhood of Harlem. Our meeting was interrupted by someone popping their head into the room to tell us the news that a plane had flown into one of the Twin Towers in lower Manhattan, just a few miles away from us. We paused briefly, a little disturbed to hear about what we assumed was a tragic accident. Then we continued our deliberations.

But when word reached us that a *second* plane had smashed into the other tower, we realized there was no point in trying to conduct business as usual. Everyone in the meeting began calling loved ones or leaving the building.

Like many people, especially those of us who were in New York on 9/11, I can remember the rest of the day vividly. Watching the news on a TV screen in an electronics store window from the sidewalk on 125th Street. Trying to figure out where my frail father was and whether he was having trouble getting back from his doctor's appointment to his apartment on 81st Street. Getting into bed that night understanding that everything had changed but not knowing what lay ahead for me, for the nonprofit organization I led, or for the world around us.

I felt profoundly inadequate to meeting the daunting challenges that lay ahead. But I would have to do my best, and a good night's sleep felt like a decent place to start. Rest might help me summon the wisdom, courage, and effort that would be required of me in the weeks ahead. That tiny first step would be the beginning of a long slog in the months that followed.

Navigating Booms and Busts

FOR A NONPROFIT LEADER, there are essentially two types of crises. One is driven by a shock experienced by a single organization. It may come from many sources: a major funder informs you that donations will cease; a damaging news story about your organization (truthful or not) hits the media; your staff revolts, and the people you hired send a collective appeal to the board to fire you; your chief financial officer absconds with half a million dollars; a major lawsuit is filed against your nonprofit. I have experienced all of these kinds of crises or witnessed colleagues attempt to navigate them.

I recall sitting with a United Nations official in New York in the early 1990s. He had performed incredibly well in Bangladesh while I was living there, which earned him a promotion to a regional leadership role in Africa. On that day, during a short trip to U.N. headquarters, he was taking some time to visit with me and Emily, and to offer her some advice about a possible job working on famine relief in Somalia.

Halfway through our meeting, the official took a phone call from his office in Nairobi. Emily and I could only hear his side of the conversation.

"Yes, I see. It's *that* bad, eh?"

He listened for a few minutes, then said, "A complete meltdown, right? Yes."

After hanging up, he continued giving Emily thoughtful career advice for another twenty minutes before returning to his work.

I soon learned that, while we'd been meeting with our friend, his world was collapsing around him. Within weeks, he would be made the scapegoat for malfeasance committed by others on his watch. I wondered at the time, and occasionally since, whether I would be able to summon such equanimity during a moment when my career was in flames due to the negligence or corruption of others.

When I wrote about some of my experiences and learnings dealing with crises in chapter nine of this book, I focused mostly on organization-specific traumas, like the one my friend at the U.N. experienced. I didn't have much to say about a second type of crisis: one caused by a systemic or environmental shock that impacts all or most of society, including nonprofits. For example, an economic downturn, a natural disaster, or a terrorist attack. Or a pandemic.

Both types of crises have some things in common, but they are also different in important ways. During an organization-specific crisis, a leader usually has a significant degree of control over their destiny, if they can figure out how to use it. On the other hand, since similar organizations are unaffected, a wounded organization can be further weakened by losing donors and talent to competitors.

During a society-wide crisis, a leader usually has considerably less control over their fate. However, peer organizations and their supporters are likely to be as negatively impacted as your nonprofit, and therefore are unlikely to be in a position to recruit your donors, social investors, or employees away from you. Like you, they are also focused on simply trying to keep their heads above water. Furthermore, it is easier to ask for support, encouragement, and ideas from one's peers when they are similarly impacted, as opposed to when your organization is experiencing a crisis of its own.

I have served as the CEO or the board chair of organizations navigating both types of traumas, and while I have made my share of mistakes and have the scars to show for them, I've also developed some battle-tested and effective approaches to leading during a crisis. But before I recount those stories and lessons, let me make two crucial points that many mission-driven leaders fail to grasp.

During good times, an organization's strengths are magnified. But during a crisis, its weaknesses are exposed and accentuated.

These statements may sound obvious. Yet their implications deserve some exploration.

When the wind is at your nonprofit's back—for example, when you're experiencing a booming economy, your issue is receiving favorable media attention, or your strategy is enjoying government support—you need to take full advantage of the positive momentum while it lasts. Don't fall into the trap of complacency during times when progress seems relatively easy. And by all means, avoid getting talked into asking for less than allies and supporters can provide because you don't want to push them too hard.

Instead, be aggressive—even relentless—in pursuing donations that can be used to attract top staff and volunteer talent and to build a rainy-day reserve fund. You'll need both during the inevitable future times when you will face strong headwinds and perhaps a crisis. On too many occasions I have heard mission-driven leaders castigate themselves for not having made the most of favorable conditions while they had the opportunity to do so. Early in my career, I made the same mistake a few times.

As I write this Epilogue, the world is grappling with the COVID-19 pandemic and the resulting social and economic fallout. You may be reading these pages while in the throes of the same ongoing crisis, or perhaps in the midst of some future disaster. If so, don't doubt that good times will come again. Grind it out now, using some of the ideas I'll offer if they seem relevant to your situation. Just as important, be ready to be hyper-aggressive in bringing in money and talent to replenish and fortify your organization when conditions are more favorable, because those positive circumstances won't last indefinitely either.

Summoning the Better Leader Within

LET'S GO BACK TO THE AFTERMATH of the 9/11 terror attacks with which I started this Epilogue.

On the morning of September 12, 2001, I needed to get back to Washington, D.C., where I lived at the time. Reports about the availability of train seats and the reliability of schedules were all over the map. I just packed a bag and jumped on the subway, heading for Penn Station, not sure whether I would end up travelling by bus, plane, or rental car instead of by Amtrak. Such are the uncertainties that follow a sudden national crisis.

It turned out that the trains were on schedule and I was easily able to get a ticket. As I headed towards my office at the Grameen Foundation, which was exactly three blocks from the now heavily-guarded White House, I grew increasingly anxious about whether I could lead my team through this crisis. My worries were well founded. In the hours, days, and months that followed, this shock exposed organizational weaknesses that included pitifully low levels of financial reserves and a board of directors that was only gradually outgrowing serving as a rubber stamp for whatever I wanted.

My immediate focus was on organizational survival, and that meant raising money. I sat at my desk coming up with some rather dumb ideas. One was to tap into the widespread liberal feeling that, in the wake of a terror attack launched by radical Islamists, enlightened Westerners needed to show their support for moderate Muslims. To do this, I proposed sending out an urgent appeal for donations featuring the Kashf Foundation, our terrific Pakistani microfinance partner led by a charismatic local woman named Roshaneh Zafar. My chair and vice-chair wisely talked me out of that well-intended but unsound plan.

Instead, I began writing a more measured message to our donors and ran a draft by our fundraising consultant. He pointed out that my message focused too much on our internal organizational needs and too little on our still-relevant mission. It also fell short in terms of expressing concern for the psychological and emotional condition of the supporters who would receive it, many of whom lived in the New York and Washington areas that had been hit hard by the terror attacks. But his feedback mainly stuck to the big picture. "Alex," he told me over the phone, "during times like these, the public looks to nonprofit leaders like yourself for guidance, reassurance, inspiration, and wisdom. Give them some in this message, in a way that feels authentic to you."

I initially recoiled at his words. I was 34 years old, and most of the people who would get this appeal were older than I was. My anxiety about the future of Grameen Foundation and how its demise might reflect on me was palpable and at times overwhelming. But as his words sank in, I saw an opportunity to summon a better leader from within myself. I could focus less on my situation and that of the fledgling organization I had founded, and more on our poverty-fighting mission and on the thoughts and feelings of those who had invested their money and time in helping us become a force for good in the world.

I rewrote the letter, and as I arranged for it to be sent out, my anxiety abated somewhat. I began thinking less about my worries for the future and more about what my employees, board members, volunteers, and financial supporters needed from me to do their best for Grameen Foundation while attending to their own needs, whatever they might be.

Slowly and methodically, I started to focus on tasks large and small that could restore organizational stability and confidence and help ensure that we not only kept afloat, but advanced our mission. Those twin goals would require strengthening the relationships among, and deepening the emotional commitment of, people who were already involved with our organization. It took time, but we got enough right to not just recover, but to emerge stronger as an organization. Within two years, we were not only back on track, but had prepared our organization for a growth spurt that would enable us to triple in size from 2003 to 2005.

Playing the Long Game

DURING A SOCIETY-WIDE CRISIS, some of your supporters will temporarily disappear as they tend to their own needs. Resist the temptation to respond with criticism, complaints, or anger. They probably feel overstretched, overstressed, and guilty about letting you and others down. Show them some grace. When they stabilize their circumstances, they will likely remember your understanding and resume their support.

In the aftermath of the 2008 financial crisis, a donor who had invested a lot of his money with the fraudulent financier Bernie Madoff signaled that he might need to withdraw a loan guarantee commitment he had made to us. This caused panic among my staff who were involved in the affected program, and they mentioned that we had legally enforceable rights to his guarantee for another two years. One suggested that we threaten to sue him. It was a unique situation, but the basic dynamic of people feeling a sense of scarcity and a desire to blame others is something every leader should expect during a time of crisis, and one that you must attempt to transcend. After all, when times are tough, there are also people and organizations that will step forward with new support and exceptional understanding for your mission-driven group, especially if you have the courage to ask them for help.

Here's an example of what I mean. Starting during our second year, motivated by respect for our founding board member and inspirational leader Muhammad Yunus, Ted Turner's United Nations Foundation had been giving Grameen Foundation annual unrestricted grants of $10,000 each fall. In 2001, a week after 9/11, a series of letters containing spores of deadly anthrax began to be delivered all over the country, killing five people and infecting others. The ensuing panic and the security restrictions it generated caused months of significant postal delays, and a lot of our foundation mail arrived late. But under the press of other concerns, it didn't occur to me that the U.N. Foundation grant that we depended upon might be held up.

I needn't have worried. Before I even thought about the problem, an anonymous U.N. Foundation staff member somehow got into our building after hours one night and stuck a nondescript envelope with a letter and their check under the door of our office.

I'm still impressed by that thoughtful gesture. The foundation staff realized our need even though we were temporarily too disorganized to recognize it and express it to them. They acted with urgency and understanding. I have never forgotten how they were there for us when we needed them most.

During the same period, I asked Gary Hattem, then the president of the Deutsche Bank Americas Foundation, to meet with me to discuss future support. He invited me to join him for breakfast in his bank's private dining room in New York. Over the course of an hour's conversation, he agreed in principle to provide $100,000 per year for three years to fund a process for recognizing leading microfinance organizations through an annual event that would rotate to different locations in the U.S. and Europe. When I reported this success back to our staff and board, morale improved noticeably. Gary himself subsequently went on to become a friend, role model, and collaborator

These generous supporters at two important foundations doubtless had their own worries in the post 9/11 chaos and uncertainty. But they devoted some of their time and attention to assisting Grameen Foundation and me to overcome *our* challenges. I drew inspiration from their supportive gestures, and tried to channel the same spirit in how I related to people who depended on me.

And what about our donor who had suffered financially due to Madoff's criminal Ponzi scheme? I decided not to send an email threatening legal action, which probably would have made him even more agitated and resentful. Instead, I notified my board chair about the problem and asked for advice. He stated firmly that there should be no threats of lawsuits, especially against someone who had been so dedicated to our cause. Instead, our chairman called the donor and told him he would personally indemnify him against any loss in the event his loan guarantee was needed.

In other words, if the donor ever had to provide funds to make good on a loan default, our chairman would make the payment on the donor's behalf.

This gesture of generosity not only defused the crisis but created even more goodwill and solidarity throughout the organization. As it happened, the guarantee was never needed, so neither the donor nor our chairman had to part with any money.

I learned two key lessons from these stories. First, when people let you down, play the long game—extend grace to them, confident that your generosity will evoke a similar response from others.

Second, in times of crisis, be on the lookout for people who will take extraordinary measures to support you if you are willing to pursue them in a disciplined manner that is guided by urgency rather than panic.

After the onset of the 2020 pandemic, some nonprofit leaders decided that it was best to put fundraising efforts on hold out of respect for the needs of their donors. That was a big mistake. In tough times, if you still believe your organization's mission matters—and you should!—don't sell your donors and allies short by assuming they would rather not hear from you about what you are doing and what you need. Instead, reach out to them to express interest and concern, update them on what you are doing, and to ask their advice. And, by all means, request their financial support in a way that feels appropriate to the relationship and to the circumstances.

Some will turn you down for the time being, but others will step up in ways that you can barely imagine.

Appreciating the Stress Nonprofit Leaders Face

WHEN THE COVID-19 PANDEMIC HIT in March, 2020, like countless other people around the world, I had to make some tough choices about personal priorities. I decided to focus first on protecting my family's well-being, on the viability of my consulting business, and on learning how to teach my students at the University of Maryland online rather than in a classroom. I also had to figure out how to follow through on my commitment to bury my just-deceased stepfather in his family cemetery in a small town in northwestern Tennessee, as well as how to meet the needs of my octogenarian stepmother who had recently suffered grievous injuries during a bus accident.

It took me a while to get a handle on those urgent matters. Once I did, I began thinking about the stress that nonprofit leaders were also experiencing. Recalling the overwhelming sense of anxiety that visited me during various crises I faced while running Grameen Foundation and American India Foundation, I wanted to help those who were now sitting in leadership hot seats.

In this spirit, I contacted friends in positions of nonprofit leadership, expressed empathy, and offered advice if asked. I recorded a video with suggestions on my YouTube channel and posted a couple of times to my blog. Finally, in one short, hastily-written article, I took three lessons from my just-published book *When in Doubt, Ask for More*, and described how they might be relevant to someone leading an organization during the pandemic crisis. It was not my best piece of writing, but after it was included in a COVID-19 resource library for nonprofits set up on the fly by the *Chronicle of Philanthropy*, it went viral, and thousands of people read it. I was pleased to be able to provide a modicum of support to leaders who I knew were grappling with painful challenges.

One day, I came up with the idea for a new article describing what I would be doing if I were leading a nonprofit organization during the pandemic. For the purposes of the article, I assumed that some of my organization's programs would be on hold, while others were operating. I figured that, during the lockdown period, some time would be freed up that would normally have been spent commuting to work or travelling around the world. Based on my experiences during previous crises, I made a list of activities I would focus on—including, for example, brushing up on a foreign language one might need in the months and years ahead. The *Chronicle* agreed to publish the resulting article.

So far, so good. I didn't think to weigh in on the title of the article, as I was so eager to get my hopefully useful tips and wisdom out there. As is usually the case, an editor at the publication came up with the headline, which suggested that my ideas should be the priorities for *all nonprofit leaders now*—even though the article itself didn't come close to making that claim.

The article appeared on the *Chronicle* website, and within 24 hours, half a dozen readers had posted scathing comments about it. The complaints varied, but basically they accused me of being hopelessly out of touch, imagining that the pandemic lockdown was a kind of paid vacation for nonprofit leaders and ignoring the existential threats to their organizations that some of these leaders were facing. (Another commenter was mildly critical of my article while trying to promote his consulting services.)

Taken aback, I tried to engage the critics by responding with comments in which I sought common ground. I acknowledged the fact that they had not found my recommendations useful, but I also highlighted aspects of the article that they seemed to have missed and that readers in other online forums had found valuable. The commenters' rage only grew more intense. They accused me of making matters worse by responding with anything other than a flat disavowal of every word I'd written.

In previous years, while some of my controversial stands about microfinance had prompted intense criticism, I had never experienced anything quite like this. It didn't help matters that I was alone in our Maryland home while Emily was in New York caring for my stepmother. In retrospect, it should have been easy for me to shrug off the overwrought vitriol from people who claimed that they were incredibly overworked but somehow had time to write lengthy barbs directed at me. But I wasn't quite able to do that.

Eventually, I talked to my editor at the *Chronicle*, who'd been as surprised by the reaction as I was. She agreed to change the headline that seemed to have set people off. It now reads, "8

Things Nonprofit Leaders Could Do If Their Work is on Hold." The *Chronicle* also announced it would publish a second article about the reaction. I asked a few people to weigh in so there would be at least a few neutral or supportive comments. To my relief, over the next 24 hours, about a dozen supportive comments were posted, from friends and strangers alike.

Later in the year, I decided to use this experience as a teachable moment for the University of Maryland students who take my course, titled The Foundations of Nonprofit Leadership and Social Innovation. I assigned the blog post and underscored that I wanted my students to read the comments so we could discuss them together in class.

Unfortunately, my plan turned out to be impossible. When the *Chronicle* shifted its website to a new platform, all of the comments on my article were inadvertently deleted. (Or perhaps it wasn't so unfortunate after all, since the words that were lost included some of the most critical statements about me ever published.)

If I'd been able to conduct the classroom discussion as planned, I would have wanted my students, as future nonprofit leaders, to take away a number of crucial lessons.

One is that leading a mission-driven organization in a crisis, whether caused by internal mistakes or external shocks, can be a very intense and disquieting experience. Stress can bring out the best in leaders, or the worst—and, in most cases, it does a little of both. I would hope that my students would recognize the need to be graceful and forgiving when dealing with stressed-out nonprofit leaders they might donate to, volunteer for, or work with during times of crisis.

I would also encourage my students to have more grace for themselves during hard times. I'd urge them to strive for high-minded leadership focused on supporting others trying to do good while resisting the temptation to assign blame and demonize others—especially those who are trying, however imperfectly, to help. As for me, with the benefit of hindsight, I would have written the article a bit differently, and taken considerably more interest in the wording of the headline. But the most important lesson I took from the whole episode was a reminder of how the caring people who are committed to serving society experience much more pressure than usual when a crisis strikes.

The COVID-19 pandemic—compounded as it was by the Trump administration's inept response, the related economic fallout, and an overdue reckoning on racial injustice—was probably more difficult to navigate than any crisis I had experienced during my years leading nonprofits. Under the circumstances, I can only applaud all of those who are doing their best to lead mission-driven organizations under very trying circumstances.

Even in a Crisis, Self-Care is Not a Luxury

IN THE LAST THIRD OF THIS BOOK, I explored the importance of self-care for mission-driven leaders. So many hard-driving executives focused on social change neglect their personal well-being—in fact, some even brag about doing so as a kind of badge of honor. This tendency often gets exacerbated during crises, a practice that can put a leader in an even deeper hole.

I have seen those leading through a challenging time abandon exercise regimens, healthy eating habits, and diversionary hobbies while also neglecting professional, personal, and family relationships. If you neglect your well-being for a few days or even a week or two, little irreversible harm will normally result. But crises usually last longer than that, and unhealthy behaviors often outlast the crises that spawned them.

Making time for things that are healthy and that feel replenishing or even a little indulgent is *not* an unaffordable luxury. Rather, it is an absolutely essential practice for effectively navigating a crisis when in a leadership position.

During a crisis, identifying your go-to methods of stress reduction, diversion, emotional release, exercise, and nurturing important relationships—and then applying them with all the discipline you can muster—can pay big dividends. It can help you find that better leader buried inside you, the one who is able to focus on the needs, challenges, and aspirations of other people and on the larger, inspiring mission of your organization rather than on your self-centered fears or worries. And in the process, it may even, in some sort of cosmic way, lead to an unexpected check or two being slipped under your door at night.

Nine Favorite Tips for Managing a Nonprofit During a Society-Wide Crisis

1

KEEP IN FREQUENT TOUCH with your board chair and give them many opportunities to feel included, to advise you, and to contribute. Realize that they are also deeply stressed by the crisis. During this difficult time, they may see their involvement with your organization as a source of meaning and potential achievement; as a burden and a possible blot on their reputation; or, perhaps, as both. Strive to understand how they are responding to the crisis, and manage your interactions with them accordingly.

2

GATHER YOUR SENIOR TEAM frequently and your entire staff periodically to share what you are doing to overcome the crisis and why. During these sessions, also take their emotional temperatures and solicit their ideas.

3

IDENTIFY SOMEONE WHOM YOU TRUST and respect to serve as a sounding board as you ride the emotional rollercoaster of managing a nonprofit through a crisis. This might be a mentor, a wise board member, or even someone managing a peer organization who might want to unburden themselves with you after you confide in them.

4

IF YOUR ORGANIZATION IS FACING a revenue shortfall, as most do during a crisis, engage your staff in identify ways to reduce costs while minimizing negative impacts on the mission. Reward those who put forward the best ideas that you can implement.

5

MAKE TIME FOR MINDFULNESS PRACTICES, for exercise, and for hobbies—all essential investments in your well-being. You may have less time available than usual, but doing *something* along these lines is better than nothing.

6

START, RECOMMIT TO, or continue a practice of daily writing down five to ten things you are grateful for.

7

AVOID OVERREACTING. When something new goes wrong during a crisis, it is rarely as bad as you first imagine. If you learn to pause and reflect before acting in moments of crisis, frustration, and even despair, you'll discover that some problems, even ones that initially appear insoluble, resolve themselves over time.

8

A CRISIS FREQUENTLY REQUIRES BUDGET CUTS. While often painful, these moments provide an opportunity to part ways with underperforming employees or teams in a face-saving way.

9

SOMETIMES, DONORS WILL STEP FORWARD to provide emergency relief funding to help address a society-wide crisis. As a nonprofit leader, you have an opportunity to educate your benefactors about the root causes of the problems, not just the symptoms that were exacerbated by the crisis. You also have a responsibility to turn down funding that you are not in a good position to use, even if it will help plug critical budget gaps.

Acknowledgments

ALMOST EXACTLY FIVE YEARS AGO, I stared at a blank screen and began to write this book. It came off the rails many times. Somehow it crossed the finish line.

I have a long list of people to thank for helping me complete it, and an even greater number who helped teach me things that I have applied and then written about in these pages.

Let me start with my editor and publisher, Karl Weber. I have admired the terrific work he has done collaborating with Muhammad Yunus on his last three books. In my case, he transformed 800 pages I had written into a final manuscript that was so much cleaner and more compelling than the sprawling mess I handed him in November 2018. He was also fun to work with and taught me a lot. My writing coach Mark Levy was an important source of ideas and wisdom; I am indebted to Grameen Foundation's first board chair, Reed Oppenheimer, for financially supporting the original workshop I took with Mark that helped make me a better writer. Nebil Mahmud worked tirelessly to advance this project in many ways, including by tracking down some hard-to-find historical records from the archives of Grameen Foundation. John Sturm has been incredibly supportive of all my recent books.

Morgan Nelson, the daughter of my dear friends Donna and Joel, playfully and helpfully badgered me for years to get this done. Okay, Morgan—I did it. Now lay off already! Her parents let me stay in their home in Key West for three months so I could focus on writing the first, very imperfect draft of this book. In fact, all of my friends in our nation's southernmost town, or whom I have met there, have been impossibly supportive of me and of this project. A very incomplete list includes Charlie Anderson, Eddie

Baker, Charlie Bauer, Bill Blue, Danny, Tim and Cindy Carter, Adam Chaffins, Jeff Clark, Brenda Donnelly, John and Gay Dougherty, Candace Estep, Claire Finley, Sally Galbraith, Valerie Garner Gavasto, Carolyn Guarini, Gail Hardy, Mark Hanna, George Harper, Dan Hogberg, Ericson Holt, Elisabeth and Darrin Van Houten, Deb Hudson, Art Levin, Alain and Marci Majeau, Steve Mellette, Emalyn Mercer, Tony Mezzacappa, Randy Morrow, Suzanne Mounger, Cindy Plume, Alicia Renner, Joan Robbins, Ross Sermons, Dann Sherrill, Rhonda Skains, Cassidy Smith, Ted Thompson, Mark and Deanna Vernon, Carl and Erin Wagoner, Cindy Walker, Randy and Christine West, Andy Westcott and Brian Wisor. And joining Morgan as people who provided vital encouragement for me to finish this project include Susan Davis, Margo Jacobs, Katja Kurz, and Camilla Nestor.

My family has been an essential source of support. My bride Emily, to whom this book is dedicated, has been a loving ally through it all. My departed father and in-laws were kind, loving, and taught me so much, mainly through how they lived their lives. My mother's love, and the quirky ways she expresses it, has enveloped me every day of my life and occasionally overwhelmed me. I have, hands down, the two best stepparents in world history: Norma Counts and John Fox. My elder brother Doug, a gifted social worker and therapist, my younger brother Michael, an acclaimed artist, and my late sister Pam, who left this earth too early but at least on her own terms, all helped make me the person I am today. My brother and sisters in law, and my nephews Wilder, Dashiell, Benjamin and Nicholas have brought more joy into my life than I could ever have imagined.

My colleagues at Grameen Foundation, those who served on the board and in other volunteer roles, and its donors gave me the support I needed to contribute, grow, and learn. They tended to forgive my mistakes and celebrate what I got right—something I remain grateful for. Many served the organization as if they themselves had founded it. A very partial list of those who went the extra mile to make this poverty-fighting organization what it became and were strong allies of mine and in some also cases mentors (and not mentioned elsewhere in this book) includes Sandra Adams, Nurul Alam, Julia Arnold, Tania Ashraf, Julia Assad, Dustin Buehler, Deb Burand, Anwarul K. Chowdhury, Sherita Coates, Erin Connor, George Conard, Darwin Cruz, Manon Cypher, James Dailey, Kimberly Davies, Katherine Devine, Jennifer Drogula, Leslie Enright, Ian Davis, Sean DeWitt, Andrea Findley, Brianne Fischer, Gigi Gatti, Arcelia Gomez, Andrea Gray, Kate Griffin, Ken Fox, Kari Hammett-Caster, Heather Henyon, Kay Hixson, Beverly Jackson, David Keogh, Lisa Kienzle, Joseph Kotun, Nelson Mattos, Fiona McDowell, Kate McElligott, Hayley Mickelson, Cheri Mitchell, Camilla Nestor, Khuloud Odeh, Chandni Orhi, Jimmy Ossman, Astha Parmar, Vlad Petrov, Taylor Robinson, Rosanna Ramos-Velita, David Russell, Betty Sams, Rob Sassor, Marshall Saunders, Melissa Scudo, Manisha Shah, Stephanie Simpson, Ven Suresh, Christopher "Happy" Tan, Leo Tobias, Joshua Tripp, Elizebeth Tucker, Emily Tucker, Si White, Cathy Yi, and Liselle Yorke

Professor Muhammad Yunus has been impossibly generous to me from the moment he received my first letter in 1987, seeing potential in me far beyond what I or perhaps anyone could. That is one of his greatest gifts, and he extends it to everyone he meets. His wife Afrozi and his daughters Monica and Deena have long treated me as family. I have too many friends and teachers in Bangladesh to list, most of whom are or have been affiliated with Grameen, but I must mention the following individuals (most of whom are not named in this book): Shofiqul Alam, Shamim Anwar, Salahuddin Azizee, Dipal Barua, Aleya Begum, Nurjahan Begum, Chitta Ranjan Chaki, Nurjahan Chakladar, Sheikh Abdud Daiyan, Abul Hossain, Mostafa Kamal, Jibon Chandra Kha, H.I. Latifee, Lamiya Morshed, Sanat Kumar Saha, Abdus Shaheen, Khalid Shams, and the late Abdul Mannan Talukdar.

Sam Daley-Harris has long been a source of inspiration, wisdom and support, and still is. His organization Civic Courage is taking important ideals he has always promoted to an entirely new level. Michael Rigby, the gifted man Sam asked to supervise me when I was an intern at RESULTS in 1987, played a pivotal role in shaping my career and for that, and much more, I will be forever grateful.

My closest friends have always seen me in the most favorable light while also helping me to enjoy life and laugh at its absurdities. Schiller Ambroise, Nick Arena, Alex Badia, Rohit Bakshi, Tim and Danny Carter, Kelvin Chan, Sam Daley-Harris, Susan Davis, Ralph D'Onofrio, Howie Erichson, Craig Fishman, Paul Hilal, Bobby, Jenny and Julie Freiman, Arcelia and Javier Gomez, Adam Goodman, Dave Kratka, Zaher Al Munajjed, Joel and Donna Nelson, Karen and Jeff O'Malley, Bob Philips, Peter Pierce, Michael Rigby, Joan Robbins, Jennifer Robey, Nicole and Paul Doria-Rose, Peter Rose, David and Amanda Schnetzer, Barb Scott, Julia Soyars, Michael Stafford, Peter Tzendalian, Lee and Sherry Waldrep, Julie and David Wallace, the late Dave (Waxy) Waxenberg, and Chuck and Laura Woolery have done more for me than I can even begin to contemplate much less adequately express.

I have been fortunate to have been able to serve in exciting and meaningful volunteer roles with a number of terrific organizations, including Fonkoze, the Center for Financial Inclusion, the Court Appointed Special Advocate (CASA) program of Prince George's County, RESULTS, the Washington Seminar Center, Katalysis, Project Enterprise, and She's the First. People in all those organizations taught me tons and have done so much good!

I have enjoyed teaching at the School of Public Policy at the University of Maryland, which among other gifts gave me the chance to test out some of the ideas in this book with my students. Bob Grimm, the dynamic founder of the Do Good Institute, and Assistant Dean Nina Harris, one of the most dedicated university administrators anywhere, have been pleasures to work with. And I am also grateful to my students and my teaching assistants, especially Kate Raulin, Theresa Montgomery, Julia Clark, Meg Lanthier, and Ryan Grimm.

My consulting clients—AIF, Arogya World, Indiaspora, the India Philanthropy Alliance, Kiva, Magic Bus USA, Shire House, and the SME Finance Forum—are not just changing the world in positive ways, but they have also helped change and shape me and the work I am doing at this point in my career.

I met many terrific people during my time at the American India Foundation. Thanks especially to Bhawna Chawla, Katrina Dikkers, Drew Foxman, Mugdha Gangopadhyay, Nirmala Garimella, Pradeep Kashyap, Lata Krishnan, Katja Kurz, Ash Lilani, Victor Menezes, Nishant Pandey, Raj Sharma, Preena Soni, Pratibha Srinivasan, and Geoff Stewart.

Friends around the world jumped in at different stages to help review and comment on the manuscript. Among those who added the most value were Chitra Aiyer, Elana Bloom, Sam Daley-Harris, Bob Eichfeld, Jason Hahn, Marilyn Kodish, Karen O'Malley, Venky Raghavendra, Brooke Raymond, Paul Rippey, Sally Stoecker, Barb Weber, and Matt Weiller. Julian, Karen, and Brooke were especially generous with their time and advice. Liselle Yorke and Max Silverman pitched in valiantly with promoting and marketing this book.

I have valued working in many coalitions, and none more than the Microfinance CEO Working Group. I so appreciate the collaborative spirit and trust in me demonstrated by Shamaran Abed, Scott Brown, Sharlene Brown, Bridget Dougherty, Meghan Greene, Anne Hastings, Lauren Hendricks, Steve Hollingworth, Mary Ellen Iskendarian, Rosario Perez, Michael Schlein, Rupert Scofield, and David Simms. I have experienced the same kind of camaraderie in the India Philanthropy Alliance.

The chairs of Grameen Foundation each, in their own way, helped make me the person and professional I am today: Reed Oppenheimer, Jim Sams, Susan Davis, Paul Maritz, Bob Eichfeld and Peter Cowhey. The vice-chairs, including Yvette Neier and Rick Helfer, were all very active and added immense value. These leaders moved mountains to advance Grameen Foundation's bold vision of a poverty-free world.

I have been able to study up close the leadership strength of a few great moral leaders besides Muhammad Yunus. They include Fazle Abed, Ajay Banga, Ann Marie Binser, David Gibbons,

Anne Hastings, Father Joseph Philippe, Wayne Silby, and Tammy Tibbetts. They have enriched my life and those of countless others. Among the many social intrepreneurs I have admired and learned from are Linda Boucard, Christen Brandt, Kara Bundy, Leigh Carter, and Katie Riley.

Quite a few consultants, paid and pro bono, helped me come to valuable insights that course through the veins of this book, not least Nick Craig, Meredith Kimbell, Bill Rentz, and Cedric Richner. I can't even begin to name all the pro bono lawyers who helped us, but you know who you are—thank you!

I am indebted to the Elisabeth Morrow School, the Brigantine, NJ public school system, Public School Six in New York City, the Lenox Hill Neighborhood Association, Horace Mann School, Cornell University, and the Fulbright program for helping to educate me, and to the taxpayers and family that underwrote the costs of doing so. Capitol Hill Presbyterian Church and my spiritual advisers Erin Keys, Mitali and Rob Perkins, Father Charlie Poole, Kim Rodrigue, Andy and Peg Walton, and Scott Wilson have let me see important aspects of life that I otherwise would have missed. I have drawn strength and insight from other faith traditions, including Judaism, Hinduism, Islam, Mormonism, and Buddhism and am grateful for those who helped educate me about each of these religions' powerful elements.

I have been trying to keep a gratitude journal for the last few years, writing down all the things and people I am grateful for at any given moment. I almost wish I could reproduce that list here. Suffice it to say that I did not write this book, or become the person I am today, alone. Thanks to everyone who has joined me on this journey.

I alone am responsible for any errors or omissions in this book.

Alex Counts
Hyattsville, Maryland
April 2019

Index

ABBA, 221-222
Abed, Fazle, 80
Accion, 177, 211, 213
Aiyer, Chitra, 86, 141-142
Alcoholics Anonymous, 137
Ali, Shomit, 86
American India Foundation (AIF), 160, 258, 273, 284
Anderson, John, 155, 219, 242-244
Anderson, Walker, 84
Andhra Pradesh, India, 171
Anwar, Shamim, 47
Arena, Nick, 263
Ashoka, 72
Austin People's Fund, 209
Avon, 209

Badan Kredit Kecamatan, 25
Bakshi, Rohit, 22
Balitsaris, Matt, 160-161
Banga, Ajay, 160
Banker's Trust, 202
Bankers without Borders (BwB), 205-206
Barua, Dipal, 47
Begum, Amena, 73

Begum, Fulzan, 73
Bhatt, Ela, 179
Biggar, Nigel, 208, 244-246
Bill and Melinda Gates Foundation, 104, 233-234, 269
Billingsley, Lucy, 104-107, 125, 158
Bladin, Peter, 142, 164, 219
Blakely, Mitch, 198-199
Bombardier, Gary, 19
Boyer, Dominique, 160
BRAC, 79-80
Braganza, Royston, 209
Bridges, Tricia, 106
Brigham Young University, 83
Brooks, Stacy, 271
Bush, President George H. W., 58, 65, 67

Cable, Ed, 207-208
CARE, 76-80, 169
Carter, Danny, 29, 223, 255, 271
Carter, President Jimmy, 57
Carter, Joanne, 62, 69
Carter, Tim, 29, 223, 255, 271
Carter Brothers Band, 223, 231
CBS News, 168

298   INDEX

Center for Creative Non-Violence (CCNV), 1
Center for Financial Inclusion, 177, 213
Chronicle of Philanthropy, 284-286
Chowdhury, Sadia, 79
Citibank, 203
City of Joy, 42
Clark, John, 37
Clinton Global Initiative, 196
Cohen, Sandy, 125
Community Knowledge Worker program, 210
Congressional Hunger Center, 206
Cornell University, 15-16, 19-22, 32, 36, 103
Counts, Emily, 4-5, 69-72, 75-83, 168, 221-223, 225, 236, 257, 261, 263, 270
Court-Appointed Special Advocate (CASA), 233
COVID-19, 278, 283-287
Cowhey, Peter, 208
Craig, Heidi, 155
Craig, Nick, 155

Daiyan, Sheikh Abdud, 48
Daley-Harris, Sam, 16, 21, 23, 24, 32, 57, 65, 69, 77, 130-131, 149-150, 252-253
Dallas City Homes, 209
D'Amato, Senator Alfonse, 34
Darling, Chris, 67-68
Davis, Geofff, 82-83, 86
Davis, Susan, 52, 54. 93-94, 96, 124, 141, 145-146, 157, 169, 183, 188, 192-197, 256, 263

DeConcini, Senator Dennis, 25, 34
Deutsche Bank, 202, 282
DeWitt, Sean, 273
Dhaka, Bangladesh, 36-39, 46-47, 51-52, 225
Different Drum, The, 32
DLA Piper, 214
Doerr, John, 106-107, 119-124, 159
DoGood Institute, 232
Doubleday (publisher), 71
Drayton, Bill, 72
Drogula, Jennifer, 101
Drucker, Geoff, 81
Drucker, Jacki *see* Lippman, Jacki
Duncan, Cameron, 17
DuPart, Omiyale, 75-76

Earth Summit, 67-69
eBay, 102, 120
Economic Support Fund, 68
Economist, The, 95, 196
Edelstein, David, 173, 189, 271
Eichfeld, Bob, 123, 166, 196, 203-204, 263, 270-272
Erichson, Howie, 3-4

Fascell, Representative Dante, 24, 25
Feighan, Representative Ed, 24
Fisher, Leah, 36
Fishman, Craig, 22, 24
Fishman, Joel, 71-72
Fonkoze, 160-162, 212
Foose, Laura, 256-257
Ford Foundation, 52, 54, 195
Freedom from Hunger, 273

INDEX

Fulbright scholarship, 1, 31, 35-37, 39, 55, 64, 66, 195, 252
Full Circle Fund, 73
Fund for Innovation and Public Service, 72

"Gary" (Grameen Foundation board member), 188-189
Gates, Bill, 59-61, 104, 143, 159. *Also see* Bill and Melinda Gates Foundation
Gates, Bill, Sr., 60
Gates, Melinda, 59-61, 104. *Also see* Bill and Melinda Gates Foundation
Ghosh, Nonibala, 73
Gilman, Representative Ben, 21, 24
Give and Take, 254
Give Us Credit, 71-78, 82, 84
Google, 120, 159
Grameen America, 209-210
Grameen Bank, 1, 5, 16, 23, 25, 27, 30-31, 38-54, 71-74, 76-77, 80, 82, 156, 168-172, 207, 260-261, 279-283
Grameen Capital India (GCI), 203-204, 209, 273
Grameen Check, 85-87
Grameen Fisheries Foundation, 207
Grameen Foundation (GF), 2-3, 7, 12, 57-63, 70, 78, 80, 218-220, 230-231, 239-246, 258-260
   board of, 182-197
   Counts's departure from, 268-273
   decision-making at, 153-162

   fundraising for, 91-109
   launch of, 81-87
   leadership challenges at, 134-152, 168-181
   partnerships with, 198-214
   relationships with donors, 110-133
   success at, 163-181
Grameen Impact Investment India, 203-204, 209
Grameen-Jameel Pan-Arab Microfinance, 209-210
GrameenPhone, 85
Grameen Shakti (Energy), 207
Grameen Technology Center, 61
Grameen Telecom, 99-101, 207, 230
Grameen Uddyog (Rural Initiatives), 86-87
Grant, Adam, 254
Graubert, Steve, 230-231
Greenberg, Jim, 201-204
Greenberg, Lisa, 201
Groundhog Day, 198
Growth Guarantees, 208

Haber, Ilene, 115-116
Habitat for Humanity, 208
Halder, Shandna Rani, 73
Hammock, John, 115
Harvard Club, 196-197
Harvard University, 209
Haryopratomo, Aldi, 209
Hasina, Sheikh, 171, 175
Hassler, Patti, 52-54
Hastings, Anne, 212
Hattem, Gary, 282
Hendricks, Lauren, 169, 206, 273

Hilal, Paul, 11-12
Hoffman, Ruth, 86-87
Hollingworth, Steve, 206, 271, 273
Hossain, Mir Akhtar, 170
Huq, Muzammel, 47

ICICI Bank, 95, 203
Innovations for Poverty Action (IPA), 173, 177-178, 208
Institute for International Education (IIE), 36
InterAction, 271
International Fund for Agricultural Development (IFAD), 21, 23

Jackson, Walter, 35-36
Jamal Poverty Action Lab (JPAL), 177
Jameel, Mohammad, 204, 209
"James" (Grameen Foundation colleague), 151-152
"Joanne" (Grameen Foundation colleague), 145-146
Johns Hopkins University, 79
J.P. Morgan, 205
"Judy" (Grameen Foundation colleague), 165-167
Jung, Andrea, 209

Kabir, Humayan, 35
Kabir, Ruma, 35
Kane, Paul, 139, 183
Karlan, Dean, 173-178, 208
Kashf Foundation, 279
Kendua-Madhupur, Bangladesh, 43-49, 52-54

Keogh, David, 156
Kha, Jibon Chandra, 46
Khatoon, Rezia, 45
Khosla, Vinod, 120, 123
Khosru, Amir, 39
Kimbell, Meredith, 58
King, Martin Luther, Jr., 13-14
Kiva, 268-269
"Kripon, Mr." (frugal persona), 259-260

La Loma restaurant, 267-268
Lapierre, Dominique, 42
Lawson, Dorsey, 33
Lippman, Jacki, 81, 83, 86, 259
Locke, Governor Gary, 59
Loevinsohn, Ernie, 23
London Microfinance Club, 213

Madhupur, *see* Kendua-Madhupur
Madoff, Bernie, 191, 281-282
Mahmood, Asad, 211-212
Mahmood, Zeba, 79
Majid, M.L., 86-87
Mamma Mia!, 221-222
Mandela, Nelson, 59-61
Maritz, Paul, 189, 197, 208, 269
Maryland, University of, 232, 258, 286
MasterCard, 160
Maynard, Shannon, 205-206
McCaw, Craig, 59-61, 102
McCaw, Susan, 59-61, 102
McConnell, Senator Mitch, 252
McHugh, Representative Matthew, 18-19
McKinley, Janet, 93-98, 105, 120, 123

McMullen, Lynn, 70-71, 83
Meehan, Jennifer, 164
Mercer, Emalyn, 255-256
Mercy Corps, 80
Microcredit Summit, 77, 82-83, 253
Microfinance CEO Working Group (MCWG), 213-214
Microsoft, 60, 142-143, 164
Mifos, 207-208
Miller, George, 96
Mitchell, John, 37
Mobile Midwife initiative, 210
Mobile Technology for Community Health (MOTECH), 143
Mohammad Mortuza, 39
Morshed, Lamiya, 63
Motley Fool, 201
MTN (Uganda), 156
Myrvhold, Nathan, 60

Nag, Ratan, 39
National Audubon Society, 67-68
National CASA Association, 233
Neier, Aryeh, 99-102
Neier, Yvette, 101, 192-193
Nelson, Donna, 263
Nestor, Camilla, 164
Newaz, Shah, 209
New Yorker magazine, 121
New York Times, 135
Nordeen, Randi, 105-106
Northwestern University, 173

Obey, Representative David, 66
O'Malley, Jeff, 224-225
O'Malley, Karen, 135, 263

Omidyar, Pierre, 96-97, 102-104, 107, 121, 124, 159, 164
Opportunity International, 77
Oprah Winfrey Show, 66
Owens, Representative Wayne, 68-69
Oxfam, 14-15, 37, 68, 114-115

Padilla, Mrs. (fifth-grade teacher), 115-116
Page, Larry, 121, 159
Pandey, Nishant, 273
Paperin, Stewart, 101
Pappalardo, Sal, 205
Parade magazine, 84
Partnership for Responsible Financial Inclusion, 213
Pascucci, Chris, 129
Pascucci, Michael, 108-109, 128-129
Peace Corps, 86, 130
Peachey, Julie, 203, 208
Peck, M. Scott, 32-33
Philadelphia Flyers, 224
Philadelphia Phillies, 224
Philippine Development Forum, 66
Pitt/Khandker studies (microcredit), 175-176
PLAN Fund, 209
Plotnik, Julia, 16-19
Poole, Father Charlie, 266-267
Poverty Probability Index, 208
Presidential Commission on World Hunger, 57
Progress out of Poverty Index (PPI), 208

Quaraishi, Sabrina, 205

Rana Plaza disaster, 85
Random House, 72-76, 78
Rangel, Representative Charles, 24
Raulin, Kate, 232
RESULTS, 1, 16-27, 29-34, 36-38, 62, 64-71, 82, 130-131, 155, 251-253
Rhyne, Beth, 177
Richner, Cedric, 92
Rigby, Michael, 23, 24, 30-31, 34
Road Less Travelled, The, 32-33
Robbins, Joan, 255-256
Robey, Jennifer, 169
Rockefeller, Nelson, 202
Rockefeller, Steve, Jr., 3, 117, 182, 202, 219
Roenen, Carine, 160
Rubinstein, Michael, 69
RUMA, 209, 273
Ryan, Michael, 84

Sadie Nash Leadership Project, 142
Safer, Morley, 52-54
Sams, Jim, 92, 204
Sarsony, Craig, 219
Schatzki, Nick, 17-18
Schlein, Michael, 211-214
Schnetzer, David, 28
Schreiner, Mark, 208
Schroeder, Julian, 161-162
Scott, Barb, 70-71
Self-Employed Women's Association of India, 179
Sen, Amartya, 169

Shah, Premal, 268-269
Shams, Khalid, 86
SHARE Microfin, 94-95
Shaymganj Deloutpur, Bangladesh, 73
Silby, Wayne, 272
Sixteen Decisions, 44
60 Minutes, 51-54, 188
SKS (India), 170-171
Skymall magazine, 87
Small Loans, Big Dreams, 78
Smith Kline Beecham, 121
Snyder, Mitch, 1-2, 33
Sobhan, Sharmi, 203
Social Business Day, 61-63
Social Performance Task Force, 256
Soros, George, 99-102
Soyars, Julia, 184, 263
"Stan" (Oxfam board member), 114-115
Stanford University, 112
Stephanopoulos, George, 24
Summit for Children, 65-66
Sun Microsystems, 120

Talukdar, Abdul Mannan, 72, 84
Talukdar, Babar Ali, 53
Tangail, Bangladesh, 43, 72-73
Taroworks, 208, 273
"Tim" (Grameen Foundation ally), 239-240
Tonina, Norm, 193
Tufts University, 103
Turner, Ted, 281

UNICEF, 77

Universal Standards for Social Performance Management, 214
USAID, 25, 52, 65, 80
USA Today, 67
Valdivia, Mabel, 160
"Vikram" (Grameen Foundation colleague), 135-138
Village Phone Uganda (VPU), 156
Voorhies, Roger, 234

Wagner, Eleanor, 190
Wainright, Duane, 266-267
Wainright, Mary, 266-267
Wallace Global Fund, 72
Washington Post, 66
Weber, Barb, 102-103, 120-124, 159, 196, 219
Weiller, John, 28
Wendt, Henry, 121-122
When in Doubt, Ask for More, 284
Where Credit Is Due, 65
Whitehead, John C., 182-183
Women's Self-Employment Project (WSEP), 73
Wood, Tim, 143

World Bank, 175-176
World Development Movement, 37
World Food Prize, 81
World2Market, 87
World Vision, 80
Worsley, Robert, 87

Yariv, Danielle, 65
Yunus, Afrozi, 48
Yunus, Muhammad, 1-2, 16, 23, 27, 30-33, 40-43, 57, 61-62, 81-82, 85-87, 99-101, 120, 122, 129-130, 131, 149-150, 153, 159, 199, 207, 209, 230, 257, 260-261, 268, 281
   conflict with Bangladeshi authorities, 171-172
   Nobel Peace Prize, 5, 76, 78, 168-170, 178-179
   60 Minutes interview, 51-54
Yunus Centre, 63, 207
Yunus Social Business, 207

Zafar, Roshaneh, 279

About the Author

ALEX COUNTS FOUNDED GRAMEEN FOUNDATION and became its president and CEO in 1997. A Cornell University graduate, Counts's commitment to poverty eradication deepened as a Fulbright scholar in Bangladesh, where he trained under Professor Muhammad Yunus, the founder and managing director of Grameen Bank, and co-recipient of the 2006 Nobel Peace Prize. Since its modest beginnings, Grameen Foundation has grown to become a leading international humanitarian organization.

Counts is the author of *Small Loans, Big Dreams: How Nobel Prize Winner Muhammad Yunus and Microfinance Are Changing the World* and numerous articles in the *Stanford Social Innovation Review*, the *Washington Post*, and other publications. Today he is an independent consultant to nonprofit organizations and an adjunct professor at the School of Public Policy at the University of Maryland College Park.

Also by Alex Counts

When in Doubt, Ask for More

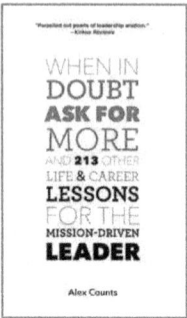

Leading a nonprofit organization is challenging, stressful work—yet it can also be richly rewarding. Alex Counts mastered the art of mission-driven leadership through decades of trial and error. Now he shares 214 of the most powerful lessons he discovered along the way—life and career secrets you'll never learn in school.

Frank, quirky, counterintuitive, and ultimately inspiring, these nuggets of wisdom cover the toughest challenges nonprofit leaders face:

- On defining your organization's mission: "Be bold, but be grounded."
- On running a meeting: "Agendas are made to be bent."
- On surviving business travel: "Check the seat pocket one more time."
- On people management: "It's okay to have a few enemies."
- On capturing an audience's attention: "Start with your conclusion."
- And on the art of fundraising: "Stop talking."

"Each tiny lesson is a self-contained, salient observation that shines a light on a specific aspect of leadership. . . . Whatever the subject, the author condenses a meaningful pronouncement into its simplest, most elegant form, using high-impact prose to make his point. . . . Parceled out pearls of leadership wisdom."—*Kirkus Reviews*

**AVAILABLE ON AMAZON, ON B&N.COM,
AND AT BOOKSELLERS EVERYWHERE**

CPSIA information can be obtained
at www.ICGtesting.com
Printed in the USA
LVHW111620200521
688017LV00001B/160